NOVELL'S

Introduction to
Networking

NOVELL'S

Introduction
to Networking

CHERYL C. CURRID AND ARCH D. CURRID

Novell Press, San Jose

Novell's Introduction to Networking
Published by
Novell Press
2180 Fortune Drive
San Jose, CA 95131

Library of Congress Catalog Card No.: 96-79758

10 9 8 7 6 5 4 3

ISBN: 0-7645-4525-6

Printed in the United States of America

Distributed in the United States by IDG Books Worldwide, Inc.

Distributed by Macmillan Canada for Canada; by Contemporanea de Ediciones for Venezuela; by Distribuidora Cuspide for Argentina; by CITEC for Brazil; by Ediciones ZETA S.C.R. Ltda. for Peru; by Editorial Limusa SA for Mexico; by Transworld Publishers Limited in the United Kingdom and Europe; by Academic Bookshop for Egypt; by Levant Distributors S.A.R.L. for Lebanon; by Al Jassim for Saudi Arabia; by Simron Pty. Ltd. for South Africa; by Pustak Mahal for India; by The Computer Bookshop for India; by Toppan Company Ltd. for Japan; by Addison Wesley Publishing Company for Korea; by Longman Singapore Publishers Ltd. for Singapore, Malaysia, Thailand, and Indonesia; by Unalis Corporation for Taiwan; by WS Computer Publishing Company, Inc. for the Philippines; by WoodsLane Pty. Ltd. for Australia; by WoodsLane Enterprises Ltd. for New Zealand. Authorized Sales Agent: Anthony Rudkin Associates for the Middle East and North Africa.

For general information on IDG Books Worldwide's books in the U.S., contact our Consumer Customer Service department at 800-762-2974. For reseller information, including discounts and premium sales, contact our Reseller Customer Service department at 800-434-3422.

For information on where to purchase IDG Books Worldwide's books outside the U.S., contact our International Sales department at 415-655-3078 or fax 415-655-3281.

For information on foreign language translations, contact our Foreign & Subsidiary Rights department at 415-655-3018 or fax 415-655-3281.

For sales inquiries and special prices for bulk quantities, contact our Sales department at 415-655-3200 or write to the address above.

For information on using IDG Books Worldwide's books in the classroom or for ordering examination copies, contact our Educational Sales department at 800-434-2086 or fax 817-251-8174.

For authorization to photocopy items for corporate, personal, or educational use, contact the Copyright Clearance Center, 222 Rosewood Drive, Danvers, MA 01923, or fax 508-750-4470.

For general information on Novell Press books in the U.S., including information on discounts and premiums, contact IDG Books at 800-434-3422 or 415-655-3200. For information on where to purchase Novell Press books outside the U.S., contact IDG Books International at 415-655-3021 or fax 415-655-3295.

John Kilcullen, *CEO, IDG Books Worldwide, Inc.*
Brenda McLaughlin, *Senior Vice President & Group Publisher, IDG Books Worldwide, Inc.*
The IDG Books Worldwide logo is a trademark under exclusive license to IDG Books Worldwide, Inc., from International Data Group, Inc.

Rosalie Kearsley, *Publisher, Novell Press, Inc.*
Novell Press and the Novell Press logo are trademarks of Novell, Inc.

Welcome to Novell Press

Novell Press, the world's leading provider of networking books, is the premier source for the most timely and useful information in the networking industry. Novell Press books cover fundamental networking issues as they emerge — from today's Novell and third-party products to the concepts and strategies that will guide the industry's future. The result is a broad spectrum of titles for the benefit of those involved in networking at any level: end-user, department administrator, developer, systems manager, or network architect.

Novell Press books are written by experts with the full participation of Novell's technical, managerial, and marketing staff. The books are exhaustively reviewed by Novell's own technicians and are published only on the basis of final released software, never on prereleased versions. Novell Press at IDG Books Worldwide is an exciting partnership between two companies at the forefront of the knowledge and communications revolution. The Press is implementing an ambitious publishing program to develop new networking titles centered on the current IntranetWare version of NetWare and on Novell's GroupWise and other popular groupware products.

Novell Press books are translated into 12 languages and are available at bookstores around the world.

Rosalie Kearsley, Publisher, Novell, Inc.
David Kolodney, Associate Publisher, IDG Books Worldwide, Inc.

Novell Press

Publisher
Rosalie Kearsley

Associate Publishers
Colleen Bluhm
David Kolodney

Acquisitions Editor
Jim Sumser

Managing Editor
Terry Somerson

Development Editor
Stefan Grünwedel

Copy Editor
Lothlórien Baerenwald

Technical Editor
Eric Burkholder

Editorial Assistant
Sharon Eames

Production Director
Andrew Walker

Supervisor of Page Layout
Craig Harrison

Media/Archive Coordination
Leslie Popplewell
Melissa Stauffer

Project Coordinator
Katy German

Graphics Coordination
Kurt Krames

Production Staff
Mario Amador
Ritchie Durdin

Proofreader
Jon Weidlich

Indexer
David Heiret

About the Authors

Popular columnist and author Cheryl Currid is president of Houston-based Currid & Company, a research and advisory firm specializing in connectivity and information technology. This marks her thirteenth book.

Arch Currid is an industry analyst at Currid & Company with over ten years of information technology experience. He specializes in training and education.

Preface

Novell's Introduction to Networking is the first place to turn to for beginning-level, accessible information about network technology. It highlights the reasons for networking, the resources available to you, and applications to assist you, as well as introducing you to the interesting possibilities that the Internet and intranets can give you and your business. Besides giving you pointers for creating a network and choosing the best hardware, we also describe appropriate networking software. Finally, we cover the responsibility of managing a network once it is put in place and give you pointers on management tools, security measures, and troubleshooting tactics. The appendix gives you recommended sites for accessing more networking information on the World Wide Web. The glossary explains unfamiliar terms. We hope you enjoy reading this book and have great success in implementing your network system.

Acknowledgments

Every book turns into a team effort with a single goal: Put together something to be proud of. This work — its concept and its cast of characters — is no exception.

Thanks must first go to Diane Bolin at Currid & Company and Stefan Grünwedel at IDG Books Worldwide who have worked together on five books in the last four years. Although they have never met in person, they work together as effectively as any team sitting side by side. I sometimes call them the dynamic duo — in a virtual sense. Together they combed and scoured the pages to make sure each concept was explained clearly. My hat is off to them for their professionalism and good spirits throughout the project.

I'd also like to acknowledge Bill Hargrove and Tim Constance for their contributions to several of the chapters. Joining us for the first time, Tim and Bill stood ready to share their experiences and advice on getting network principles translated into English. As you will soon see, we cover a lot of ground in the book, and borrowing the special insights of Bill and Tim proved especially helpful.

I'd also like to acknowledge and thank Anne Hamilton of IDG Books Worldwide for getting this project off the ground. She moved through the acquisition process quickly and professionally and helped develop the original tone of this book.

Finally, I would like to welcome Arch Currid, co-author of this work, to his first book-length project. Arch pitched in when the original co-author became unavailable to complete the work. He'd never written a book before and this experience became his trial by fire. He weathered it well.

— Cheryl Currid, President
Currid & Company

Contents at a Glance

Contents

PART I

Network Advantages
and Resources

CHAPTER 1

Why Network?

If, as a child, you ever connected cups with a string to make a play telephone, you've already installed your first network. You found that you could send and receive messages, secrets, and jokes with your friends. Chances are that you were both delighted and frustrated with the results.

Initially you were thrilled to receive a message from someone on the other end of the string. While you may have noticed some distortion, messages came through mostly intact. It felt like a technical triumph. If you tried to expand your network, say, with a longer string or more than two cups, you probably began to encounter technical difficulties. Moreover, to get the message through, both you and your friend had to be online (or "onstring") at the same time.

Luckily, with today's advanced technologies, computer networks aren't quite so limited. If you use the right combinations of computer and communications hardware, and good design techniques when planning your connections, then you can expand your network to almost anywhere. And because technology lets you store messages, neither you nor your friend have to be at either end of the string at the same time.

Today you can link up with many friends and coworkers by connecting to their computers within a workgroup, office building, or anyplace in the outside world, just like with the cups and string. This chapter begins a journey into the world of networking. It will take you on a tour following two tracks — a philosophical track (why network) and a practical or technical track (how to network).

People build networks so they can share devices, resources, files, messages, and ultimately knowledge. Sharing knowledge makes people smarter and better able to make business decisions. Businesses can justify building networks because it saves money when workers share devices, such as printers, fax machines, modems, scanners, and other *peripherals*. (A peripheral is any device used in conjunction with a computer, whether internally or externally.) But evidence suggests the biggest benefits are in the new ways networks enable people to do business.

Yesterday's Networks

Experts disagree on when the first computer networks arrived for business applications. Some like to think that vintage mainframe computers with terminals were the start of network computing. Before the advent of the personal computer a decade ago, computer systems usually consisted of only one real computer (a large *central processing unit* or CPU), with attached printers and display terminals. Unlike today's networks, the CPU did all the calculating, sorting, storing, and data retrieval, and then sent the requested information down to the terminal as characters that appeared on the screen. The processing seemed to happen quickly, but it had to be managed very carefully.

At the time, computers were very large, very expensive, hard to learn, and difficult to use. Companies created data processing departments to control and set priorities for work the computer would do. Specially trained operators and programmers worked day and night to schedule computing jobs so the system would run efficiently. Every effort was expended to conserve expensive computer power, which was measured in *millions of instructions per second* (MIPS). The mainframe computer of 1980 cost $250,000 per MIPS.

Slow communication lines compounded the problems of expense and organization. Up to the 1980s, mainframe communication lines usually ran at 4,800 to 9,600 *bits per second* (bps).

Minicomputers were developed during the 1970s. These computers were less expensive, but less powerful. They were useful for small departments or groups of people. The architecture of mainframes and minicomputer systems were basically the same, as shown in Figure 1.1. Each was based on the notion that one central computer could manage everything: applications, printers, terminals, and other resources. The terminals displayed the data on the screen, but didn't process anything.

In the beginning, terminals were used more for inputting information than obtaining anything from the CPU. That's what paper reports were for — reams and reams of paper reports. Generally these reports took hours for mainframes to produce (called *batch processing*), and the addition of a new kind of report required many extra hours to rewrite the programs and include it in the batch.

These "host-terminal" computer systems provided the only way to compute large sets of numbers and business analyses until the very early 1980s, when the *personal computer* (PC) arrived on the scene. These small computers based on newly invented, inexpensive microprocessor chips changed all the rules of data processing. Because PCs actually had the power to compute independently, people could perform some work without waiting for the mainframe system batch program to run.

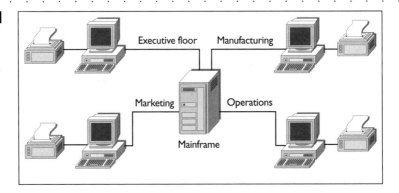

For both mainframe and minicomputer systems, all work was performed by the CPU. Attached printers and terminals did not do any processing.

Then came easy-to-use software. Mainframe and minicomputers required difficult-to-learn programming languages. It frequently took months, if not years, to train a specialist to operate and program a computer. Not so with microcomputers. Early computer spreadsheets such as VisiCalc and Lotus 1-2-3 were simple and gave everyday businesspeople the power to do their work independently.

Initially most companies installed PCs in separate PC workrooms. Those who needed to use the computer would gather up their work and proceed to the workroom. As PCs grew in popularity, getting a time slot in the PC workroom became more difficult, but the excitement over stand-alone PCs was short lived. Even though these relatively low-cost computers helped workers get their jobs done, the problem of developing and sharing information was far from solved. Scheduling time on a PC turned into a hassle, and before long few people felt they were saving time by taking information off printed reports from the mainframe computer and rekeying it in their PC's spreadsheets. What's more, when the work was done, they had to rely on old-fashioned copying and mailing to disseminate their information. Even if a businessperson could create quick results with a spreadsheet analysis, he or she couldn't share it instantly.

By the mid-1980s businesspeople were ready for a change. All the benefits brought by personal computers seemed wasted because it was so hard to share the results. Also, PC peripherals, such as printers and large fixed disks, were expensive. Most companies refused to buy an expensive, high-quality laser printer for each PC, nor were they willing to spend thousands of dollars for extra disk storage space. While computer work was faster, the arduous process of sharing results made personal computers an inefficient option for businesses.

Still, the enormous cost differences between host-based systems and PCs were too compelling to ignore. *Local area networks* (LANs) emerged as an experimental technology. A LAN is a high-speed communications system designed to link together computers, peripherals, fixed disks for storage, and communication devices, usually within a small geographic area. LANs were designed originally for connecting the computers within a workgroup, department, or a single floor. Several LANs can be interconnected within a building or campus of buildings, as well, to extend connectivity.

To put it kindly, early attempts at networking personal computers were technically challenging. Crudely designed equipment sometimes never made it through installation and went up in a puff of blue smoke on the first try. Few standards existed, so it was difficult to buy parts from one vendor if another had quality problems. Even when the networks did work, there were only limited diagnostic tools available to determine if they were working well. Sometimes a faulty pin or plug from the wire of a single connection could bring the entire network to its knees.

Also, few well-trained technicians existed. Because the technology was very new, most people learned it on the job. Long-time data processing professionals who were unfamiliar with PC technology tended to dismiss the new networks as error-prone and unstable. Usually it was their unwillingness to learn how the technology worked that made PC networking problems a foregone conclusion — making other companies shy away from the technology.

EARLY NETWORK PIONEERS

Despite the challenges of early network technology, pioneering companies built up networks almost as quickly as the products were brought to market. The benefits of networking people and their computers into more effective teams overshadowed the problems.

Companies like UPS, Coca-Cola Foods, and Manufacturers Hanover Trust Company (now Chemical Bank) were among the first to experience the power of a connected workplace. In each case, users reported productivity improvements after the installation of LANs.

By putting PCs on the desks of individual workers and connecting the computers through a network, businesspeople started working together differently. They shared information differently, coworked more projects, and armed with more analysis, seemed to make decisions faster. While cost savings from sharing resources did occur, the real benefits came from people finding better ways to do their jobs. These early, successful efforts to connect computers made headlines in the mid-1980s.

In the early days, LANs were also used because they could be assembled quickly. For example, The Democratic National Party, in 1988, marked the first use of networks in the hectic political process. Technicians installed ten LANs, hooking up more than three hundred PC workstations, to handle the 1988 convention. The networks ran several types of applications, from counting delegate votes to keeping track of party invitations. The system worked without a hitch.

That same year, the ABC television network (not to be confused with a computer network) tied together 126 PCs in a LAN to cover the Olympic games. The LAN helped coordinate everything from athletes' statistics to travel arrangements. ABC also maintained a video library of twenty thousand tapes for quick retrieval and on-air use.

Network technology went to war in 1991 during Operation Desert Shield and Desert Storm. Such heavy reliance on computer power in military conflicts was previously unheard of, and though it's hard to say that computers won the war, many credit the military's quick access to information as a major influence in the outcome.

LESSONS LEARNED

Networking technology served as a platform from which many different applications grew. Previously, computer systems like minicomputers followed one specific task, such as processing a certain type of data or processing words.

The practice of one computer/one application had interesting results. In some companies, the sheer number of computer terminals made it impossible for anyone to sit at a desk. For example, workers in a Houston-based oil company took pictures of their desks and showed them to their management to make them understand the difficulties. Some desks contained as many as four terminals — one for access to the company mainframe, one for the department accounting system, one for the database, and one for the personal computer.

With PC-based LANs, a worker could run all the applications needed on a PC that was connected to the company CPU. It certainly cleaned up desk space.

Certain LAN applications, namely electronic mail (e-mail), also cleaned up the phone lines by providing another way to contact people than telephone tag.

Early networks also put vast amounts of data and information within easy reach of people who needed it to make better decisions. As workers learned to share files, spreadsheets, reports, and databases with each other, many were able, for the first time, to get to the information that helped them make smart recommendations or decisions. This, then, was what the early attempts at networking taught the business world: Connecting people to information and to each other makes them work smarter.

Today's Networks

The computer networking industry can be measured in dog years. Since the first signs of popularity in the mid-1980s, LAN technology has already progressed through several generations. Most business-oriented networks were originally designed as solutions for people in workgroups. The average network consisted of one server (or master PC) that provided file storage and print services for about ten to twelve personal computers.

Today, there's nothing local about LANs. Servers can host hundreds of users from a single location. Most organizations that build LANs are really building enterprise computing networks that span not only the local workgroup, but the entire organization, and because organizations are not always located in one physical place anymore, these networks have been expanded with special equipment, such as hubs, bridges, routers, and switches, which tie together LANs with not-so-local networks. Similarly, as the business world embraces the global Internet, more and more organizations discover their networks are part of a global computing environment.

The software that directs the activities of a network, known as network operating systems (NOS), have matured to support a wide variety of configuration needs. For example, NetWare 4.x has been demonstrated hosting up to two thousand users on a single server. Users can share printers, files, and even applications across the network. Realistically, however, most networks today consist of several servers that are optimized to either perform certain tasks or handle the needs of certain users. In that case, the NOS must give an aura of transparency to the users. The user shouldn't know or care exactly what server he or she has accessed. Instead, the user only expects appropriate access to system resources, files, and applications.

LANs by Other Names

Over the short history of network computers, LANs have taken on more than one name and definition. Table 1.1 lists some of the other acronyms that have grown from original LAN technology.

New acronyms often spring up. We the authors coined terms for two more emerging types of networks: TANs and FANs. TANs are *tiny area networks* that connect the computers in very small offices with perhaps two to five PCs. FAN stands for *family area network*. These networks are emerging as families begin to buy more than one PC per household. By the year 2000, for example, PCs are expected to be found in half of all households in the United States, and almost half of those households will have more than one computer. In fact, many families are already approaching a ratio of one PC per person.

Justifying Business Networks

Businesses have many justifications for using LANs. These include reduced cost, higher worker productivity, and smaller increases in overhead during growth periods. Increased productivity is the most common justification. With today's acceptance of information technology in the workplace, many companies have abandoned cost-justification requirements for the existence of the network. Managers feel that building a LAN is simply a requirement of doing business. The PC connected to the network is a common, company-issue item, much like a desk, chair, and telephone.

TABLE 1.1	ACRONYM	MEANING
Network Acronyms	LAN	Local area network — Refers to a network that services a work group or department within an organization.
	WAN	Wide area network — Two or more LANs that are housed in physically different spaces. A WAN can exist when LANs are connected across different towns, states, time zones, or countries.
	CAN	Campus area network — A network of two or more LANs that span several buildings in the same physical location, such as universities, office parks, or large companies with several nearby buildings. CANs are usually connected with wires (copper or fiber-optic) or without wires, through microwave technology or laser repeaters.
	MAN	Metropolitan area network — Two or more LANs connected within a few miles. MANs commonly extend across public roads, highways, or external areas, so they're usually connected wirelessly. Sometimes microwave dishes can be used if there is a line of sight between buildings.
	GAN	Global area network — Many LANs around the world connected together.

LANs are also less costly than stand-alone computers. For example, support for commonly used individual software applications, such as word processors, spreadsheets, databases, and presentation creators, is more cost effective on a network. For stand-alone computing, a business organization would spend hundreds of dollars per PC buying the software, and a similar amount paying for annual upgrades. The same goes for the purchase and maintenance charges associated with individual printers, copy machines, fax machines, modems, and scanners, just to name a few. Add to that the labor charges for technicians to maintain all of the disparate computerized devices. Some experts estimate that 70 percent of the cost of owning technology falls into support.

A network reduces cost. Rather than several dissimilar software applications on each PC, each PC can share a master copy of the same suite of applications from the network (barring licensing restrictions). When upgrades arrive, the master copy, not each individual PC, receives the upgrade; consequently, labor costs for installation are reduced.

Networks also enable workers to share office hardware. For instance, rather than have scanners (or any other peripheral) for every individual PC, one scanner can be accessible through the network to all PCs. Money is thereby saved on maintenance costs as well as paper, because network scanners can distribute documents through e-mail systems to everyone in your office more efficiently than passing out stapled reports.

From a cost analysis point of view, perhaps the largest gain by networking computers is in freeing up employees' time to accomplish more work. A network can cut down on the time employees spend attending to the copy machine, sharing CD-ROM applications from a single PC, or linking up different word processor applications to churn out consistent reports. Less time spent dealing with tedious processes begets more time to accomplish important work. This means more value for the salary dollar.

Evolution of Network Uses

After deciding that the figurative and literal cost of a network is justifiable, it is time to choose a network configuration. To do this, it is helpful to understand how networks have evolved, so you can see where your company or organization fits in.

Ever since people started moving work away from the big iron mainframes, networks have expanded in usage and complexity. It began as a simple way to share files and print services in a workgroup, but network-connected PCs have evolved into nodes on large corporate networks that sometimes connect millions of computers both publicly (Internet) or privately (intranet).

FILE AND PRINT SERVICES NETWORKS

The original network plan, file and print service is where it all began. A single PC stores work through an NOS. The NOS creates the connection to various PCs and peripherals spread out through the office or enterprise (many offices). Different NOSs are available from a number of companies, including Novell NetWare, IBM OS/2, and Microsoft NT and LAN Manager, just to name a few.

Printers, fax machines, voice mail, scanners, and the like can be linked between two PCs or hundreds. The distances vary from a few feet in a small office using a

LAN to hundreds of miles using a WAN. The server (the single PC that runs the NOS) is usually expensive at the outset but pays for itself in worker productivity and the increased functionality of existing peripherals.

Sometimes, however, the complexity and expense of dedicated servers is overkill for small businesses. In an effort to provide for the *small office/home office* (SOHO) market as well as for those with a lower out-of-pocket start-up migration path, *peer-to-peer networking* was developed as an alternate NOS.

SMALL OFFICE COMPUTING

While the rise in file and print service networks was skyrocketing, so too were the numbers of small and home-based businesses. This statistic, combined with rapidly falling prices for PCs and their counterparts, created a market for an NOS specifically for SOHOs. Peer-to-peer networking is for those who need to share files and printers and pass e-mail, but do not need the processing power of the server-based network.

Peer-to-peer networking provides SOHOs with the advantages of larger networks without the associative costs of dedicating a PC as a server. The only significant expenditure is for the necessary wiring and NIC. Commonly available peer-to-peer NOSs include Novell Personal NetWare, Microsoft Windows for Workgroups, and AppleTalk.

During the evolution of these different NOSs, the increase in power and decrease in price of PCs and their related hardware gave many companies the opportunity to save costs in both real estate and utility overhead by encouraging people to work at home.

REMOTE ACCESS

With modem speeds exceeding 28,800bps it is no wonder *telecommuting* is one of the fastest growing segments of business productivity today. Telecommuting means, essentially, to work from home yet still be connected to the office network. This is accomplished through specialized software and modems which create a simulation of the desktop at work on the desktop at home.

There are three basic methods to maintain office connectivity. The primary one is e-mail. Typically an e-mail server stationed at the office has an attached modem that allows for dialing in and transferring mail from the home PC. Thus, any e-mail (or appointments or schedules) received from coworkers are downloaded to the home PC when the user dials in.

The second method is through remote control. A PC at the office serves as a host to the remote PC (the one at home). Once the two machines are connected over the phone lines, the remote PC can do and see everything that the host PC can.

The third dial-up connection for telecommuting workers is called remote node, which enables a remote PC to use all of the resources on the office LAN as if it were actually at the office. This includes file, application, and printer access.

Prime examples of companies taking advantage of telecommuting include computer industry help desks, sales staff from all industries, and medical personnel that must alternate between clinics while maintaining access to the computer resources of the main hospital.

Companies utilize telecommuting to save the rental costs of office space, enjoy higher worker productivity, and decrease commute time. Because employees benefit by spending more time with families and the companies benefit by trimming their overhead, the number of companies connecting to a corporate network remotely is on the rise and will continue to grow.

The increased use of remote connectivity technology has led in part to the incredible growth of the Internet and World Wide Web.

THE INTERNET

The *Internet* is the global network that has taken the software, marketing, and business world by storm. Millions of PCs, thousands of networks, all connected by a single communication means that is as simplistic in nature as our telephone numbering system. The Internet can be thought of as an extension of the file and print services and peer-to-peer LANs that permeate the landscape of the business world — with one hundred times the available information and accessibility, twenty-four hours a day, seven days a week.

Every topic known to humanity can be found on the Internet. It has become the driving force behind the computer industry in the last two years, and barring any breakthrough technology, will continue to be for at least the remainder of the decade.

For example, it is estimated that if current trends continue, there could be close to one hundred million people worldwide with access to the Internet by the year 2000.

The *World Wide Web* (WWW) is the graphical user interface to the Internet in much the same way that Microsoft Windows is to a PC. Don't be fooled — the Internet is not just a place for the technically savvy computer geek. All major product vendors from Sony to General Motors have sites on the WWW, as well as normally paper-based publications such as *Time* magazine and *The Wall Street Journal.* Many companies are even using it to lower their costs in other areas. For example, in 1996, overnight delivery companies created web pages that enabled customers to track their packages based on their tracking number, thereby significantly reducing the number of calls to their 1-800 lines.

Other burgeoning Internet-related technologies include real-time conversations with anyone in the world (without long distance charges), video teleconferences, and secure banking and financial transactions, as well as an endless supply of demographic data for every category in existence.

What makes the Internet so appealing? Its accessibility. It is not linked to any one type of PC or software product. Any type of PC (Intel, RISC, or Macintosh) running any operating system (UNIX, Windows, System 7) can access the Internet.

And, as a consequence of the simplistic yet powerful features that make up the Internet, corporations are now developing and refining their own version of the Internet, called *intranets.*

INTRANETS

An *intranet* is a scaled-down version of the Internet. It is used primarily for the employees of a company who are spread out geographically or spend a lot of time traveling. By using the principles of the Internet, such as web browsers and e-mail, corporations can provide access to all aspects of their resources to their users.

Intranets sprung up almost overnight, as an important part of corporate computing. Researchers at Boston Research Group estimate that early in 1994 fewer than 11 percent of large business organizations had an intranet. By 1996 that number had risen to over 50 percent, and as the number of large corporations increase, small- to mid-sized firms are also finding the benefits of putting people together on networks.

A key reason for companies to join the intranet generation is the ease of implementation. Intranets have become the cyberspace equivalent of water coolers for getting the news, views, and clues about company activity.

Technically, intranets are secured by private lines rather than run across the same network as the Internet. For example, the sales force headquartered in Houston can access marketing material headquartered in London through real-time interaction across entirely secure lines that are controlled by the corporation itself. Thus, company information such as phone lists that were previously only available on paper and may never be up to date are now obtainable by the click of a mouse and never more than a week or so old. In addition, scheduling meetings, seminars, vacations, and conferences can be coordinated through a single interface without ever touching the telephone to call someone or worrying about time zone conflicts, because all the information is truly right at your fingertips.

Summary

When all is said and done, the benefits of networking computers far outweigh both the material and opportunity costs. Networks based on LAN technology let people connect, communicate, and share through their computers. When you consider the benefits of optimizing people, the decision to network becomes compelling.

CHAPTER 2

Networked Resources

Some people like to think of PC networks in the same way as condominium ownership. If you own a condominium apartment, you own the interior walls of your apartment and an undivided interest in the rest of the facility. Generally a management company maintains the hallways outside your door, grounds, and facilities. While you are free to decorate your living room any way you choose, you don't have complete control over the remainder of the building and grounds. You share the pool, exercise room, lobby, and other amenities with other condominium owners.

Similarly, with a PC network users are free to work on any independent application — spreadsheet, word processing, database, e-mail, and so on — as needed. A well-designed network confines most application processing to the local PC with little impact on the rest of the users of the network. To print to a network printer, send e-mail, query a large database, or store files on a network disk, however, users must use a shared resource — a network device. They don't have complete control over how these devices are set up and configured, and usually leave the maintenance and upkeep tasks to a network management organization, such as an information services department.

This chapter, the first of two devoted to how networks work, focuses attention on how networks handle shared devices and resources. It covers the fundamentals in both theory and execution.

Starting with a brief description of how networked devices operate, we lay the groundwork for understanding what and how devices are connected. The *Open System Interconnection Model* (OSI Model), developed by the *International Standards Organization* (ISO), sets the standard for services that LANs should provide. Today, most networking devices adhere to the principles, if not the exact letter, of the OSI Model.

Next, we discuss what is required to connect a device to a network, focusing on how devices are recognized by the network. Finally, we turn to examples of shared network devices to give you an idea of some of what equipment available.

Understanding the OSI Model from the Bottom Up

In 1977, the ISO started a process of defining standards for network products. This standardization guide, the OSI Model, enabled network hardware and software vendors to conform to specifics that would enable most of their products to work together.

As illustrated in Figure 2.1, the OSI Model has seven layers that explain logically and sequentially how computers communicate to one another on the network.

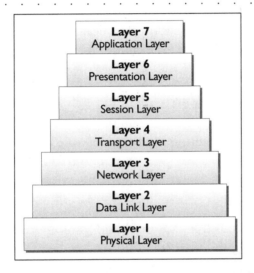

The model can be thought of as a seven-layer cake or stairs like those leading up to a pyramid. You may have also noticed that as you move from layer one to layer seven, the steps get progressively smaller.

In terms of priority, the requirements of each layer must be met from the bottom to the top. For example, it doesn't help to implement a signaling scheme (layer two) or a data link (layer three) unless your cables are connected (layer one). This model provides the building blocks for every network today. Understanding where activity takes place will help you understand why certain network components work.

THE PHYSICAL LAYER

Layer one includes all of the communicating hardware devices on the network. For example, all the specifications for how the NICs and serial ports for modems communicate are contained in the OSI's Physical layer. Since cabling is required for these devices to communicate, all of the wiring, connectors, and rules concerning how cable should be placed are included here.

THE DATA LINK LAYER

The Data Link layer addresses how each signaling scheme, such as contention or token passing, determines how and when data travels and arrives. It also shows how errors (when signals don't arrive) are dealt with. Ethernet, Token Ring, and ARCnet are just a few of the items included in this section.

THE NETWORK LAYER

Sometimes large networks have more than one signaling scheme transmitting across the wires. For example, many large corporate networks have both Ethernet and Token Ring data links. The third layer of the OSI Model, the Network layer, addresses this potential conflict by providing rules on how disparate signals should communicate.

THE TRANSPORT LAYER

For both large and small networks the Transport layer is paramount. It's at this stage that all of the various network protocols communicate their packets of data to all the different nodes of the network.

THE SESSION LAYER

Layer five is where the user finally has meaningful interaction with the network. The Session layer is named as such since it is at this point that the user establishes a session with the network by logging in a user name and password where they are then verified by the network operating system's various security measures.

THE PRESENTATION LAYER

The Presentation layer supports the conversion of data from the form in which it is sent over the network into a representation that the computer understands. For example, *external data representation* (XDR) use ensures that an Apple computer and a Sun computer can both understand each other despite the fact that, internally, each computer represents data differently.

Included in this layer are compression algorithms, which make files smaller so they take up less network traffic space. An analogy would be the ability to press a button on a Chevy Suburban and shrink it to the size of a Toyota Corolla, but still leaving its six-passenger capacity, color TV, CD changer, full-size spare tire, and leather seats.

THE APPLICATION LAYER

The top of the OSI Model is the application layer. Based on the name, you might think of software, but actually this layer deals with print services, database queries, and e-mail. This is where everything starts.

Connecting Devices to a Network

To connect any device to a network, the device needs to be physically connected to the network wire, enabling the device to send out an electrical signal alerting other network resources to its existence. Following the bottom layers of the OSI Model, layers one and two must be in place before anything else will work.

To a network, at this primitive level, all devices are created equal. Whether it is a PC, a printer, a server, or a connection to the mainframe — the network sees it as a node. The importance of the node isn't determined until later.

The device, such as a PC or printer, may have an NIC physically inside it, or it may be part of another device (such as a printer connected to a PC) that has an NIC. Network interface capabilities come pre-installed in some computers and printers. There's usually a built-in port on the back of the unit, as shown in Figure 2.2. If you need to add networking capabilities, you must purchase an NIC and add it to the device. The NIC must be designed to work with that device — for example, an NIC for a PC won't work in a printer. Also, not all NICs work in the expansion slots of a PC. Double-check before buying one.

As seen in Figure 2.3, an NIC is a piece of hardware that transmits signals, proclaiming its existence across a network . If you imagine the NIC as a homing signal, you've got the right idea. In addition to the signal the NIC sends out, it also has a predetermined address that makes it unique from any other device on the network. The number is actually referred to as a *MAC address,* which is discussed in Chapter 4.

Some printers and other devices intended to run on networks come with pre-installed ports for your network.

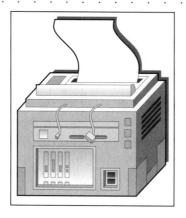

A network interface card fits into such devices as PCs, printers, and modems.

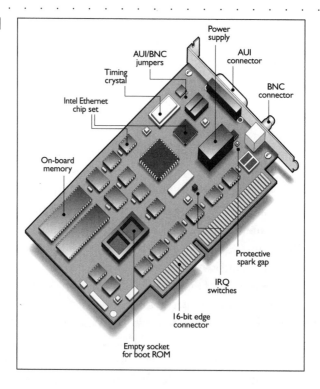

In addition to the NIC, a device needs an NOS to make itself visible to other devices on the network. You could imagine the NOS as a language. Network devices may recognize a newly added device, but won't understand it unless it speaks the same language they do.

The next part of the equation is purely subjective — naming the devices. Each resource that is shared on a network must have a distinct name so that it is identifiable to the NOS. For example, Susie's hard drive in a peer-to-peer network could be called "susies_driveC," just as the 4th floor LaserJet printer could be called "4th_floor_laserjet." This may seem redundant, but giving shared resources names detailing their physical location makes for quick work if problems arise.

Examples of Shared Resources and Devices

The advantages of sharing resources across the network include, but are not limited to, decreased cost of ownership for software applications (only one package has to be purchased for everyone to use), lower maintenance fees on peripherals (several people can share one printer rather than everyone having their own), and most importantly, the ability to create data that everyone can use on the network (such as a spreadsheet for the budget), rather than having multiple copies.

FILE SHARING

This is the holy grail of networking. Having the ability to distribute a document, like the budget spreadsheet mentioned earlier, to a central location on the network, where all the appropriate people can access it and use the information without changing the original, is what data sharing is all about. Related to file sharing is application sharing, which is what software applications consist of: many, many files working in concert to perform a certain function, like word-processing. Since the crux of network software applications are covered in the following chapter, it is sufficient to say that sharing applications across the network is not only cheaper due to their one-time fee, but also because it costs less for someone to support and manage than having multiple copies of different software applications on each person's PC.

DRIVE SHARING (FIXED DISKS AND CD-ROMS)

Your next question should be how these files and applications are shared. Aside from the NIC and NOS discussed earlier, files are shared on different types of drives. The most common are hard drives that can hold over 1 *gigabyte* (1 billion bytes) of information, CD-ROMs that carry around 600 *megabytes* (1 million bytes), or floppy drives that can generally only carry 1.44 megabytes (although higher capacity floppy drives are becoming more prevalent). These drives are shared through networked PCs, servers, and CD-ROM towers, which are the devices that actually contain the NICs. Another important type of shared drive is the tape drive. Tape drives are used on a network to create backups of the data and applications installed on hard drives. Tape drives, too, are more efficient when shared between many PCs rather than having one on each PC individually.

VOICE MAIL ON THE LAN

Rather than rely on third-party service providers for voice mail, with a network you can have, control, and monitor all aspects of it yourself. This opens many doors for information tracking. For example, with your own voice mail server, numbers dialed out can be recorded for auditing procedures, your phone answering system can be automated to page users when voice mail is left, and long distance charges can be tracked through the use of codes for each user.

NETWORK SCANNERS

Network scanners also aid in improving communication by disseminating information more efficiently — transferring paper-based documents to electronic ones. These network scanners enable you to share electronic versions of snail mail (postal mail), incoming faxes, magazine articles, and the like. Through software, individual electronic copies of the information can be sent via e-mail to all pertinent users or stored in a single location on the network shared drive. Either way, paper, and therefore money, is saved.

SHARED MODEMS

A great help in worker productivity is the network pool of modems. From a user's workstation, through various proprietary software, anyone on the network can use pagers, access online services for research, query bulletin board databases, and configure a PC for dialing in from home. Having a pool of modems, rather than a modem on every PC, cuts down on costs. Only a few modems have to be purchased and everyone uses the same communications software. Some have the ability to redirect open serial ports on workstations to communicate the link across standard network wires, and others simply serve as terminal-based links to a modem to the outside world. Another huge benefit is security.

SHARED FAX

Sharing a fax machine through a network may seem redundant, considering most offices share a single, centrally located fax machine anyway. However, the amount of time wasted printing documents from the computer, carrying them to the fax machine, and then waiting for the connection to be made and processed is significant.

A LAN-based fax machine enables everyone on the network to send faxes from their workstations. That means no printing is required, tons of money is saved on paper, and worker productivity moves up a notch.

No, we're not referring to a fax/modem on every PC. You can install a fax server, which operates much like a network printer. It accepts and processes each item in the order received, with the additional capability of sending a confirmation message back to the user. You can also redial on busy signals, and you can even have more than one phone line attached to the fax server.

NETWORK PRINTING

Of course, sometimes the printed word just can't be beat. Next to sharing files across the LAN, sharing printers has got to be one of the most advantageous benefits of networking. Since printers can cost anywhere from hundreds to thousands of dollars, placing one on the network for everyone in the office to use is definitely cost efficient. Plus, there are so many different kinds of printers now, that it is possible to have one of each and still allow all the users to access them.

For example, there are printers that are specifically designed to produce color. Others output several pages per minute in high quality. Some even create the complex engineering diagrams typically produced by computer-aided design software.

There are many companies that produce network-capable printers, such as Hewlett-Packard, Lexmark, Epson, Panasonic, and Tektronix. Although more costly, the printers that come with the NIC already installed are the simplest to configure on the network because they typically use their own software to configure themselves.

Summary

With all of the potential ways to share information on a network, the increases in communication and decreases in cost seem almost boundless. Each new generation of technology presents tools and options for sharing or individualizing resources, so your configuration decisions are likely to change over time.

CHAPTER 3

Networked Applications

Picture this: A fax comes through the centrally located fax machine for a department — a document relevant to the entire company. The department administrative assistant scans it into a network scanner and forwards it to everyone across the network through electronic mail. Or, after scanning it, she places it into a shared directory on the network and notifies everyone of its existence through a single voice mail message which is replicated to all the relevant personnel. Because of the importance of the information received, she also tags the voice mail message to page each of the recipients so that they are instantly aware of the need to check their voice mail.

Once the message has been received and viewed, managers decide that a meeting should be called. Instead of calling the participants of the meeting, however, the administrative assistant uses an electronic scheduling program with links to e-mail to reserve the conference room, overhead projector, and coffee bar. Since all the participants' electronic schedules are available on the system, the administrative assistant can easily find a time clear for tomorrow afternoon. She sends a meeting request, marks each schedule accordingly, and awaits their confirmation. To help everyone prepare for the meeting, she pastes electronic copies of the documents to be discussed to the appointment e-mail so that it can be edited and approved online. She also creates a quick presentation with the documents and files it on the network, so the managers can pull it up on their networked laptop computers and review it during the meeting. She includes the scanned images of the original documents so that the people in the meeting can review it online using the PC and projector in the conference room.

Did you notice that the only piece of paper mentioned in this scenario was the original? While we'd hesitate to say that a networked office is a paperless office, it may well be a "less paper" office. When information travels over the network there is less need to use paper, and the process of "print out, make copies, and file in cabinet" turns into a matter of "read on-screen, e-mail to others, and file on disk."

Today's networking technology enables almost any office to operate as we just described. People, products, and processes are all linked together to make business more efficient. That is the goal of networking.

Almost any computing application can be networked, whether it needs to be or not. Some applications, however, cannot exist without networks. These are the applications we discuss first. If networking promotes sharing, and a big part of sharing involves messages, then e-mail should top the list of important network applications.

In a network user's view, e-mail becomes part of the fabric of networking. No other application brings functionality quite as fast or quite as far-reaching. Beyond e-mail, applications such as scheduling, bulletin boards, or groupware, round out the ability for people to use networks for sharing.

Electronic Mail

For many people, e-mail turns into one of the most important (and most popular) applications available on a computer. E-mail provides people with a way to communicate, escaping the constraints of time, space, and location. Its business benefits can be so far-reaching that Intel's energetic president, Andy Grove, once quipped that e-mail is a "killer application" because once you've got it, you can't live without it. Lots of e-mail advocates agree.

Network users can communicate information via e-mail when they need to and receive answers when it is convenient. E-mail puts an end to time-robbing phone tag and paper-chasing memos that circulate around until, forgotten, they find a final resting place in an already too-full file drawer. (Even though electronic in-boxes can get pretty full, many e-mail systems sort mail automatically, so your messages are better organized than they'd be as a stack of memos on your desk.)

HOW E-MAIL WORKS

In most mail systems (electronic or manual), there is a post office to store and forward the mail, a mailbox for each person, and a vehicle to deliver mail. In good electronic mail systems, there are extra conveniences, such as the ability to attach another file (a spreadsheet, document, or other information) to your message, as seen in Figure 3.1; the option of requiring a return receipt notice; and the possibility of storing your mail in folders, which can be shared with others. With a specially equipped multimedia PC, you can even add voice annotations to your e-mail.

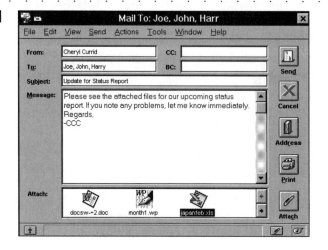

Here is an e-mail message created in Novell GroupWise that includes several attached files. Notice that the icons for the programs that created the documents, as well as the document name, appear in the attachment window.

ESTABLISHING E-MAIL ROLES

Because the computers do most of the work, with e-mail you won't need a fleet of trucks to move the mail, a team of sorters to sort it, a mail carrier to deliver it, or clerks to file it after it's read.

To establish a successful e-mail system, you do need to define roles for an e-mail *administrator* and a group of mail *users*.

The mail administrator sets up the system and periodically performs maintenance chores. For networks of less than fifty people, this is not a difficult or time-consuming task, but for networks with hundreds of users, it can easily turn into a full time job.

Most e-mail administration tasks include the following duties:

▸ Creating the post office

▸ Assigning post office passwords

▸ Adding/changing/deleting mailboxes and users

▸ Monitoring disk space on the post office

▶ Backing up files on the post office

▶ Maintaining the e-mail system files

▶ Troubleshooting problems

Also, the tasks of training and providing everyday end-user support must be done. Sometimes these duties also rest with the e-mail administrator, while in other organizations, training and support comes from another area within the company.

People must *use* an e-mail system in order to get any benefit from it. This is a key point. Some individuals and groups may have to make adjustments in their organizational culture to get the full benefits of e-mail. E-mail users will have to check into the e-mail system frequently, reply promptly to their mail, delete unnecessary messages, and adjust their personal habits to accommodate e-mail's advantages.

BEST PRACTICES FOR E-MAIL IMPLEMENTATION

Since each e-mail package has its own idiosyncratic methods of installation, this section focuses on best practices in general terms for successful e-mail implementation.

The first consideration is disk space. As messages are sent and forwarded between users, disk space is quickly absorbed. Some users will not use more than 100K of disk space for their mailboxes, while others will use much more. Given an average work environment, 1MB per user is a safe number to start with if your network users are unfamiliar with e-mail. If your e-mail users are experienced, or if they expect eventually to link into other e-mail systems, you should allocate 2MB per user from the very beginning. These disk space guidelines are for the post office data only, and do not figure in the amount you'll need for the various e-mail server software and other related applications.

E-mail packages distinguish users by their mailbox name, which must be unique for every user. Before you add the first user, you should establish conventions for making user names and mailbox names unique. Many mail administrators fall into the trap of using everyone's first or last name as their e-mail address. We suggest you don't. Some first names are so common that duplicates will likely occur. It is best to use the first initial followed by the last name. In addition to identifying post office users when it comes to administration, their Internet e-mail addresses will be easier for them to remember. Many e-mail packages support network names as well, and so make things easier for the administrator and users alike because there is only one name to remember.

While we're on the subject of naming conventions, the post office name should also be considered especially as it relates to Internet mail. Remember, simple is always better. Regardless of the e-mail package used, when naming and setting up the e-mail post office, try to keep it limited to the name of the company. Complex Internet e-mail addresses only spell confusion for users, too much space taken up on business cards, and hassles for the network/e-mail administrator.

E-MAIL ETIQUETTE

Regular users of e-mail develop their own set of customs. Many e-mail messages take on a much less formal tone than traditional business correspondence. The main purpose is to get a thought across, so messages are often very short. E-mail users also frequently use abbreviations and *emoticons,* which are combinations of symbols that convey facial expressions. (You have to turn your head to the side to see them as they're intended). For a list of the most common abbreviations and emoticons, see Table 3.1.

TABLE 3.1	ABBREVIATION	MEANING
Common E-mail Abbreviations	BTW	By the way
	FWIW	For what it's worth
	FYI	For your information
	IMHO	In my humble opinion
	IOW	In other words
	:-)	Happy smiley face
	;-)	Wink
	:-o	Surprised face
	:-(	Sad face
	\<grin\>	(Sheepish) grin
	\<xxx\>	Sigh or snarl

E-MAIL AND THE PAPERLESS TRAIL

If you consider that today's networked office is one with less paper flowing, then e-mail is a critical application. A good e-mail system can provide a paperless trail for documentation of any kind. As shown in Figure 3.2, a good e-mail system can help you track where your document is, when it was delivered, and when it was opened.

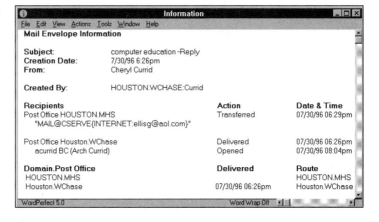

FIGURE 3.2

This screen from the outbox of GroupWise appears when an e-mail is opened by the addressee.

Consider this example: Marketing gets three new employees in one week. As the designated human resources representative, your duty is to get these people acclimated to the company through mandatory training, parking, W-2 forms, etc. With e-mail not only can you create a traceable dialog with each of the prospective departments, but you don't have to rely on "telephone tag. With e-mail, you send it and it's there. It's also traceable, meaning that if for any reason a discrepancy arises and it appears that a ball has been dropped somewhere along the process, you have an electronic paper trail detailing and covering every single exchange that has taken place with all the various individuals involved. Best of all, this paper trail is not misfiled in some rickety old filing cabinet that never has been organized to begin with. It is safely stored in an electronic folder residing in your e-mail basket, which is backed up every night.

Group Scheduling Electronically

Like e-mail, a computer-assisted appointment book can become an indispensable tool for today's network member. Manual appointment systems take too much time, are inefficient, and frequently cause people to resort to keeping multiple calendars. How many times have you seen a busy executive with a leather-bound calendar on his desk and a secretary with an almost identical copy? Everything is fine until the phone starts ringing and the schedule starts changing. Before you know it, the calendars get out of sync and nobody is sure what to do, where to go, or when to do it. The problem becomes worse with more people. Getting together for team meetings or bringing in new team members can be a major ordeal to coordinate.

Do electronic scheduling programs really make things easier? After all, there have been scheduling programs available on computers for a number of years. It hasn't seemed to help that much.

The problem with "first generation" computer calendar programs was that they were oriented to the personal user on unconnected computers. This simply doesn't add much to an office environment where people work together. The solution starts with software that is designed for people to share information.

WHAT YOU CAN DO WITH ELECTRONIC SCHEDULES

Electronic schedules of any variety serve three primary functions, all centered around managing and maintaining your projects and day-to-day work. The functions include appointments which maintain your calendar and a planner that schedules meetings, group events, and tasks.

Schedulers typically go where you do. You can work with them on your desktop computer or export files to a laptop or pocket-style computer. This is a great convenience for busy professionals who work both in and out of the office.

Network scheduling programs typically interact closely with their proprietary e-mail system, so users can share schedules and access copies of each other's schedule information. As shown in Figure 3.3, a good scheduling application will let you look into the availability of several people at one time. This is called a *busy search,* and can save a lot of time.

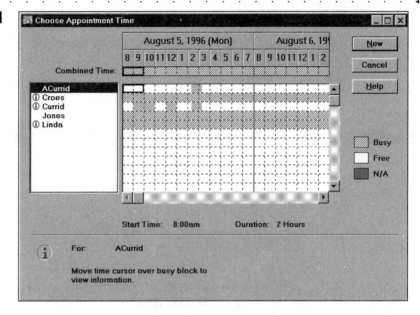

FIGURE 3.3

A GroupWise screen showing the availability of five people for a meeting

Security is compensated for by granting different levels of access to different members of your organization. For example, you can allow some people to make your appointments for you; permit others to just view your appointments; allow still others to just see whether you are busy at certain times, but not your activities; and prevent others from seeing anything at all.

You can also use the program to schedule use of common resources, such as conference rooms, audio-visual equipment, or even other computers.

HOW ELECTRONIC SCHEDULING WORKS WITH E-MAIL

Typically, electronic schedules and e-mail work hand in hand. For example, in Novell GroupWise, both functions come in the same package. Usually they share the post office directory list of names and the same users' passwords. When an appointment is made through a scheduler, typically an e-mail is sent through the network to the other attendees asking their response to the invitation.

Recall the scenario mentioned at the beginning of the chapter, with the administrative assistant organizing a meeting? How do you think the participants were all brought together? If each person on a network is using a group electronic scheduling package, then individual schedules are viewable by all. One look at all ten directors' schedules and a time can be found and a meeting set in minutes, rather than the hours normally given to playing phone tag. Don't forget about the problems typically associated with reserving a conference room, audio-visual equipment, or even PCs for presentations. All of these items can be placed into network scheduling software too. Some applications do a good job of putting all information on a single screen or printed page, as shown in Figure 3.4.

FIGURE 3.4

A view of projects, notes, appointments, and mail folders for one day

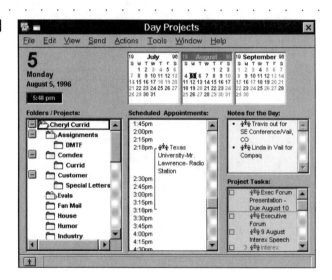

Groupware: When to Go Beyond E-mail

Fundamentally, there's a big difference between e-mail and groupware. E-mail is basically one-to-one messaging. Joe sends Sue an e-mail. Sue sends Joe a reply. Easy enough.

Of course e-mail can be expanded to share the message with many people. Let's say Joe sends Sue an e-mail and copies the marketing team. Sue sends Joe a reply and copies the marketing team. Basically, the conversation is still between Joe and Sue, but this time they send their messages in public. Carol and Carl can also provide their comments, and take the message to a completely different topic, but that's where e-mail tends to go awry. If Carol and Carl, Sam and Sandy all want to add their two cents worth, they should take their discussion to groupware.

A groupware discussion resembles an electronic bulletin board or a meeting without a moderator. It resembles many-to-many conversations. Everyone can participate, all at the same time or individually as new thoughts surface. Products like IBM's Lotus Notes or Attachmate's OpenMind started as group-oriented products.

The e-mail systems of today have conveniently stretched to accommodate the needs of groups by performing like bulletin boards. Imagine a set of electronic bulletin boards viewable on the computer screen at work. Each bulletin board is designated for a certain type of information. Company phone lists, medical plans, retirement plans, and upcoming social events can all be distributed and viewed on today's e-mail system. For example, specifically, how up-to-date is your company's employee phone and pager list? If it was centrally located within the e-mail bulletin board system, it could easily be updated daily.

The prior examples only address the internal workings of a company. There is an entire world out there, just waiting to be contacted, communicated with, or sold something. Anyone who has Internet-enabled electronic mail can communicate with anyone else who has the same technology.

Best of all, e-mail is a whole lot cheaper than the cost of a stamp, envelope, paper and the labor to put it together. The average postal letter in the United States costs $1.50 to $2.50 to create (including the cost of labor). An e-mail, by contrast, might cost as little as 50¢. It's more personal, too, because there is an etiquette involved in writing business e-mail.

Flip on the computer, pick the e-mail address of an acquaintance, and away you go. Want to add your comments to a group discussion? Just tap out your thoughts and push the send key. E-mail and groupware makes networking what it always should have been-easy.

Office Automation

While it is true that many applications don't require networks, all should be networkable, because the end product of most work must be shared with someone — the boss, colleagues, subordinates, customers, suppliers, and so on. Electronic documents are the way to go. In addition to electronically creating documents once done by hand, today's office automation software all work in conjunction with each other. In other words, numbers crunched in spreadsheets can be applied to charts and graphs in presentation software, as well as databases and word-processing documents. Furthermore, data from any of the applications can be imbedded into any of the other applications in the suite. The newest function of office software is for the creation of pages on the World Wide Web. Instead of sharing documents across the LAN or through e-mail, as mentioned earlier, they will be placed on controlled corporate intranet sites, which is covered in Chapter 5. Office automation *suites,* as they're called, typically include at least a word processor, spreadsheet, database, and graphics software used for presentations.

WORD PROCESSING

The year 1995 marked the end of an era for the typewriter when Smith-Corona filed for Chapter 11 reorganization. The once strong maker of dedicated, single function typewriters was among the last to go. The executioner? Word processing. Over the years, the versatility of word processors has increased to the point that an untrained person can now produce better documents in less time than a trained person on a typewriter.

Modern day word-processing programs have not only replaced the typewriter, but the specially trained typist too. With standard features such as spell checking, revision editing, tables, columns, and automatic outline and table of contents creation it is no wonder that word processors are one of the leading software packages purchased every year.

Word-processing software on a network has the added functionality of sharing documents in real time with coworkers for editing and collaborative creation, which saves time and money. For example, using standard templates, electronic highlighting, and notations in the margins, all on-screen, are possible without ever printing out the type-written page. Perhaps best of all, with a multitude of file formats in which to save a word-processing document (everything from Microsoft Word to basic text), your work can easily be shared with other companies or clients by attaching these files to e-mail messages just as you would through the office.

PRESENTATION SOFTWARE

Another way to enhance productivity is with presentation software. It produces multimedia presentations that can be run from your computer to a projection screen in a conference room. That's right — no more creating or paying for those expensive, frail transparencies. Plus, as an added benefit, most current presentation software enables you to display the presentation on a computer screen in front of a large group of people. The presentation never has to be printed to be used.

Networks expand the ease-of-use for presentations by making the files available on the network servers. They can be shared, edited by others, or sent via e-mail to another person or location.

SPREADSHEET SOFTWARE

A tool that fundamentally changed the world is the spreadsheet. Aside from giving people a quick way to add up numbers, it gave them the ability to perform countless what-if analyses in a short time. This leads to people making more informed decisions because they can look at a problem any number of ways.

Also, by compiling the numbers and statistics saved in a spreadsheet, the software can automatically create bar graphs, pie charts, and xy plots. Not to mention the fact that people can now retire their ledgers, calculators or, if any still exist, slide rules. A spreadsheet can do it all when it comes to numbers. Spreadsheet software, just to name a few features, can automatically add, subtract, divide, multiply, and perform statistical analysis and even actuaries.

Networks make spreadsheets more powerful by letting people share files and information. In the case of a spreadsheet with graphs, the individual user or someone else on the team can pull just the pertinent graphs into presentation software. In fact, users can create live links between the data and reports. Say for example Fred updates his quarterly estimates in a spreadsheet. When his boss wants to update her presentation, she can create a link to Fred's spreadsheet so that each time she pulls up her presentation she has the most current numbers.

DATABASES

For some people, data and analysis spreadsheets are too limiting. For instance, say a user needs to be able to query (search) for all the dates that a client has been late for payment, arranged quarter by quarter to view a trend. Database software can do all of that. Maybe your business is market or medical research. There is no easier tool with which to produce standard survey forms. These forms can be e-mailed to clients or put on a web site, and when returned, the data can be entered into the database for statistical analysis, trends, and even financial forecasting.

Database software is among the most powerful software on networks. Properly configured, a database lets people share and update records efficiently. Can you imagine an airline trying to assign seats from the ticket counter, reservations desk, and gate area without a real-time, multiuser, seat selection database? Sure it can be done, but not with nearly the same ease and accuracy as with a network.

Applications for the Network Administrator

Now back to the needs of a network administrator for a minute. You may be thinking, "If I have to manage a network with so many resources, PCs, and applications, how do I keep track of it all?" Easy. Look into the utilities and the network operating system itself. For example, with a NetWare 4.x network operating system, everything on the LAN can be efficiently tracked and maintained. The extensive database even includes a way to track where users sit and their phone numbers, departments, and titles. The database, called *NetWare Directory Services* (NDS), maintains all the information related to the network, including user access, printer specifications, file rights, and which user has supervisory access to manage all the resources. NDS also acts as a security guard by maintaining the strictest of access privileges. Thus, the company budget spreadsheet, while shareable on the network, is only viewable by those users with the correct access rights as determined by the network administrator and enforced by NDS. These enforceable rights include permitting admittance to use the various applications on the network as well. Detailed information about rights can be found in Chapter 12.

Should Every Application Be Networked?

While it isn't necessary for every single application to reside on network servers or shared disks, you should consider every application before dismissing it. When it comes to helping people share information, lowering the cost of licenses (when concurrent-use licenses are available), or simply finding the easiest way to centrally update and maintain software — networks look pretty attractive.

Networking applications usually help keep installation, support, and maintenance hassles to a minimum. Keep in mind, however, that individual products do vary. Some applications are written in such a manner that they constantly call sub-programs, which may cause too much traffic on an already busy network. In other cases, software installations are not network-friendly and force files to a local drive. It is best to read the package or contact the software maker's technical support desk if you are unsure.

Summary

Throughout this chapter, three recurring themes present themselves. First is sharing. Networks help people share their work, information, knowledge, and wisdom. Make sure you design your network strategy to share as much as possible. Second, applications should conform to standards. For the benefits to be realized, office automation standardization must take place. Unless end users are very mature and can support special configurations of their own software applications, it helps to choose one set of office automation tools and install them in the same manner, consistently. Third, before purchasing or upgrading, always remember to document and test, test, test software to verify that it will serve your needs.

CHAPTER 4

The Internet and Intranets

For fifty years, people could only dream of having a universal information source that put the world's knowledge within an arm's reach of desire. Today it's available, and for those who have the right connections, the path to endless information lies only a few mouse clicks away.

It's the Internet, and access to it is free — well, almost. Access costs actually vary widely based on your existing technology infrastructure. It may cost as little as a few hundred dollars for equipment, plus monthly charges for additional telephone lines and an Internet service provider (ISP). Or you could spend thousands to hundreds of thousands of dollars retrofitting your existing network to accommodate the new traffic. Once you do connect your company's LAN to the Internet, you and your colleagues can pursue either or both of two paths for traffic: marketing and learning.

The marketing path will lead you to assembling your organization's presence on the Internet. You'll want to stake your company's place in cyberspace, so to speak. For this, you'll need to assemble quite a few skilled workers, from artistic Web page designers to network engineers familiar with setting up servers, network gear, and communications options. Alternatively you can outsource most, if not all the work by using consultants to build your site and host it on someone else's computer. Cyberspace is a virtual world so nothing is location-dependent. For example, Web page designers don't care whether the host computer is across the hall or across the country. With the right communications in place, it doesn't matter.

The learning path takes you in a slightly different direction. If all your organization wants is to improve its ability to learn, you only need to concentrate on providing information access. Your technical architecture can be different, and you won't require an in-house server or a team of Web page creators. Instead, you'll focus on getting solid, reliable, high-speed access to all your colleagues all of the time. You should also help your colleagues find the right training and support for their individual information needs. Most professionals are excited to see the extensive — and inexpensive — research resources on the Internet. Most information there is free or low cost. But without a road map, people end up wasting more than they save by fumbling around using the wrong search engines or asking the wrong questions.

This chapter introduces the Internet and intranets (the homespun, in-house version for your organization's insiders). We start with a little history and define the necessary terms that you need to know about sources and resources. If you've been looking for a guide to the fundamentals of the Internet and World Wide Web *(the Web* or *WWW)*, then this chapter should give you a reference for how things work. If you are already familiar with the Internet and intranets, but want to know how to connect to it, then skip to "How to Access the Internet and the Web" towards the end of the chapter.

What Is the Internet?

While its root technology was developed during the cold war back in the 1950s and '60s, the Internet was hardly a household word before the early 1990s. Things just fell into place, and suddenly it was a modern day gold rush. As the initial stampede continues, people are trying to assess the Internet's value to business. Most likely, its ramifications won't be known for years.

If you've already started your journey into the online world, you've probably found the Internet to be an indispensable resource. Those just starting their trek may find the new frontier a bit daunting, but still remarkable.

The word *Internet* literally means *network of networks*. In itself, the Internet is comprised of thousands of smaller regional networks scattered throughout the globe. On any given day it connects roughly 40 million users in over 160 countries, and more are added daily.

Science-fiction writer Bruce Sterling describes the Internet as *functional anarchy*. It works, it functions, but it has no controls. No one owns the Internet, and though it has coordinators and groups to suggest standards, there's no real boss.

Some try to describe the Internet as a group of teenagers hanging out at the mall. Since they're all peers, no one member tells the others what to do. Despite occasional squabbles, they tend to stick together. What makes this mode of existence endure is this: funding. Thanks to their moms and dads, these kids have no worries. They can play, be curious, investigate, invest, or throw away the products of their activity. Creativity soars, as does the tab.

The Internet today is like that giddy mall-crawling group. It is a sociotechnical entity that evolved because no one had to worry about paying for it. For the Internet, the parent was the U.S. government under the perceived threat of the space race forty years ago. It was the Department of Defense who sponsored the *Advanced Research Projects Agency* (ARPA) and gave it the charter, funding, and the challenge to invent an indestructible network. And that's exactly what it did. ARPA built a network designed so well, it now carries millions of times more activity than those wild kids (err... designers) ever imagined it could.

The Internet's architecture has no center, hub, or master. Theoretically, no single outage could take it down. If something broke (or was bombed), the network would fix itself and messages would simply find another route, as shown in Figure 4.1.

▶ • ◀

FIGURE 4.1

The Internet was built so that no single point of failure would disrupt all communications. If any host goes down, the traffic is rerouted.

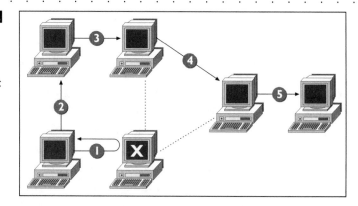

Previously, the Internet existed as a product of the government, universities and selected companies that worked on government projects. The network was built to share resources, never go down, and move information from anywhere to anywhere.

That's where the cosmic-collision theory comes in. In a few short years, the efforts of many teams working under no single master came together.

Among the events:

- ▶ Opening the Internet to commercial sites

- ▶ Development of *Wide Area Information Servers* (WAIS), making information electronically searchable

- ▶ Upgrade of the Internet backbone so it supports speeds of 44.7MBps

- ▶ Establishment of high-profile sites like the U.S. White House

- ▶ First Internet audio multicast (March 1992) followed by video multicast (November 1992)

▸ Creation of the InterNIC in 1993 to provide specific Internet services; namely, directory and database services, registration services, and information services

▸ Release of Mosaic software in 1993 by the National Center for Supercomputing Applications in Illinois released Mosaic software (a browser that allowed PCs and other desktop computers to access the Web with a graphical point and click tool)

NOTE **President Bill Clinton is the first U.S. president to have a public e-mail address, `president@whitehouse.gov`. Vice President Al Gore can be contacted at `vice-president@whitehouse.gov`, and First Lady Hillary Clinton's e-mail is `root@whitehouse.gov`.**

Once commercial sites were granted access to the Internet, the number of Internet hosts increased greatly — by over four hundred percent over the past two years.

What Is the Web?

To help differentiate the Internet and the World Wide Web, it helps to think of them as two different parts of the same object. The Internet refers to the physical structure of millions of computers cabled together worldwide. It's the hardware, topology, and technical part. The Web is the content — at least in terms of the snazzy graphics, colorful text, and hyperlinked structure.

Given the Web's early enthusiastic acceptance, many people believe its rapid growth provides yet another early warning sign of its potential to change the way people work, learn, and live. Several organizations have taken the challenge to chart its growth and changes, and you can find surveys announcing its breathtaking growth almost quarterly.

After reviewing many research documents, we decided to provide you with selected summary information to give you a sense of what's happening on the Web, and who is using it. We believe that with time the population of the Web will look more like the general population. In a nutshell, everybody will be there.

GVU STUDIES

Among the most widely respected survey instruments is the GVU WWW User Survey, a product of researchers at Georgia Tech University. The survey is conducted approximately every six months, attracts from four thousand to twelve thousand participants, and asks basically the same questions each time. Recent surveys have expanded its scope, but we find interesting historical value in comparing the first to the most recent survey. Table 4.1 summarizes some key findings from the surveys.

TABLE 4.1	FACTOR	1994	1996
Internet/Web usage statistics, 1994 and 1996	Age	N/A	33
	Female use	6%	31.5 %
	U.S. use	69%	73.4%
	Frequency of use	36%: >10 hrs./wk. 42%: 0–5 hrs./wk.	>80%: daily
	Instead of watching TV	N/A	36%
	Household income	N/A	$59,000

NETWORK WORLD 1996 INTERNET STUDY

According to the 1996 Network World 500 Internet study, which surveyed 500 companies using Internet/intranet technologies, strong corporate interest was seen. Even allowing for the obvious bias of these corporate respondents, the results are impressive:

- Eighty-nine percent have or will implement an intranet strategy within the next year.

- Eighty-five percent have Web servers in their organizations for Internet applications, seventy-three percent for intranets.

- Twenty-eight percent use Internet/intranet applications for some kind of electronic commerce transaction with their customers and forty-eight percent plan to within twelve months.

> ▸ Eighty-three percent use the Internet for communications such as e-mail and file sharing.

> ▸ Seventy-eight percent use the Internet for research — accessing electronic information.

According to Colin Ungaro, Network World's president and CEO, "The Network World 500 study clearly indicates that the Internet/intranets will revolutionize our lives. It will be driven as businesses integrate Internet technologies into their corporate networks. As networking enters the cyber age, it will create new electronic commerce opportunities on the Internet, increasing general acceptance and demand."

NIELSEN INTERNET SURVEY

The Internet continues to grow by leaps and bounds. A few more fascinating facts from researchers at Nielsen:

In January 1988, Internet traffic consisted of eighty-five million packets. In December 1994, Internet traffic had grown to more than eighty-six billion packets — an increase of 1,000 percent in seven years.

For the first time ever, in 1995, more e-mail messages were delivered in the US than regular postal messages — ten billion more!

1995 saw an explosion of corporate and commercial sites on the Internet. On December 31, 1994, there where only 29,000 commercial organizations on the Internet in the U.S. By January 5, 1996, the number had grown to over 170,000! Four months later on April 12, the number grew to 276,400.

How to Access the Internet and Web

Accessing information on the Internet and the Web is a very simple process. The most complex part will only occur one time, and that involves hooking up the LAN to the Internet. Once that's done, everyone has access. There's no need to configure separate modems for each desktop computer.

BASIC SOFTWARE

For many users, the only software that's needed is an Internet browser and a few add-in modules for special processing of audio or video information. Products like Netscape Navigator or Microsoft Internet Explorer are easy to set up and provide one access point for all applications.

Once a desktop PC has accessed the Internet, other capabilities, such as transferring files, are accommodated by the browser. No other specialized software is generally required. The search engine software resides on the server, as does most of the file-transfer capabilities. Even some mail capabilities are incorporated into browsers or tightly integrated in links. This architecture is especially helpful to new or infrequent users. They don't need to learn separate tools to accomplish each task.

TEXT-BASED INTERNET ACCESS TOOLS

While most of today's research and development efforts go into graphical Web-based tools, the Internet's long heritage makes it rich with text tools. Even if you've already moved to a graphical interface and use a Web browser, you still can get to many text-based tools and download files with file transfer protocol (FTP) sites.

Text-based tools can pull resources from around the globe that aren't programmed to show up on a Web page. Knowing about these tools could help for many types of research. A quick list and description of these tools includes:

> ► **Archie.** A search capability developed at McGill University's School of Computer Science, in Montreal, Canada, an Archie server tracks the content of FTP sites throughout the world and indexes the file names. To use Archie, you simply enter the names of files you need, and the software returns with a list of FTP addresses where those files can be found. This is fine so long as you know specific file names. Archie does not search the text within files. If the proposal for flat-screen panels is located in a file called SC97PNL.TXT, you have to call it by name. There's no facility to search for the words "flat" or "screen" or "panels."

▶ **Standalone FTP programs.** FTP is one of the Internet's original protocols for moving files from one computer to another. While your browser can now handle uploads and downloads, some people consider standalone FTP programs faster. Most FTP sites have a facility for passersby to download files. Since the Internet was originally created to freely share information, anonymous FTP was created to give any user access to public sites without having to obtain a specific login ID or password to the host computer. Instead, you simply log in as "anonymous," and use your e-mail address for a password. (You only have to authenticate yourself to access more specific material.)

▶ **Gopher.** This is a good tool with an on-screen pointer that enables you to access network resources. Originally developed at the University of Minnesota, Gopher lets you sift through text, WAIS databases, Telnet sites, and other data by letting you enter a key word.

▶ **Veronica.** This helps you search public-access gopher menus using key words. It is a little like Archie (which searches FTP sites), only for gophers. If you were looking for files about ergonomics, Veronica would look at all the gophers it knows about, and then returns, with a gopher menu of choices. Unfortunately, Veronica has the same drawback of Archie, it searches through the index of file names, and not the contents or text within the files.

▶ **WAIS.** The Wide Area Information Server took a giant technological leap by providing search capabilities for the full text of Internet databases. WAIS conducts searches of databases for key words and returns a list of files based on the relevance of the files returned (determined with algorithms). You can then refine your search with more keywords, if necessary. Many Web sites today use WAIS technology, although they may not advertise as such. To see an example of how it works, try *The Encyclopaedia Britannica* on the Web using WAIS.

Putting Your Organization on the Net

If you've been given the project of putting your company on the Internet, don't run for your keyboard to update your secret file, RESUME.DOC. Consider the project as an adventure! Depending on your budget, you can even outsource the adventure to a computer consultant or outside organization that specializes in making good Internet connections.

If you'd rather learn first-hand about putting your organization on the Internet, we can help. Simply open up your word processor software (or project management or spreadsheet software) and lay out your plan. Here's our quick ten-step task list:

1 • Choose your access method (dedicated, dial-up, line speed, etc.).

2 • Decide on your organization's server and browser software.

3 • Locate an ISP.

4 • Order your telephone line(s) and schedule installation.

5 • Confirm what your needs are regarding connection hardware.

6 • Register your domain name.

7 • Install the phone lines and hardware.

8 • Get connected to the ISP.

9 • Install the browser and server software.

10 • Educate yourself and enjoy the Internet!

CHOOSE YOUR ACCESS METHOD

You need to look carefully at your options to access the Internet. Since the Web is increasingly graphics and multimedia oriented, let us suggest two simple rules of thumb:

▶ Buy as much bandwidth as you can afford.

▶ Use a dedicated line (not dial-up).

Increased bandwidth makes a lot of difference to users. When they experience snappy response time, they tend to use the Internet more productively for more things. They take that extra step to seek another source for information, or feel more comfortable double checking the facts.

You'll more than justify the added costs for faster lines when you consider the cost of people's time awaiting slow graphics screens to repaint. Plus, people will produce higher quality work if they can avoid the anxiety imposed by slow response.

You'll also need to decide if your organization supports two way traffic. If you plan to host your own Web server as well as give your in-house employees access, then you should seek advice on capacity planning.

Watch out for surprises! Even if you are a small business, if your organization has many mobile workers or telecommuters, you may find one high speed connection isn't enough. If you are trying to accommodate inbound traffic to your web server, and outbound traffic of your employees to the Web, you could start to slow down your connection quickly. Noticeable speed degradation takes place when only 20 percent of the bandwidth is occupied.

Guides for Web server capacity planning are available on the Internet. For example, Sun Microsystems, among other computer makers, generally keeps current planning worksheets posted on its web site.

If you work in a large organization and are planning the needs for hundreds or thousands of users, we recommend that you call in some expert help. It never hurts to get a second (or third) opinion.

When it comes to ordering your lines, shop carefully. Because of the many communications technologies available to make the connection, intensive price competition exists among suppliers. Depending on the size and complexity of your infrastructure, you may spend a week to a month searching out your options. Table 4.2 shows the differences in bandwidth and throughput among line types from old 9.6 (or 9600bps) modems all the way up to new ATM technology. Keep in mind that certain compression methods can make the line speed act much faster. For example, using a compression technology called LAP-M, a 28.8Kbps modem can achieve upwards of 230Kbps — ten times faster then the modem speed! For additional details on lines, refer to Chapter 5.

DECIDE ON YOUR ORGANIZATION'S SERVER AND BROWSER SOFTWARE

If your organization doesn't have a standard set for server and/or browser software, you should take some time reviewing the market. There are many packages to choose from, and you should understand the tradeoffs. For example, using the Netscape browser and server software, you will likely encounter many third-party add-ins or enhancements. Netscape designs an architecture that many other software developers support. If you choose a product such as Microsoft NT Server and Internet Explorer, you will likely have to rely on Microsoft for enhancements. This differentiation continues to evolve.

	NETWORK CONNECTION	BANDWIDTH	THROUGHPUT
TABLE 4.2 *Bandwidth and throughput comparisons for different line types. Bandwidth units are kilobits per second (Kbps). Throughput units are HTTP operations per second for a network technology transferring a 1K file*	POTS — 9.6Kbps modem	9.6	1.2
	POTS — 14.4Kbps modem	14.4	1.8
	POTS — 28.8Kbps modem	28.8	3.6
	POTS — 56Kbps modem	56	7
	56K frame relay modem	56	7
	ISDN 1	64	8
	ISDN 2	128	16
	T1	1,536	187.5
	Ethernet 10BaseT	10,240	1,250
	T3	46,080	5,625
	Ethernet 100BaseT	102,400	12,500
	ATM 155Mbps	158,720	19,375
	ATM 622Mbps	636,928	77,750

LOCATE AN INTERNET SERVICE PROVIDER

The ISP provides you with a tap, or connection to the Internet. This differs from obtaining an access line, or pipe.

Initially, most organizations used different companies; however, that practice isn't always the best. Now that telephone service is deregulated, you'll find both old and new faces when you begin to look for a good ISP. Some telephone companies, such as AT&T, MCI, and Sprint, will sell you both services.

Don't choose your ISP on price or purchasing convenience only. Make sure your ISP has a good reputation, maintains its equipment well, and has a good track record with existing customers. You may even want to visit existing customers to see how they are set up.

Make sure you try to sample their services and call clients for references. Changing ISPs along the way is possible, but a hassle. Since you must first connect to your ISP, then to the Internet, your connection is only as reliable as your ISP. Ask for performance statistics — if the ISP doesn't maintain any, then find someone who does.

Larger sites may wish to host their own access to the Internet; however, it is expensive and complex. You'll need to call in a team of experts to help if you choose to make a direct connection.

ORDER YOUR TELEPHONE LINE(S) AND SCHEDULE INSTALLATION

Once you've confirmed your needs and selected an ISP, you are ready to order your telephone lines and schedule the installation date. Double check your plans and coordinate other activities to take place in a rapid sequence. You can begin to install client software, such as browsers, even before the lines are active.

CONFIRM YOUR NEEDS FOR CONNECTION HARDWARE

You need to provide hardware for your connection. At the very least you need a terminal adapter or router to connect your LAN to the new lines. Your ISP will likely help you plan and select your hardware. In some cases the ISP makes this hardware a part of the deal.

REGISTER YOUR DOMAIN NAME

To register a new domain name, you need to go through several steps. The InterNIC provides the following seven-step list on their Web site at

`http://rs.internic.net/help/domain/new-domain-reg.html`

We recommend that you review them here, then access the InterNIC directly online for any updated information and for your forms and templates. The seven steps are:

1 • Review the appropriate policies.

2 • Determine whether your selected name is already in use.

3 • Coordinate for primary and secondary *domain name service* (DNS) for the name.

4 • Obtain a domain name registration template.

5 • Review the template.

6 • Review the most common errors made in the process.

7 • Submit the template.

You may track the status of your application once you receive a response from the InterNIC. An invoice for one hundred dollars per domain name will be mailed within ten days of completion of registration. This registers you for two years. You will receive subsequent invoices annually at the rate of fifty dollars per domain name.

Creating Your Organization's Domain Name

If you use an outside ISP to give you access to the Internet, you do not need a domain name. Many organizations find it useful to have one anyway, so that their employee's e-mail addresses and the organization's electronic address are similar to the company name.

You should use *Whois* to research the domain name you'd like to register. It can be accessed on the web at:

```
http://rs.internic.net/cgi-bin/whois
```

The InterNIC's Whois service provides a way of finding e-mail addresses, postal addresses, and telephone numbers of those who have registered objects with the InterNIC. Using Whois, you can also determine whether the domain name you desire is already in use.

If the name you want is in use, your Whois query will return a list including information about the organization who holds the name, the name servers, and the contacts responsible for administering it. If it is not in use, the answer you receive will be: "No match for 'YOURNAME.TLD'."

Web Naming Conventions

When you first set up your organization on the Internet and the Web, you'll have to register your organization. The process lets you establish an electronic name and address. This is done by filling out a template and submitting it to the InterNIC organization.

You must register domain names and modifications electronically. This is done by filling out an electronic template and sending it via e-mail to:

```
hostmaster@internic.net.
```

Your application is processed electronically, so the information you send to InterNIC is entered into the database exactly as it was submitted on the domain name template. (So, if there is a mistake, you made it.) This also saves time and effort rekeying information. Hard copy registrations of any kind are not accepted.

A domain name can be up to twenty-six characters long, including the four characters used to identify the top level domain (.net, .com, .org, .edu or .gov). The following is a description of these designations:

- ▶ **.com** is for commercial, for-profit organizations.

- ▶ **.org** is for miscellaneous, usually non-profit organizations.

- ▶ **.net** is for network infrastructure machines and organizations.

- ▶ **.edu** is for degree-granting institutions.

- ▶ **.gov** is for United States federal government agencies.

Most organizations like to use the organization's name as the Domain name. If the organization goes by its initials or an acronym, it makes a convenient Domain name.

Remember, although your domain name isn't the same as your electronic address, it is used to make up the address. The electronic address or *uniform resource locator* (URL) is how Web browsers access different places on the Web. For example, International Business Machines (IBM) goes by the electronic address of: `http://www.ibm.com`. Same goes for Hewlett-Packard, which uses `http://www.hp.com`. Experience says that your domain name is as important as your company name and its physical address. Make it easy for customers and suppliers to remember.

INSTALL THE PHONE LINES AND HARDWARE

Your activities will increase on installation day. While the telephone company is going to be busy actually installing the lines, you need to coordinate other activities. Depending on how you purchased the service, you may or may not get help from the phone company after your line is installed.

For example, if you decide on an ISDN connection and purchase it through your local telephone company, the service may stop when the installer gets the line working. Historically, the regional Bell operating companies do not install your equipment for you. They only guarantee that the line is working. That practice may change with increased competition in the industry.

Unless you've made other arrangements, however, the hard part starts when the line goes in. You must install the connection hardware and then configure it.

GET CONNECTED TO THE ISP

Between your line provider and your ISP, you have plenty of numbers to deal with. At this time you also need to install your router. Your ISP will provide you with special TCP/IP addresses that identify your server (if you have one) and two domain name servers.

INSTALL THE BROWSER AND SERVER SOFTWARE

If you are not hosting your own Web server, then you only need to install browser software on each desktop. Many LAN administrators install the software on a server and either force it to each desktop automatically or make an icon available so that users who want the software can easily install it themselves.

Browser software needs some configuration, but that is usually limited to creating identification information or e-mail addresses.

If you choose to provide content to the Web, you will want to choose a Web authoring tool. While it is possible to create Web pages by using a Notepad-like utility and adding your own *hypertext markup language* (HTML) tags, we don't recommend it. Check out popular word-processing programs like Corel WordPerfect or Microsoft Word — both can create Web pages. For even more control over your Web page development, use a tool like Microsoft FrontPage, Sausage Software's HotDog, or some other HTML authoring software. You will also need to install server software on the computer designated as the Web server. Novell InternetWare makes an excellent choice for server software.

EDUCATE YOURSELF AND ENJOY THE INTERNET

Voilá! You did it. Now, just one more task before you sit back and enjoy all the benefits of the Internet. That's end-user training and education. While we discuss general training programs in a later chapter, we want you to make sure that you put "education" up front on your task list.

Without giving end users an effective education program, all your work putting up an Internet connection goes to waste. It's akin to turning over the keys to your brand new car to an untrained (unlicensed) teenager. It's not a matter of "if" they'll have a problem, it's a matter of "when."

Internet Code of Ethics

Among the things every Internet user should know is how to be a good *netizen*. Citizens of cyberspace sometimes take their new-found freedom and misuse it. The newly connected should all get the indoctrination and wisdom of those who pioneered the Internet.

In January 1989, the *Internet Activities Board* (IAB) issued a document titled "Ethics and the Internet." The simple and eloquently stated five key messages establish sensible and responsible behavior. The following are unethical and unacceptable:

Any activity which purposely

- seeks to gain unauthorized access to the resources of the Internet

- disrupts the intended use of the Internet

- wastes resources (people, capacity, computer) through such actions

- destroys the integrity of computer-based information

- compromises the privacy of users

For the most part, participants on the Internet follow this code of ethics; however, everyone goes through a learning curve when first going out on the Web. Studies show that you'll reduce that curve by a factor of two or three times if you offer end-user training. We strongly recommend it.

Intranets

Intranets are simply a private version of the Internet. Starting in 1995, people began to take Internet and Web development tools and apply them for local applications. Since many companies already had the infrastructure (LANs and WANs), once they added the TCP/IP protocol for the Web, it was easy to build a private network; hence, the name *intranet* as the internal version of the Internet. (TCP/IP is discussed in depth in Chapter 6.)

Once the technology is installed and the first applications go up, intranet-based applications begin to grow and multiply almost by themselves. Because Web authoring tools are so easy to use, almost anyone can set up an internal version of a discussion group or post project status reports on a Web-formatted page.

Intranets have proven to be useful from the start. For example, U.S. federal government workers have started pilot programs to share information within and among different government agencies. Intranets solved the "too hard to do" problem caused previously by cumbersome incompatible computer systems that people tried to kludge together. Quick benefits were seen as the technology started breaking down the limitations of physical walls, space, and buildings. Now agencies can share information with each other and with other organizations.

High-profile early adopters started sharing their stories of success. Some examples:

- **Columbia/HCA Healthcare.** In keeping with its goal to find more effective ways of conducting business and servicing customers, Columbia/HCA Healthcare found it could more effectively reach its internal associates with an intranet. Columbia launched its intranet in January 1996, and within months it contained content from more than a quarter of the company. With over 275,000 employees, the company needed a more timely and cost-effective way to handle communications. Paper (and the cost to process it) used up too much money that would otherwise be spent on improving health care. Columbia/HCA's intranet hosts a variety of information sources, including an up-to-date corporate directory, reports, and posts collected from the threaded newsgroups where employees exchange information about process improvements and other topics.

- **John Deere.** This equipment manufacturer installed an intranet so staff members could access an online catalog of equipment and integrate data from multiple sources. The system provides company-wide access to results from remote test sites, furnishes technical documentation to employees, offers a visual front end to all parts of the database, and integrates corporate information with agricultural data on the Web.

▸ **Booz Allen & Hamilton.** As a leading international management and technology consulting firm with over six thousand staff members in more than eighty offices around the globe, Booz Allen & Hamilton's main asset is knowledge. To facilitate sharing that hard earned asset, the company developed an online information system called Knowledge On-Line (or KOL). The system gives internal staff members around the globe easy and immediate access to the company's current information and best thinking. It lets associates link to company's experts on various topics. More than a dozen applications in four key areas put people within a short reach of valuable information. These include:

- ▸ **Knowledge Repository.** Reviews of more than four thousand knowledge-content documents cross-filed by topic, industry, and locations where the information originates and is applied.

- ▸ **Expert Skills Directory.** Using commercial server software search engines, this system inventories the skills of staff members.

- ▸ **KOLaborate.** A type of bulletin board collaborative tool that allows for both public and private messaging.

- ▸ **Access to Legacy Systems.** The intranet provides a gateway to existing corporate information, such as varied booking systems, human resources, and personnel information.

Another advantage of intranets is that they enable workers to use a browser to access information in a data warehouse. This idea seems to be catching on because it shifts the burden of platform compatibility to the browser vendors and not tool vendors or corporate in-house developers. It also provides a universal client so that the same server application can be easily accessed by both employees and customers. Better yet, it is a low-cost option because Web browsers are only a fraction of the cost of online application programming client tools.

Summary

In this chapter we took a high-level view of the options for building an intranet or Internet presence. Included was a short description of what's available on the Internet and a discussion of how a local version — an intranet — can be conceived. We focused on the practical how-to aspects of putting together an intranet (or access to the Internet). There are many options, and your own investigation will likely lead you to many places. We recommend you steer clear of less traveled roads here. Stick with major products from reliable companies. Once you are connected, enjoy cyberspace!

PART II

Creating a Network

CHAPTER 5

Network Design

By the very nature of connecting computers, devices, data, and applications, networks represent endless opportunities. In theory, you should be able to connect to, use, view, or update any device or bit of information anywhere. Your success at doing just that will vary depending on how well your network is designed and installed.

Good network design will allow your network to grow as large as you need it to, but bad design, followed by slipshod installation, will plague you and your users forever. The system may work, but it won't work well. And when the inevitable needs for upgrades surface, you'll be faced with hit or miss results. Some additions will be easy, and others simply won't work.

We cannot overemphasize the need for comprehensive planning and design. Of course, few people have the budgets to put top-of-the-line components at every twist and turn of the cable, and even if they do, rapidly changing technology can make those components obsolete almost overnight; nonetheless, we stress that you familiarize yourself with the consequences your decisions create in selecting network components.

In this chapter we provide detailed descriptions of the various network topologies to consider when planning a network strategy, as well as comprehensive suggestions for selecting actual cable types from today's market. To round out the chapter, we close with a look at dial-up capabilities and other connection options for wide areas.

The Need for Cabling

Everything electric emits electronic signals. These signals can conflict with each other if allowed to coexist on the same plane. In other words, two objects cannot occupy the same space at the same time. A perfect example is when you travel between two cities and get bits and pieces of two different radio stations on the same channel. The problem is only solved when your car moves completely out of range of one station and into the range of the other. Thus, it is important for network cable to have the resiliency to thwart such interference. After all, we don't want radio and TV signals interrupting and possibly corrupting data traveling over our network cable. By the same token, we don't want our data signals leaking from the cables only to be intercepted by those devious enough to capture our valuable information for their own use.

Another very important consideration is installing enough cable in the beginning. There's nothing worse than beginning the installation of additional equipment and discovering you don't have enough spare cable to support it. In the long run, doubling the amount of cable is very cost-efficient. Even if you don't foresee your network having much immediate growth, you can count on significant expansion over time. Remember that it is not the cable itself but the labor that is usually the most expensive part of the cable installation. Installing ample cable to begin with will save you money and time.

The type of cable you choose will hinge on your preferences for security, data reliability, and topology.

Cable Topology

As you may have guessed by now, there is a lot of organization that goes into networking computers. For cabling (wiring) purposes, there are three main schemes in which to organize how the cable connects to the nodes: linear-bus, star-shaped, and ring topology.

Unlike the phone system in your home or business, network wiring must be installed in a certain pattern in order to quickly diagnose malfunctioning cables and to compensate for the signaling pattern of certain network communication.

LINEAR-BUS TOPOLOGY

As seen in Figure 5.1, in a *linear-bus* arrangement a single cable called the *bus* or *trunk*, is installed — usually along a cable path in the ceiling or wall — and terminated at each node on the network. *Daisy chain* is another description for linear-bus. A good analogy for how this topology works is to think of electrical extension cords. Whether stringing lights for the holidays or linking those orange extension cords when edging the yard, you are using a linear-bus topology. The plug-in points are the terminators.

▶ · ◀

The bus is a single, branching cable that serves each node.

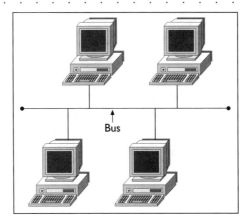

T-*connectors,* shown in Figure 5.2, are T-shaped metal tubes that serve as connection points for each network node. They work in conjunction with the terminators, which are placed at the beginning and end of the cable (the first and the last PC).

▶ · ◀

This T-connector resembles a T-joint used by plumbers to join three separate lengths of pipe at one location.

As you can imagine, linear-bus topology is low-cost and simple to design. Assuming you can keep track of the primary cable, it is easy to set up additional PCs by simply tapping into and expanding the trunk cable (like adding more holiday lights to the rooftop). Since each PC is attached directly to the cable, there is no need to purchase additional hardware such as hubs or wire centers. Another advantage is that you will use less cable than with the star-shaped option, discussed next, because the length of cable only has to connect to the next device on the network.

Unfortunately, any break in the cable can cause the entire network, or a good part of it, to fail. A failure can be caused by one end or the other losing proper termination, which can be caused by a pinched cable, loose T-connector, or malfunctioning terminator. As with the holiday lights, these failures can be difficult to diagnose.

Convenient and inexpensive, a linear-bus topology is appropriate for very small workgroups of between three and ten members.

STAR-SHAPED TOPOLOGY

In a *star-shaped* arrangement, an individual wire is run from each PC to a central location, as shown in Figure 5.3. Here all the wires are connected to a hub device, which completes the electronic connections. Although they will be covered in detail in a later chapter, you can think of a hub in a star-shaped topology as a Greyhound bus stop. It provides a central location for all of the signals to meet and then branch out to their individual destinations.

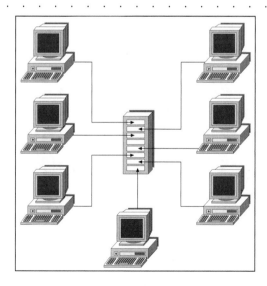

FIGURE 5.3

A star-shaped topology runs a cable from each PC to a central location.

Star-shaped wiring uses more cable than linear-bus wiring, but has several important benefits. Since each PC's cable is unique to that machine, if there is a cable fault, only the PC attached to the broken cable is likely to be affected. For example, if you start with a star-shaped network cabled with common unshielded twisted pair (UTP) wiring for Ethernet (covered later in this chapter), and then later decide to replace the Ethernet with Token Ring (covered in Chapter 6), you won't have to rewire your offices.

Star-shaped topology is easier to manage and administer than linear-bus. Once it is set up, it can be easily documented. Most hubs that connect star-shaped networks contain some form of status lights that assist you with locating and diagnosing faults.

The disadvantage of a star-shaped configuration is cost. More cable is needed, as well as a hub to connect all the wires together. However, if greater control over cable network faults is what you're looking for, it may be well worth it to consider this type of network topology.

TOKEN RING TOPOLOGY

Ring topology networks, where the cable is laid in a circle, are nearly extinct. Although you may hear the word *ring* used as a synonym for networking, it is mostly used to refer to a media standard such as *Token Ring,* as seen in Figure 5.4. While token ring networks do actually use a ring topology in the signaling scheme (each signal has to pass by each node sequentially in the ring), they are typically configured with a specialized star-shaped topology.

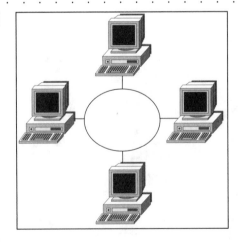

F I G U R E 5.4

A Token Ring topology lays the cable in a circle.

Cable Types

Once you've decided on the topology, you're ready to select the wiring to be used. There are several types of wiring that network electrical impulses will travel over. Each type has physical differences, length requirements, preferred topologies and signaling mechanisms, and a range of pricing structures. The following section will provide both the technical information referred to above as well as descriptions of the most commonly used in peer-to-peer and client-server networks.

COAXIAL CABLE

Coaxial cable infrastructure accounts for 5 percent of the computer networks in the United States. Illustrated in Figure 5.5, the coaxial communicates across the network on a single strand of copper wire that is protected from electronic eavesdropping and interference by either more copper wire or foil similar in appearance to that used in your kitchen, surrounding the original strand in a weaved pattern. The topology of choice for coaxial is a linear-bus, and consequently is used mostly for peer-to-peer networks.

FIGURE 5.5

Thinnet coaxial cable resembles the cable used for your TV.

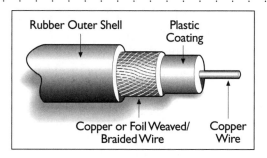

Rubber Outer Shell   Plastic Coating

Copper or Foil Weaved/   Copper
Braided Wire   Wire

There are two types of coaxial cable: *thinnet,* which looks like the kind used for cable TV, and *thicknet,* as shown in Figure 5.6. Their main differences include size, price, ease of installation, resiliency to electromagnetic interference, and effective signaling distances.

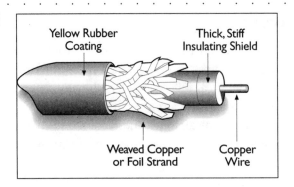

F I G U R E   5.6

Thicknet is sometimes referred to as "frozen garden hose" because it's often yellow and rigid.

Yellow Rubber Coating

Thick, Stiff Insulating Shield

Weaved Copper or Foil Strand

Copper Wire

Thicknet Coaxial Cable

Thicknet is commonly referred to as frozen yellow garden hose because of its color and stiff texture; nonetheless, it has the same basic physical make up as thinnet, only with a much thicker protective shielding. Thicknet's inherent installation limitations (It's difficult to put in walls, around corners, and so on.) have made it the least popular choice in recent years. Its primary uses today are between buildings, floors of buildings, or areas with high levels of electromagnetic radiation, such as factories and warehouses. Thicknet's ability to carry a signal approximately 541 yards without a repeater (Chapter 7) make it especially appealing for use in the factory or warehouse setting. It typically connects to the desktop through an *attachment unit interface* (AUI) connector, which looks similar to a serial port. From the desktop, the AUI cable hooks into the thicknet with what are called vampire connectors, and can be very touchy if not attached within a few inches of the designated marks along the cable. It is for these reasons thinnet is the more popular of the two.

Thinnet Coaxial Cable

From the outside, *thinnet* (also called *cheapernet* because it's less expensive than thicknet) looks exactly like the cable used for cable TV. But don't let appearances deceive you, they're completely different. The correct type of thinnet cable is labeled RG-58 for Ethernet and RG-62 for ARCnet, both or which are described later in this chapter.

Another similarity thinnet has with cable TV coaxial is the connecting ends. The ends of the cable have what are called *BNC connectors*, shown in Figure 5.7. Affixing these connectors to the cable requires no more than a wire stripper and a pair of pliers. Another difference between cable TV wiring and that used for networking is that cable TV wiring can't be connected to network devices.

F I G U R E   5.7

A close-up view of a BNC coaxial connector

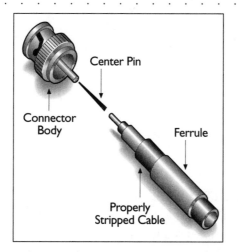

Think of T-connectors as though they are pipe fittings used in plumbing. Data flowing into one connection point continues and flows out of the other two connection points in equal amounts. These connectors aren't valves, but rather three-way converging points, as seen in Figure 5.8, and must occur at every signaling base. In other words, on the back of every network interface card there must be a T-connector in order to branch the connection. Otherwise the signal passing inside the wire will continue on without an opportunity for the node to transmit its data.

Thinnet can support data streams up to 200 yards without a repeater. Granted, this is considerably shorter than the 541 yards of thicknet, but with its more pliable exterior, thinnet is easier to install. Naturally, the type of T-connector is also important. There are many inexpensive imitations available, so make sure they match military specification UG-274.

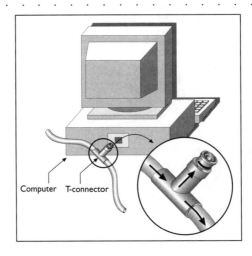

F I G U R E   5.8

Thinnet coaxial cable must terminate into T-connectors at the node.

Computer   T-connector

SHIELDED TWISTED PAIR

Next to coaxial, *shielded twisted pair* (STP) is the most electromagnetically resistant copper-based cable used in LANs. Like coaxial, the main data conducting wires are protected with woven copper or metallic foil, as shown in Figure 5.9. In addition to that, the wires are twisted around each other, thus providing the most protection from interfering signals (coming or going) and giving it its name. One pair of wires is used for receiving data while the other pair is used for sending data. STP can be used in both peer-to-peer or client-server networks. However, because of its higher cost of purchase and installation, it is generally only used in large client-server based networks with star-shaped topology and a Token Ring signaling scheme.

As part of the increased shielding properties, STP requires specialized connectors to the various nodes (PCs, printers, and so forth). Rather than the cable being attached to a single connector that then attaches to the NIC (as on coaxial cable), STP cable requires a D-shell connector to the NIC and an IBM data connector to the *medium attachment unit* (MAU) whose end then goes into the wall towards the hub, as seen in Figure 5.10.

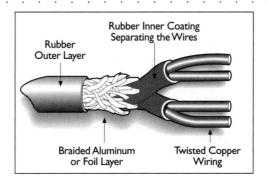

FIGURE 5.9

STP is protected by copper or aluminum shielding as well as the twisting of the main copper wires.

Rubber Outer Layer

Rubber Inner Coating Separating the Wires

Braided Aluminum or Foil Layer

Twisted Copper Wiring

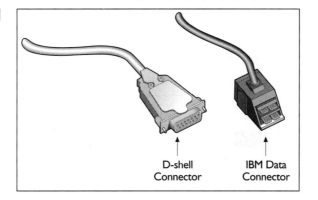

FIGURE 5.10

The difference between the D-shell connector and the IBM data connector

D-shell Connector

IBM Data Connector

To prevent data loss from cable deterioration or human error (cutting the cable), as well as crashing the entire network, STP is installed independently between each workstation, server, and wiring hub. In other words, rather than have one long, extended coaxial cable, STP is split between each connection point. As illustrated in Figure 5.11, the extra cable between the nodes and its relative thickness means it quickly fills up the wiring conduits in the walls. All in all, both the purchase and the installation of STP is more expensive than coaxial.

UNSHIELDED TWISTED PAIR

For low cost, an abundance of qualified installation experts, and an installed base of 90 percent within the United States, *unshielded twisted pair* (UTP) is a great choice for cable. However, UTP is not without complexities. For example, unlike a coaxial cable which runs directly from PC to server, UTP must have an intermediary in the form of a hub, shown in Figure 5.12. This can be expensive depending on how many connections it supports. Furthermore, the installers' "rule of thumb" suggests limiting UTP to 330 feet between the network node and a hub, almost half the usable distance of Ethernet coaxial (550 feet).

F I G U R E   5.11

Because of its thicker, less pliable outer surface, STP can be more difficult to install than coaxial.

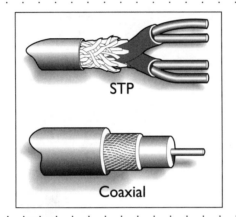

F I G U R E   5.12

An eight-port hub is connected to four nodes.

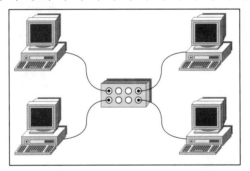

UTP looks deceptively like regular telephone line, although UTP cable is slightly thicker. Also, UTP uses RJ-45 connectors whereas telephone wires require RJ-11 connectors, shown in Figure 5.13. Telephone-grade twisted-pair cable is composed of two wires twisted together at six turns per inch to provide electrical interference shielding and consistent impedance (electrical resistance). Because existing buildings usually contain plenty of this wire, it is often used as an inexpensive, easy way to link computers.

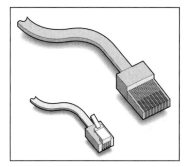

F I G U R E   5.13

Without comparing the number of wires inside the cable, the easiest way tell the difference between network (top) and UTP phone cable (bottom) is the number of connectors.

However, using telephone wire for your network, especially when it is already in place, can lead to several major problems. First, unshielded twisted-pair cable is sensitive to electromagnetic interference. In addition, low-quality twisted-pair cables have a varying number of twists per inch, which can distort the expected electrical resistance. Though this cable is usually quite adequate for most telephone communications, network data transmission demands much smaller tolerances.

Also it is important to note that telephone wire is not always run in straight lines. Cable that appears to run a relatively short distance between two offices might actually run through half the building to get from one to the other. A misjudgment could cause you to exceed the maximum cable length specifications.

The technical terms for the differences between UTP types are the category levels. Category 3 is typical phone line and Categories 3 to 5 are network-grade. The differences are in both the speed and amount of data they can conceivably carry. Category 3 has been tested at 16 *megahertz* (MHz) for attenuation (which describes the rate at which the signal becomes weaker the further it travels) with data capabilities up to 16 *megabits per second* (Mbps). Category 4 has been tested at 20MHz but has a low *installed base* (number of users), because most people usually move from Category 3 straight to Category 5 when upgrading. Category 5 cable is capable of bandwidth speeds up to 100MHz and can handle up to 100Mbps, which is important when we discuss Fast Ethernet later in this chapter.

While not as shielded as coaxial or STP, all UTP wiring is doubly protected from encroachment by insulation over the copper wires as well as twisting every pair of the wires together, shown in Figure 5.14. The plastic sheath provides absolutely no electromagnetic shielding, although the twists in the wire provide more protection than if it were untwisted.

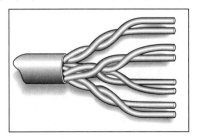

*UTP is primarily protected
by a thin plastic sheath and
by the twisting of the
conductive copper wires.*

In short, unshielded twisted-pair cable is inexpensive, easy to install, and provides a variety of uses. But be careful: The money that you save may be offset by additional costs later if the network doesn't function properly. To better determine if UTP is worth using, hire an experienced wiring or cable installation contractor to test the signal quality and actual cable lengths of the wiring in your building. This will add to the cost of your network, but it is the best way to avoid cable-quality problems later on.

FIBER-OPTIC CABLE

Fiber-optic cable, the most expensive, uses pulses of laser light to transmit data over glass cables, as shown in Figure 5.15. It is not subject to electrical noise and can handle exceedingly high data rates. While the price of fiber-optic cable has decreased over the years, it still requires skill and expertise to ensure proper connections. The ends of the fiber must be polished with precision to correctly transmit data.

*Fiber-optic cable can handle
extremely high data rates.*

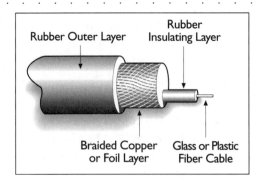

Rubber Outer Layer

Rubber
Insulating Layer

Braided Copper
or Foil Layer

Glass or Plastic
Fiber Cable

There are two types of fiber-optic cable, multimode and single mode. The multimode is glass and is used for shorter lengths, requiring a less powerful laser light. The single mode is made of plastic or glass and has a larger diameter, requiring a much stronger laser. The light on single-mode fiber is so powerful it will burn the retinal tissue of anyone who comes into direct visual contact with an actively transmitting cable. Fiber-optic cable usually carries several warnings. Read and follow warning labels carefully.

Fiber-optic cable has a significant advantage over all metallic cable options. Fiber-optic cable is more reliable because it is not susceptible to packet loss through electromagnetic or radio interference. This feature makes fiber-optic cable appropriate for those who need a high level of security and for electromagnetically noisy environments. Because the light pulses that carry the data are restricted to the cable itself, it is virtually impossible to surreptitiously tap into the medium without getting down into the actual core of the cable. In electromagnetically noisy environments, like those around large cranes and massive mechanical equipment, fiber-optic cable is often used to bypass the interference caused by engines and generators.

Fiber-optic cable is also very thin and flexible, making it easier to move than the heavier copper cables. Because signal losses while traversing the medium are less than those associated with metallic conductors, fiber-optic cable can support network segments up to 3.5 kilometers (approximately 2.2 miles) apart. Where long runs or links between buildings are required, fiber-optic cable is often the only viable choice.

While it is likely that you or someone on your staff is competent at cable installation for any of the wire-based types, we strongly recommend that you allow only qualified professionals to install fiber-optic cables. Not only does the technology demand close tolerances for tapping and termination, it also requires sophisticated, expensive test equipment to test the quality of the fiber-optic lines installed.

In addition to the preceding examples, there are options available for LANs that are more secure and have higher throughput (the amount of data that passes through). Due to their high costs, however, they're usually reserved for MANs or WANs, where ends are separated by miles rather than feet.

Peer-to-Peer vs. Client-Server

Although it's easy to understand the concept of sharing resources and applications across a network, it's also important to understand several different approaches. Basically, networks conform to one of two methods: peer-to-peer and client-server.

PEER-TO-PEER

In some networks, especially very small ones with just a few computers attached, people simply attach each computer to the network wires and set themselves up to share their individual devices. There's no central server to administer sharing. While this approach seems easy and straightforward, it does have limitations. NOSs designed for peer-to-peer networks include Novell Personal NetWare, Microsoft NT Workstation, Windows for Workgroups, Windows 95, IBM OS/2, and all of the Apple Macintosh systems.

Sharing Information

As a user on a peer-to-peer network, your experience is similar to having multiple disk drives. Your computer's hard disk is defined as drive C, and you also have access to a directory on Stan's hard disk as drive D, Pam's as drive E, and Jo's as drive F.

CD-ROM drives are also shared in the workgroup setting. Whole applications will not run from CD-ROM titles, but files such as clip art can certainly be accessed and taken advantage of by everyone on the peer-to-peer network. Through these means everyone in the workgroup can easily share data between computers.

Sharing Printers

Printer sharing is a very cost effective and versatile use of printing resources. In a peer-to-peer network, Pam can configure the printer attached to her computer as a sharable device, as illustrated in Figure 5.16. Then if Stan in the office next door wants to use Pam's printer, he ensures the correct print driver is loaded on his computer and sets his default printer destination to Pam's printer. From then on (until he changes it) every time Stan wants to print, his work will go to Pam's printer.

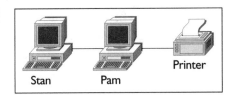

FIGURE 5.16

Through a peer-to-peer network, printers connected parallel to workstations can be shared with other workstations.

Stan   Pam   Printer

Peer-to-Peer Caveats and Kudos

Peer-to-peer networks differ from traditional file-server or client-server networks in several important ways. Because peer-to-peer networks allow each computer to share its resources, there is no need for an expensive dedicated file server. This allows groups of very small sizes (three to ten people) to justify networking. Peer-to-peer networks are easy to set up. It is a simple matter of installing network adapter cards and connecting cables, and then configuring the software. Administration of peer-to-peer networks promises to be simpler than other networks because each user controls access to his or her computer, eliminating the need for a full-time LAN administrator.

Theoretically, peer-to-peer networks can handle hundreds of connected PCs. Realistically, most are quite a bit smaller, containing fewer than five or six computers. If a peer-to-peer network grows larger, it can (and should) be reconfigured to include a dedicated file server. Also, peer-to-peer is deceptively simple. If someone's computer is turned off or crashes while you're trying to print, a peer-to-peer system may not handle it gracefully. Instead it gives users error messages which users often don't know how to fix.

Application sharing is difficult, if not impossible, on peer-to-peer networks. Just because Pam has spreadsheet software installed on her computer, and Stan has access to the directory, doesn't necessarily mean he can use her software. Unless Stan installs the software on his own computer, or uses a configuration to use Pam's computer as a server, most software is unlikely to run correctly.

Even disk, data, and printer sharing has limitations. Let's say Stan's computer holds the data files for the accounting system. Pam won't be able to work on the accounting records if he's gone on vacation and turned off his computer. Likewise for Stan if he tries to print to Pam's printer and she's gone home for the day and turned off her PC. However, even if all the shared devices are turned on and configured properly for sharing, performance is another issue. For instance, if Stan is printing to Pam's printer, she will probably notice a significant degradation in the usual speed that her PC performs while the print job is being processed. The same principle applies to data sharing. If Pam is accessing large clip-art files from Stan's shared CD-ROM, then he, too, will notice slower response times from whatever application he is using on his computer.

Minimum Requirements for Peer-to-Peer

Each peer-to-peer network operating system will have its own minimum requirements for installation, setup, and hardware requirements (disk space, memory, etc.). Thus, the least you need for the simplest peer-to-peer network is an NIC for each PC you plan to connect, coaxial cable with terminators and connectors for every workstation, and of course, the NOS.

As we've watched people try to work with peer-to-peer networks over the years, we've come to the conclusion that they are not suitable for day-to-day office work. With the lowering price of servers, it's more expedient to look at client-server-based approaches.

CLIENT-SERVER NETWORKING

Client-server networks can be thought of as high-powered peer-to-peer networks. There are still PCs and printers connected and communicating through wires like peer-to-peers, but there are fewer, if any, limitations. Printers don't need a PC attached to be shared with other users, which means it can always be powered on and also won't drain a user's productivity by involving the processor of their workstation. Client-server hard disks and CD-ROMs are both larger in size, and faster than those found in peer-to-peer. Consequently, this allows for greater data and application sharing. As illustrated in Figure 5.17, the concepts are the same except that instead of PCs acting as both client and server, there are specific machines that act only as servers, freeing up the client to do the everyday work.

Evolution of Client-Server

So far, client-server has been explained in terms of its differences and similarities to peer-to-peer, but there's more to say than that. Client-server was originally based on a single server with multiple clients. The classic example of client-server is that of Novell NetWare 2.x and 3.x. All of the shared applications, database engines, and e-mail software ran from the server's hard disks. The server's job was to handle and distribute the various file and print requests regarding the applications (see Figure 5.18). Once the client workstations received the files in its memory, the brunt of the file processing occurred on the workstation.

FIGURE 5.17

Client-server networks include all of the basics of peer-to-peer sharing, but have higher capacities and the ability to expand.

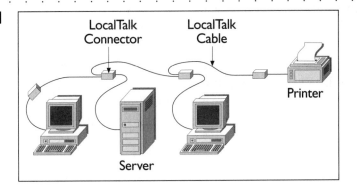

LocalTalk Connector LocalTalk Cable

Printer

Server

FIGURE 5.18

A client-server network has separate servers designed for file and print services, database engines, and e-mail systems all transferring data independently to clients.

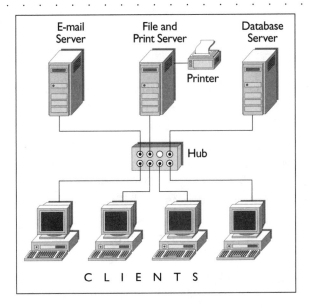

E-mail Server   File and Print Server   Database Server

Printer

Hub

C L I E N T S

Due to the constant transferring of files between server and workstation, this scenario was not conducive to controlling network traffic, but it was cost effective in that there was only one server. The need for better management of network traffic and larger, more robust databases and applications, led to the next step in client-server.

In order to decrease network traffic, the database transactions needed to occur mainly on the server (much like they did with mainframes), then once complete, be returned to the client PC. For example, a client PC (workstation) at a hospital requests all of the data regarding patients that had late payments for the first two quarters of the last two years. The data for this information is kept in raw form (not organized) on the database server and consequently must be organized into the requested format. Once the information is organized, as ordered, the results are sent back to the client PC. Another way to think of this scenario is to imagine the client as the front end and the server as the back end. The front end refers to the client because it is actually what the user sees. The back end refers to the server because it is where all the work is performed. An analogy would be that the front end, or client, is a hand puppet and the back end, or server, is the hand inside the puppet providing life to the client. After all, without the information from the server, the client is worthless.

However, to do this, the *back-end servers,* as they're called, had to be just as loaded in hardware (if not more so) as the more traditional file and print servers. The result was the need for one dedicated server with high memory (16–32MB of RAM), fast disk drives, and a 486 or better processor per application.

We don't mean to imply that decreasing network traffic was the only justification for the more expensive hardware platform. With the advent of increasingly powerful database engines and applications, the hardware had to match the requirements of the software. These database engines, while still performing within the boundaries of the NOS, can be of different types. Some examples of vendors in this category include Microsoft, Oracle, and Sybase.

On the plus side, back-end servers are not limited to certain platforms or operating systems. A *platform* is a general term for the type of hardware system on which the PC operates, such as Intel, RISC, Macintosh, and so on. Back-end servers sometimes also need to use operating systems independent of the surrounding NOS to enable its higher processing duties. Some examples include Windows NT, NeXT, and UNIX.

Surprisingly, these differences are actually beneficial for the development of the network. Why? Because the client PC operating system and platform is not tied to that of the server. This creates an environment with infinite means to continually add products and services to the network without jeopardizing the original investment in PCs and network structure (including the NOS). This type of setup is commonly referred to as a *multivendor* or *heterogeneous network.* For these reasons, client-server computing can really be thought of as the parents of the Internet and intranets.

Currently, there is no one particular type of back end or client. The Internet and all the many intranets contain thousands of different back ends. Perhaps an example will help.

Remember our discussion in Chapter 3 about e-mail, both LAN and Internet based? This is a perfect instance of how client-server computing can be likened to the Internet, which, so far, is the current end of the client-server evolution.

On the LAN, each client PC has a front end, like Novell Groupwise, that let's the user read and send e-mail messages. On the Groupwise server, requests are taken from other users on the LAN and held until the user's client requests them. Now, think a little larger. Imagine that the company is world-wide and has small LAN-based e-mail client-server setups everywhere. If Nigel is in London and wants to send Nicole in New York an e-mail, he types a message from his client workstation and sends it to the e-mail server in London. If setup on an intranet, the message is forwarded from the London e-mail server through the secure "cloud" shown in Figure 5.19 to the e-mail server in New York. When Nicole's workstation e-mail client requests her new messages, the NY server transfers them. Internet e-mail works exactly the same, with the exception that there is no controlling cloud; e-mail can be sent and received from anyone in the world.

The native LAN-based, client-server e-mail arrangement can easily be expanded to include both Internet and intranet uses.

Nicole's PC   New York
E-mail Server

Internet/
Intranet

London   Nigel's PC
E-mail Server

Minimum Requirements for Client-Server Networks

Once again, the various NOSs truly dictate the minimum server hardware requirements. Considering the increased complexity and potential for growth, more care and planning is required to implement any client-server network than a peer-to-peer. However, whether installing a single file and print-based server solution or several database servers, you will need various cables, NICs, and a very detailed agenda. Chapter 6 will aid in the creation and understanding of that agenda.

Whether you choose peer-to-peer or some variation of client-server, the important decision will lay in the planning considerations of future growth for your network. Considering all aspects of your network needs, present and future, allows you to lay the groundwork that will enable you to build on top of each succeeding upgraded layer of the network, rather than tear down the past version to start anew every time a new advancement or extended communication link is wanted or needed.

Dial-up Connections

Generally, any network confined to distances measured in feet comprises a LAN, a few miles between major connections could be considered a MAN, and any network that involves ten or more miles can be thought of as a WAN. For WANs there are several wiring options. All of them can use the telephone as an analogy because all of them use phone numbers to connect.

ANALOG CONNECTIONS

Simple cable setups use standard analog modems. The modem connected to my PC dials your modem, and through specialized software I can use all of the resources on your PC. This type of connection has many uses in a network, including giving remote users access to it and transferring information between databases or e-mail systems, just to name a few. Modem speeds have peaked at 28.8bps. This type of connection is great for establishing quick links and transferring small files between the machines or using remote control to trouble shoot. Analog modems are not good for maintaining static connections, transferring large files (larger than 2MB), or if your office or home only has a single phone line, allowing for simultaneous data and voice connections. Analog modems have these limitations because in addition to transferring data they must also convert it.

While it is true that most phone lines in large metropolitan areas are digital (they transmit an electronic signal in binary code either as on/off pulses or as high/low voltages), they are only digital between the dialing central offices of the phone company. From the central offices to homes and businesses the lines are analog, so that voice can be transferred. Thus, the signal pulses that the computers communicate must be converted from digital to analog (which is the static noise you hear) so they can be converted on the receiving end from analog back to digital. For higher bandwidth, more reliable connections, faster data transfers, and a more simplistic, cleaner dial-up data exchange, *Integrated Services Digital Network* (ISDN) is the choice.

INTEGRATED SERVICES DIGITAL NETWORK (ISDN)

ISDN can transmit data up to speeds of 128 *kilobits per second* (Kbps), maintain static connections, and allow for multiple connections (data and voice). It does this by combining a total of three digital lines.

Two of the lines are for data and transmit at 64Kbps each, for a total of 128Kbps, while the third line has a speed of 16Kbps and is used for telephone communications.

Unfortunately, due to its newness, ISDN is not available everywhere. However, most major U.S. cities and practically all of California is ISDN linked. Call your local phone company for details.

T-1 AND T-3

If larger pipes of information over long distances is what you need for transferring data, then a T-1 or T-3 may be what you're looking for. Unlike analog modems or ISDN, T-carriers provide a constant connection, so no dial up is required. T-1 is a 1.544Mbps channel that can handle twenty-four voice or data channels at 64Kbps. The standard T-1 frame is 193 bits long, which holds twenty-four 8-bit voice samples and one synchronization bit; eight thousand frames are transmitted per second. T-3 is a 44.736Mbps channel that can handle 672 voice or data channels at 64Kbps. T-3 requires fiber-optic cable.

Basically, T-1 and T-3 are direct connections from one end of the country or state to another. Typically this technology is used in the medical community for the remote diagnosing of patients in hard to reach or poverty stricken areas, where families cannot afford to make the trip to a large city. It is also used as a high bandwidth solution for Internet connectivity for large businesses that can afford the exorbitant fees and require the constant connectivity to maintain competitiveness in business.

One more option worth considering is *Switched Multimegabit Data Service* (SMDS). SMDS is a high-speed, switched data communications service offered by the local telephone companies for interconnecting LANs in different geographic locations. It was introduced in 1992 and became generally available nationwide by 1995.

Connection to an SMDS service can be made from a variety of devices, including bridges, routers, and CSU/DSUs (the digital equivalent of a modem), as well as via frame relay and ATM networks. SMDS can employ various networking technologies. Most implementations use rates up to 45Mbps.

Data is framed for transmission using the *SMDS Interface Protocol* (SIP), which packages data as *Level 3 Protocol Data Units* (L3_PDU). The L3_PDU contains source and destination addresses and a data field that holds up to 9,188 bytes.

That covers the gamut of cabled options for networks. However, there is still one other option to connect PCs together with a network: wireless.

Wireless Networking

Probably the simplest form of a wireless LAN is the one that is created between a laptop and a desktop (and even a printer) using infrared technology. Basically, there is a red panel on each device that looks and acts exactly like the remote control that goes with your TV set. Some of the low-powered systems behave just like your remote control unit: The infrared ports must be in plain view of each other and within a certain minimum distance in order to transmit and receive data properly. However, high-quality, high-powered systems do not have the same line-of-sight restrictions, and will transmit around objects and over much greater distance.

The next simplest form of wireless LAN technology is that developed by such companies as Proxim and US Robotics. These products use radio frequencies to connect PCs. Unless your LAN is on a peer-to-peer network, however, most of your wireless LANs are only one part of your network as a whole, which includes cabled nodes. In other words, some of the PCs will have wired connections to the network while others will be tethered with radio waves.

Radio frequency LANs are generally much slower than cabled LANs but it is the capability of mobility that makes them attractive. For example, industries with disparate users or in structures that don't support standard wiring are prime candidates for wireless networks. In medical institutions all over the United States, doctors and nurses use hand-held wireless devices to record patient data or laptops with wireless adapter cards (PCMCIA cards) to transmit data back and forth to the servers or printers because running cable in patients' rooms is not feasible. Another good example of where wireless technology is used is in the manufacturing industry. With huge warehouses of products, networked computers are a necessity to keep track of inventory, and wireless networked computers allow merchants to transmit data to the network while staying mobile.

Sometimes, though, mobility is not the issue. Earlier we discussed the bandwidths of T-1 lines for usage with long distances and large bandwidths. Another option, and probably the ultimate in wireless networking communication is the use of satellites. Satellite communication is primarily used for WANs.

Communication satellites orbit the earth at the equator so that they are motionless relative to earth-based receivers (that way the terrestrial antennas or dishes don't have to constantly restructure themselves to point at different areas of the sky). In comparison to T-1 lines, satellite connections are more feasible for several city connections, but only for certain types of data. Because it takes a signal 0.27 seconds to make the trip from the satellite to the receiver, only data transfers like e-mail or overnight database changes are any good, although someone trying to type in real time using the 0.27 second delay wouldn't really lose much speed on their words per minute. Although the wireless world is a new one for PCs, through continual advantages they are bound to become more prolific.

Summary

Hopefully this chapter has provided you with some significant insight into the numerous options available in designing the right network for the right job. By now, you've discovered that the term *network* means much more than simply having two or more computers connected by a wire and transferring files back and forth. Network design can be as unique as the individuals sitting at each node.

CHAPTER 6

Passing Data Across a Network

This chapter builds on the concepts of network design by explaining how data travels across a network. *Signaling schemes* can be thought of as the roads across which data (information) travels. These roads differ primarily in the amount and speed of traffic they can hold. Typical examples include Ethernet, Token Ring, *Asynchronous Transfer Mode* (ATM), *Fiber Distributed Data* Interface (FDDI), and, on the broader bandwidth scale, Fast and Gigabit Ethernet.

Once you build the roads, you can put traffic on them. Electronic impulses called signals are the actual carriers of data. All protocols are carried over signals, though not all protocols are alike. Some can carry more information than others, the same way trucks and cars have different payload capacities. Protocol examples included in this chapter are TCP/IP, SPX/IPX, NetBEUI, NetBIOS, and ODI/IPX.

Network Signaling Schemes

Millions of electrical impulses traverse the nerve fibers in a human body, carrying information to the brain, tissues, and muscles. Basically, signaling and communication across a computer network operate the same way. Electrical signals travel over the wiring from PC to PC, PC to printer, and PC to server, and there are different methods for this communication. These signaling schemes come in two flavors, *contention* and *token passing*.

CONTENTION

Networks that use contention schemes, such as Ethernet and AppleTalk, listen to the network cable and wait for the line to go quiet before sending out messages. If two computers happen to send messages at the same time, these messages will inevitably collide and be garbled. When this occurs, collision-sensing electronics take note of the event and the lost messages are resent.

TOKEN PASSING

Networks that use token-passing schemes send data in a more orderly way. A *token* is a specific electronic signal that indicates a node has permission to transmit or receive. A limited number of tokens (usually one) circulate around the network

— that is, messages follow a specific order of circulation, and the last recipient in the order passes the message back to the first recipient in the order. Messages to be transmitted are held at the local workstation until a free token arrives that can pick up pending messages and deliver them to their destinations. Once properly delivered, the messages are stripped off the token, freeing it up for other messages. Both *attached resources computing* (ARCnet) and Token Ring systems use token passing, as does the high-speed FDDI.

Ethernet

Ethernet is a fast (10Mbps) and efficient signaling standard that has been adopted by a third of the computer market in the United States. Ethernet was invented in the mid-1970s by two Xerox employees, Robert Metcalfe and David Boggs. Its specification is defined by the *Institute of Electrical and Electronics Engineers* (IEEE) standard as 802.3 (pronounced "eight-oh-two-dot-three").

NOTE

IEEE is a group of electrical and electronics engineers that are at the head of their various industries — medical, manufacturing, computer chip, and so on, who meet several times a year to discuss and provide standards for the hardware everyone uses. This is done so that the myriad components of a single computer or a large network will operate together with the least amount of conflict.

Ethernet is a contention-based protocol standard. Unlike a token passing scheme, all the computers can communicate (send their data) at once. Consequently, messages sometimes collide and disintegrate before reaching their destination. To compensate, Ethernet LANs use a technique called *CSMA/CD*, which stands for Carrier Sense Multiple Access/Collision Detection. CSMA/CD listens to the wire to determine when it is not being used, then sends the message and listens again to see if the message got through. If a collision occurs, CSMA/CD waits and resends the message, as illustrated in Figure 6.1. As an analogy, consider fax machines. A fax machine will not try to send its data across the line until the other fax machine picks up. If the line is busy, the sending fax machine waits a period of time and then tries to send its data message again.

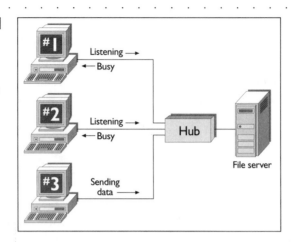

FIGURE 6.1

In this example of CSMA/CD, PCs #1 and #2 listen to the wire before sending. They're told the line is busy, because PC #3 is currently sending data.

Sometimes, however, Ethernet is not so well behaved. In certain circumstances an Ethernet NIC decides that it doesn't want to wait for an available line to send its data. Instead, the NIC broadcasts information on the network with no regard to other signals, thus causing what is referred to as a *broadcast storm*.

Broadcast storms are usually caused by protocol problems.

NOTE

Our traffic analogy works well here. You can think of CSMA/CD as a four-way traffic light with all of the Ethernet devices respectfully obeying when to stop and start sending information. A broadcast storm occurs when one of the "vehicles" ignores the traffic light and heads into the intersection, wreaking havoc with the orderly flow of traffic.

Depending on their configuration, Ethernet LANs can be very inexpensive. Since Ethernet will work in linear-bus or star-shaped topologies and run on thinnet coaxial (also called 10base2 — meaning 10Mbps at 200 meters), thicknet coaxial (also called 10base5 — meaning 10Mbps at 500 meters), twisted-pair (STP or UTP), or fiber-optic cables. Installation prices vary depending on which cable scheme is used.

Perhaps the following will help you make a choice. Ethernet is appropriate for small or large groups of users. Linear-bus-based Ethernet is a good option if cost is a primary concern, and if you have a network of fewer than twenty PCs. Ethernet in a twisted-pair topology, though a little more expensive, is a better choice for larger groups in that it provides fault isolation, better network management capability, and more room for later expansion. It might be a good choice if you are starting from scratch, too, because it provides a great deal of flexibility for both small and large networks. A 10baseT configuration (a star-shaped configuration based on UTP cable), while it may be slightly more expensive to install, will offer the most flexibility for connecting with other networks.

On the other hand, if installation price is really not an issue and you want more than Ethernet's 10Mbps, then Token Ring is the signaling scheme for you.

Token Ring

Token Ring networks were popularized in the mid-1980s when International Business Machines (IBM) began to support the Token Ring Protocol standard. A number of IBM computers, including minicomputers and mainframes, have direct connections to Token Ring. Most businesses using Token Ring today do so because they are old IBM mainframe shops from the 1970s. According to our research, Token Ring accounts for 21 percent of computer networks in the United States.

Today, the IEEE 802.5 specification defines the workings of Token Ring. There are two speeds available, 4Mbps and 16Mbps. Although Token Ring is commonly associated with IBM, there are a number of third party vendors such as Proteon, Intel, Madge, 3Com, and others that sell Token Ring products.

Token Ring uses what is known as a token passing scheme. Rather than PCs broadcasting signals at will, like in Ethernet, Token Ring signaling is more structured. A single token (electrical impulse) will pass by each device on the network. A PC's network card gives its information to the token as it passes, and then no other PC can give data to this "busy" token until it receives the information it needs. This is another way Token Ring differs from Ethernet — there can be no information collision, because only one PC can send data at a time.

Token Ring's physical topology is a cross breed of both ring- and star-shaped topologies, as shown in Figure 6.2. In other words, data flows from workstation to workstation in sequence (as in a ring network), but continually passes through a central point (as in a star network). The central wiring hub called a *Multistation Access Unit* (MAU) using a twisted wire cable. The central hub makes it easier to troubleshoot failures than a bus topology. This is a completely different type of hub than the one used in a 10BaseT twisted-pair Ethernet network.

F I G U R E   6.2

Token Ring topology has elements of both ring- and star-shaped topologies.

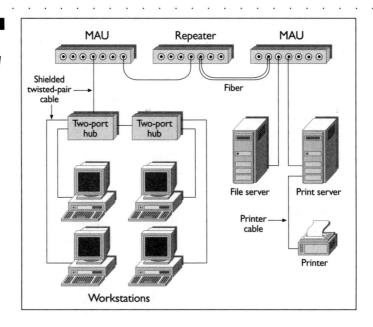

If a PC takes the token and doesn't give it back, the whole ring can crash.

NOTE

Unlike Ethernets, where one PC not communicating doesn't affect the whole network (with the exception of broadcast storms), if one PC on a Token Ring network doesn't cooperate by transferring the token on to the next station, *beaconing* occurs, thus creating a continuous signaling of error on the LAN.

Token Ring networks can run on *unshielded twisted-pair* (UTP), *shielded twisted-pair* (STP), or fiber-optic cables. They are available in two versions, supporting transmission speeds of 4Mbps or 16Mbps. Although an individual network must run at either one speed or another, networks operating at different speeds can be bridged or routed together.

Token Ring networks are reliable, even under heavy loads, and fairly easy to install. When compared to the total costs of ARCnet and Ethernet networks, however, Token Ring networks are more expensive. Fewer vendors offer Token Ring equipment than Ethernet or ARCnet equipment.

So, after all of that, is Token Ring right for your network? Token Ring is appropriate for large and small networks. Also, it is especially useful when you are connecting your network to IBM host computers, such as AS-400 minicomputer models or mainframes, because IBM supports the Token Ring Protocol standard more than any other.

If you are starting your network from scratch, and have mostly IBM minicomputers or mainframe equipment to connect to, Token Ring will provide a great deal of flexibility and support. Token Ring networks may cost a few dollars more, but are extremely reliable, and the 16Mbps version is very fast.

Increasing the Bandwidth

Neither Ethernet nor Token Ring may be fast enough if you're planning to use high resolution graphic files (MPEG and JPEG), video conferencing, and other multimedia applications across your network. *MPEG* (Motion Pictures Experts Group) is an *ISO/ITU* (International Standards Organization/International Telecommunications Union) standard for compressing video. MPEG-1, which is used in CD-ROMs and Video CDs, provides a resolution of 352 × 240 at 30fps with 24-bit color and CD-quality sound. For effective playback, MPEG-encoded material requires either a fast computer (Pentium, Pentium Pro, and so on) or a plug-in MPEG board. *JPEG* (Joint Photographic Experts Group) is an ISO/ITU standard for compressing still images. It has become very popular because it provides compression with ratios of 100:1 and higher. Both MPEG and JPEG are among the most efficient image file types — they're generally smaller than other types containing the same data (say, TIFF).

Video conferencing transfers both voice and images from one PC to another. Because it involves huge amounts of data, video conferencing has to be extremely fast or there will be a delay in the sound and movements of the person you see on the other screen.

FIBER DISTRIBUTED DATA INTERFACE

FDDI is similar to the IEEE 802.5 standard of Token Ring in the way it communicates, with one exception — there are two rings that pass through each network device. FDDI provides an optional dual counter-rotating ring topology. It contains primary and secondary rings with data flowing in opposite directions. If the line breaks, the ends of the primary and secondary rings are bridged together at the closest node to create a single ring again, as shown in Figure 6.3. Not all devices on the network have to include connections to both rings, but what you save in installation could cost you in fault tolerance.

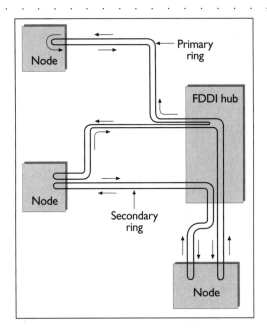

In dual counter-rotating topology, if the line breaks, the ends of the primary and secondary rings are bridged together at the closest node to create a single ring again.

Speaking of the IEEE, FDDI is not one of their standards. FDDI is part of the *American National Standards Institute* (ANSI) and its abbreviated name is ANSI X3T9.5. FDDI travels at speeds of 100Mbps, which, when compared to Ethernet or Token Ring, is no comparison.

Although the fiber portion of the FDDI name implies that the signaling scheme only works over fiber-optic cable, this isn't the case. FDDI also works over both STP and UTP. However, FDDI is typically used as a backbone for large networks or with MANs, so the mileage capability of fiber optics does come into play. An FDDI that runs across fiber optics has a signaling distance up to 2 kilometers without repeaters. It is limited to 100 meters on copper-based UTP and STP.

As you can imagine with the double-fault tolerance, high speed, and preference for fiber, FDDI is expensive to implement all the way to the workstation, though it holds 24 percent of the United States market.

ASYNCHRONOUS TRANSFER MODE

In this context, ATM has nothing to do with Automated Teller Machines. That said, what is it?

ATM is a signaling scheme that has the unique ability to simultaneously deliver both video and sound across a network. Real-world applications include the promised cable services with five hundred channels, video conferencing, and remote medical diagnosis (sometimes called telemedicine). It operates over every kind of cable, from coaxial to the twisted-pair twins (STP, UTP), to dial-up connections such as ISDN. ATM has speed and bandwidth greater than the other double-digit signaling schemes, because it has 48-byte cells that travel much smoother and quicker over the network. Some reported speeds are in excess of 155Mbps.

Currently, ATM is neither widely accepted nor implemented. According to data from 1996, ATM is only being used on the backbone side of networks, of which it only holds 5 percent of the U.S. market. It is still hotly contested as a signaling scheme up-and-comer that may or may not be able to compete with 100Mbps standards, such as *Fast Ethernet.*

FAST ETHERNET (100BASET)

If 10Mbps Ethernet is throttling your network, multiply the bandwidth by ten and use Fast Ethernet's 100Mbps signaling, called *100BaseT.* It operates exactly the same as Ethernet's 802.3 standard, except the network interface cards and hubs have to be replaced with 100BaseT models. Fast Ethernet operates over several wiring schemes including Fiber-optic, STP, and UTP (but only at the Category Five level for the TP wiring). Coaxial cable is not an option. Only recently have companies started using Fast Ethernet to upgrade existing networks, as well as build new ones from the ground up. Research data indicates that 18 percent of the U.S. market uses Fast Ethernet right to the desktop.

A relative of 100BaseT, known as 100BaseT VG (voice grade), runs on telephone twisted-pair wiring, commonly called Category 3. Bear in mind that your ability to use existing Category 3 telephone wiring in your business or home is entirely based on the quality of the installed line. When telephone wiring is installed there are four wires, even though telephones only use three. In 100BaseT VG, this extra line is used for Ethernet's error checking to ensure packet validity.

For some, even 100Mbps is not enough where video conferencing, MPEG and JPEG presentations, or x-ray images are concerned. Consequently, the never-say-die computer industry has come up with a new, as yet untested technology: Gigabit Ethernet.

GIGABIT ETHERNET

At 1,000Mbps, *Gigabit Ethernet* is the network speed of the future. It is, however, so new, that although the IEEE has a standard number for it, 802.3z, meetings are taking place among the IEEE committee members to define the standard for broad acceptability. Hopefully, it will be as simple to implement as Fast Ethernet.

ARCnet and Macintosh

Last and perhaps least in usage, statistically speaking, are ARCnet and Macintosh. Although the future isn't bright for these two products in terms of networks, they still have a loyal following.

ATTACHED RESOURCES COMPUTING (ARCNET)

ARCnet topology has been widely available since the 1970s, but according to current research, doesn't hold a significant percentage of the U.S. network market. ARCnet passes information around the network using a token passing scheme, meaning each computer has an individual turn to relay information. If this sounds similar to Token Ring, that's because it is, sort of. In Token Ring networks, a token passes around the ring topology until a PC needs it to transmit information . The token is then busy until the information requested is given back to the original requester, during which time no other PC can transmit. In ARCnet, a token is administered by a single PC designed as the controller and identified by the lowest assigned number (more on this further on). The controller passes the token through the network to each PC sequentially, based on its assigned number. Those PCs not needing to send stay quiet; those with information to pass on do so.

ARCnet can run on coaxial, UTP, or fiber-optic cable. If coaxial is used, however, it must be the RG-62 specification. ARCnet requires a topology that is a combination of star and bus, so hubs are mandatory. One of the best features of ARCnet is its traveling distance between hubs. Between active hubs, which function as signal-boosting repeaters, there is a maximum length of 2,000 feet. This is more than double that of other signaling strategies. Unfortunately, the maximum distance of the network from one end to the other is only 20,000 feet. This pigeonholes ARCnet into the small-network end of the industry.

ARCnet network interface cards use no manufactured, pre-assigned network number addresses like those of Token Ring and Ethernet. ARCnet NICs must be manually configured to give it an assigned number from 1 to 255 where, again, the PC with the lowest number serves as the controller. Thus, it is a good idea to place your most powerful PC in the number-one spot for quicker token processing.

Speaking of speed, the original 1970s version of ARCnet traveled at only 2.5Mbps which, when compared to the 4 or 16 of Token Ring or 10 of Ethernet (not to mention the 100Mbps mentioned earlier) is pale by comparison. However, Datapoint, a manufacturer of ARCnet products, has developed technology that raises the signaling speed all the way up to 20Mbps — even within the existing 2.5Mbps scenarios. (You just have to have new hubs and NICs.) So, if you're LAN has no serious growth plans, ARCnet can serve your needs for quite some time.

MACINTOSH

The good news about Macintosh computers is that they're networkable right out of the box. "Macs" (for short) use two protocols to connect across the network, AppleTalk (older computers)and EtherTalk (newer computers), both of which are contention-based signaling schemes.

AppleTalk can be used over STP or standard telephone wiring. The telephone wire version is actually called PhoneNet. PhoneNet's adapters and wiring are less expensive than LocalTalk's (another variety of AppleTalk).

Either way, both systems allow the sharing of files, e-mail, and printers. Of course the major drawback is AppleTalk's speed — 230,400bps — even slower than original ARCnet. Granted, this is still faster than modern modem speeds, which top out at 28,000bps, but it's still rather slow for true networking.

As a result, there is an Ethernet version for Macs called EtherTalk. EtherTalk has all of the usual 10Mbps speed and features of PC-based Ethernet. On the newer Macs, an EtherTalk adapter is included as standard hardware. The connection, however, is different. It isn't a 10baseT (UTP) type connector or BNC connector (thinnet coaxial cable); rather, it is called an *Apple Attachment Unit Interface* (AAUI).

An additional benefit of EtherTalk for Macs is the capability to attach to NetWare servers. Granted, PCs still can't read most Mac files, but at least printers and the few file formats that are compatible with both PCs and Macs can be shared.

Protocols: The Electronic Signals of Network Life

For data to travel across the network, regardless of the speed (2, 4, 10, 16, or 100Mbps), the methodology used (Ethernet, Token Ring, ARCnet, and so on), or the cable (UTP, STP, coaxial, or fiber-optics), there still has to be a carrier for the information. Think of it this way: Signaling speeds can be seen as speed limits (4–100Mbps) on various highways (UTP to coaxial). Regardless, there must be a transport for the data. Protocols serve as those transports. Some can carry large amounts of data, like a school bus, and some carry only smaller amounts, like a compact car.

To carry the analogy further, a protocol is not just the vehicle, it's all the different parts that make up the vehicle. Some portions transmit the data (the wheels), others ensure the data is sent correctly (the steering components), and still other parts of a protocol ensure that data arrives in one piece (the safety belts).

Some protocols carry information more efficiently than others, which is important to keep in mind when choosing a protocol.

The carriers of information include TCP/IP, SPX/IPX, ODI/IPX, NetBIOS, and NetBEUI. The following section defines the acronyms, explains their individual purposes, and gives their brief evolutionary history.

TCP/IP

Thanks to the Internet and intranets, the most popular networking protocol in the world is TCP/IP. TCP/IP also has something else that the other protocols don't have — a proprietary owner.

TCP/IP stands for *Transmission Control Protocol/Internet Protocol*. It was developed in the 1960s by the United States Department of Defense as a method for linking computers all across the world to maintain connectivity in the case of another World War. A technical definition of TCP/IP is: an industry standard suite of networking protocols, enabling dissimilar nodes in a heterogeneous environment to communicate with one another. In English, this means that TCP/IP can communicate to any PC using any desktop or network operating system anywhere in the world as long as it supports the TCP/IP suite. The military intended TCP/IP to be a routable, flexible, robust, and fault-tolerant protocol — and it is just that. Consequently, TCP/IP is the bread and butter protocol for the Internet and corporate intranets.

TCP/IP can be thought of as a special set of numbers similar to the numbers used with telephones. The same way each household and business has unique phone numbers, so must PCs using TCP/IP. However, there are two ways to do this. Either TCP/IP is configured on each PC or one PC distributes the TCP/IP numbers through what is called a *DHCP* or *BootP server* (Bootstrap Protocol), depending on your NOS.

Configuring TCP/IP

The most time-consuming tasks in large networks are installing TCP/IP communication software on each PC in the network and assigning each device its very own Internet address.

Internet addresses used with TCP/IP can be just a number or a number represented by a name. The number is split up into four *octets* with periods, such as "127.248.119.149." An octet is an eight-bit storage unit. In the international community, the term "octet" is often used instead of "byte." Alternatively, this number can be associated with a specific name, like a company (www.ibm.com) or a government institution (www.govt.nasa.gov). So, if you've been surfing the Internet, all of those Internet addresses you see are also represented by unique numbers.

The third octet is known as the *subnet*. With the typical Class C Internet address you get 253 possible numbers with each subnet. Subnets are used by businesses, for example, to separate addresses according to floors of buildings to keep the numbering schemes organized. This way, when there is a problem, it is more easily identifiable. Businesses can have more than one subnet, it just depends on how large their institution is and how much money they want to pay.

Dynamic Host Configuration Protocol

In this instance, a PC on the network is given the information for all of the available TCP/IP (also called "IP" for short) addresses. Whenever a person in the organization attempts to access an Internet related service (like the World Wide Web), the *Dynamic Host Configuration Protocol* (DHCP) server assigns an IP address upon bootup for that PC to use temporarily. This method of IP addressing is referred to as *dynamic IP addressing* because it is an active assignment. Online service providers, such as CompuServe and America Online, operate in the exact same manner. Every time you dial into these services, an IP address is assigned for your usage while accessing the Internet.

Using DHCP is simple because there is less potential for duplicating IP addresses. (Imagine two PCs have the same address and one of them happens to be the network server or another important resource. The resulting busy signal could bring the network to a screeching halt.) Also, DHCP can be cheaper in the long run because not as many addresses are needed.

If money is no object and a large network support staff is available, *static IP addressing* can be used. In this instance each PC has its own unique IP address that, when installed, must be configured so that it doesn't interfere or conflict with any other PC or device. Although static addressing is simpler than dynamic addressing, problems such as duplicate IP numbers are much more difficult to diagnose. To compensate, make the NIC number, rather than an individual's name or department, the primary associative information link in your record of IP numbers. Names and departments can be used as secondary links in your database. People and PCs are hard to keep track of in corporate America, but the NIC card number never changes. Recording the information in this manner will allow for easier tracking if duplicate addressing does occur.

 Static addressing is still the norm today.

NOTE

SPX/IPX

If Internet access or supporting many different types of PCs and operating systems is not what you want, then the SPX/IPX Protocol option may be for you. SPX/IPX is an acronym for *Sequenced Packet Exchange/Internet Packet Exchange.*

Unlike TCP/IP, SPX/IPX is a proprietary protocol, owned and developed by Novell, but also used by other network operating system companies, such as Microsoft and Banyan.

IPX is a protocol that sends data packets to requested destinations (workstations, servers, and so on). IPX addresses and routes outgoing data packets across a network. It reads the assigned addresses of returning data and directs the data to the proper area within the workstation's or network server's operating system.

SPX verifies and acknowledges successful packet delivery to any network destination by requesting a verification from the destinations that the data was received. The SPX verification must include a value that matches the value calculated from the data before transmission. By comparing these values, SPX ensures not only that the data packet made it to the destination, but that it arrived intact.

SPX can track data transmissions consisting of a series of separate packets. If an acknowledgment request brings no response within a specified time, SPX retransmits it. After a reasonable number of retransmissions fail to return a positive acknowledgment, SPX assumes the connection has failed and warns the operator of the failure.

Because IPX was first developed by Novell, the makers of NICs had to supply their own compliant IPX driver. The results were an IPX driver for each kind of NIC and a lot of hassle for network administrators to keep track of which went with which. For this reason, Novell developed the ODI/IPX communication protocol.

OPEN DATALINK INTERFACE

ODI stands for *Open Datalink Interface,* a network driver interface from Novell. It is a specification for NIC manufacturers to write a device driver for their NIC that can be used by any network protocol (for instance, SPX/IPX, TCP/IP, AppleTalk, and so on).

NETBIOS

NetBIOS stands for *Network Basic Input/Output System.* NetBIOS started out as a protocol that could communicate directly with network hardware without any other network software involved. Basically, it enables the use of naming conventions, rather than the typical numbering schemes, such as TCP/IP and IPX.

Unfortunately, NetBIOS does not contain a routing layer and is therefore unable to provide internetworking capability. Other protocols, such as IPX and IP, must be used for internetworking, though NetBIOS is often used to establish the connection.

NETBEUI

The acronym stands for NetBIOS *Extended User Interface*. Originally developed in 1985 by IBM, NetBEUI is a networking protocol that is an extension of the NetBIOS protocol. Consequently, it has the same shortcomings as NetBIOS. NetBEUI, too, does not travel across other LANs, because it can't be routed (routers are covered in Chapter 7), and is therefore recommended for linking fewer than two hundred PCs on the same segment or where bridging or switching is used to connect segments.

Summary

As this chapter illustrates, the dynamics involved in passing data across a network are complicated and they change daily with the evolution of networking. Nonetheless, understanding the most common choices available should help you decide which method best suits your networking needs. Table 6.1 provides an at-a-glance breakdown of the differences between the types of networks available.

TABLE 6.1	NETWORK TYPE	SIGNALING RATE	CABLE USED
Network Types and Their Characteristics	Ethernet	10Mbps	Coaxial (thin and thick), STP, UTP, Fiber optic
	Token Ring	4 or 16Mbps	STP, UTP
	ARCnet	2.5–20Mbps	Coaxial, STP, UTP, Fiber optic
	FDDI	100Mbps	Fiber optic
	ATM	1.5, 25, 51, 100, 155, 622Mbps and 2Gbps +	Fiber optic
	Fast Ethernet	100Mbps	Fiber optic, UTP (Cat 5)
	Gigabit Ethernet	1Gbps	UTP, Fiber optic

CHAPTER 7

Choosing Network Gear

Don't let the word *gear* in the chapter title scare you. You're not preparing for a trip through the Amazon or suiting up to climb Mount Everest. We simply replaced the overused term hardware with gear in order to bring a little change to our review of the component parts that make up an average LAN.

It seems not a day goes by that a maker of computer networking hardware (gear) doesn't introduce a new and improved device for LANs. Why? Because there are so many physical components that make up a network. This chapter takes you on a tour of the most common of those components. Depending on the topology and protocol chosen, you will need some of the following items among the gear making up your LAN.

Hubs

In Chapter 5 we introduced you to several network configuration models, or topologies. In our description of these various topologies, we briefly mentioned the hub device as a central location where all the cables come together.

Hubs in general are not unique to any one topology. They're used in Ethernet and Token Ring configurations, to name a few. Often they serve as a central connection point when adding workstations to a network or to strengthen transmission signals when longer cable segments are added between workstations and servers.

DUMB HUBS

First generation hubs, sometimes referred to as *basic* or *dumb hubs* were created to provide a basic LAN connection point for workgroups requiring access to shared resources. They're referred to as dumb because these earlier hubs lacked any control or management capability. They simply tied all of the cables together by way of a box with ports to plug cables into. In other words, a dumb hub accepts transmission signals via connected cables, then passes the signals on to other workstations connected to that hub.

Although they're being used less and less today, dumb hubs do provide an inexpensive and effective central connection point for the cables that make up a network. Because of their relative simplicity compared to today's smart hubs, dumb hubs are suitable for less complex environments. Sometimes referred to as *workgroup hubs,* dumb hubs are used to either split a transmission signal or provide a connecting point for additional workstations added to the single LAN segment. The dumb hub cannot boost a transmission signal and must be cabled directly to a workstation or smart hub for support.

SMART HUBS

Recognizing the limits of dumb hubs, manufacturers developed the second generation or *smart hub.* Smart hubs usually play the role of a signal amplifier in a typical network topology (much like a repeater, which is explained later in this chapter). These hubs provide limited management capability through software that enables the network administrator to program the way the hub operates. Smart hubs are more versatile distribution points and provide integrated support over several types of cables. You may have heard smart hubs referred to as *concentrators* because they can take the LANs capability and concentrate it into one device. Also, smart hubs sometimes take the shape of a card that fits into a slot on the server's motherboard to work jointly with network software and direct communications within the network. These are called internal or *card hubs,* and they do have limitations that external hubs do not. These include limited on-board random access memory, limited number of ports per card, a confinement to the capabilities of the buses they're plugged into, and they can slow down server speed. If you ever consider using card hubs, make sure you find out their limitations before you buy and install them.

INTELLIGENT HUBS

This is the level where hubs become significantly more task specific and advanced. Intelligent hubs are sophisticated smart hubs that support multiple LANs and topologies, provide extensive management capabilities, and can house other module types, such as routers and bridges. Intelligent hubs walk a fine line between the traditional role previously mentioned and the role of a switch, which is discussed at the end of this chapter. This fine line comes from the intelligent hub's very comprehensive network management capability and its ability to perform port switching and provide fault tolerance.

If you're considering a LAN that will eventually evolve into a WAN, then also consider investing in a top-end, intelligent hub. In a large network environment, systems administrators are well-served by hubs that offer the latest monitoring and management capability. Intelligent hubs keep tabs on the status of the network and correct problems as they occur. In our network management chapter, we tell you how intelligent hubs use management protocols to provide their sophisticated services.

Today's generation of hubs has come so far from the early first- and second-generation roots, it's hard to say how many branches the hub family tree has. Hubs from basic to intelligent come in several shapes and sizes and fall into numerous categories. In other words, not all hubs are created equal. So make sure you do some further, more extensive research on the type of hubs you need (if you need them at all) once you decide the extent of your LAN design.

As you can see, hubs — dumb, intelligent, or anywhere in between — play an essential role by providing significant flexibility in the design of a new network or by expanding the capability of an existing LAN.

Repeaters

Not to be confused with hubs, bridges, or routers, *repeaters* are the simplest form of a signal booster. A physical device designed to tie two long network cable segments together, a repeater gives the signal the added kick it needs to travel long distances in various cabling schemes. Whether or not you'll need repeaters as part of your network configuration will depend on how long the segments are. Segments consist of cables and computers combined. As mentioned in our chapter on network design, as long as the total length of the segment doesn't exceed the limit requirements for the particular type of cable used, a repeater isn't necessary, seen in Figure 7.1.

Repeaters accept information in the form of data packets sent by nodes (PCs) and other devices on the network, and basically rejuvenate (or amplify) the packet signal so it can travel a long distance without data loss. Data loss occurs when a signal gets so weak it becomes vulnerable to interference. This phenomenon, known as *attenuation*, is the sole reason repeaters exist. Weak signals that have been a little distorted by interference are fixed by the repeater before getting a shot of energy and pumped out the other side.

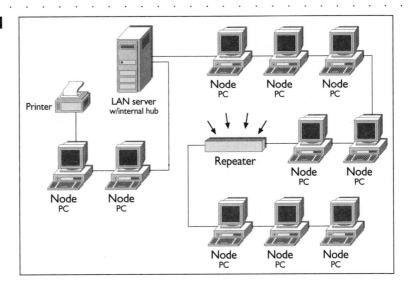

FIGURE 7.1

Repeaters are used when the total length of a segment exceeds the maximum signal length of the type of cable used.

Though this an important role, this is all repeaters do. They do not distinguish good packets from bad. They do not make computing or switching decisions. Repeaters simply receive data packets, juice them up, then send them on their way. It's as simple as that.

Well, almost. Some repeaters are choosy when it comes to which network signal they will accept on any given LAN. For instance, a repeater designed for an Ethernet network will only accept and pass Ethernet packets; a repeater designed for ARCnet will only pass ARCnet packets, and so on. Ethernet repeaters also help control data wrecks. Because Ethernet sends packets after only briefly checking to see if the path is clear, sometimes the checking process doesn't work. Sometimes the network segment is so long, a data packet that is using the cable may not be seen by an Ethernet workstation that's checking it. The workstation, assuming the cable is empty, then sends its packet. The two packets using the same path collide, resulting in a data-wreck. Repeaters designed specifically for Ethernet networks can assist in preventing wrecks by shortening the network. The segments required to accommodate multiple workstations on the network are thus shorter and allow the Ethernet card to see all data packs on the network at any given time.

These days, repeaters used on Token Ring networks are not stand-alone devices, but usually part of the hub device. Since hubs come in different network signaling configurations, there isn't much thought to the process of which complementing repeater to buy.

Repeaters are not choosy when it comes to cable, however. Most repeaters have the ability to link up disparate cable types. They accept data packets from coaxial, UTP, or STP cables on the same LAN and usually come with connectors for all three types.

One last important note about repeaters. No network should have or require more than four repeaters total. Why? Because each time data packets enter a repeater, they are taken apart and reassembled in their original form before they're released. This process, though done quickly, does delay the packet. Now imagine the packet traveling through this process more than four times. Probably not enough to notice, right? Wrong. If the sending workstation does not get a receipt signal back from a packet's destination in a certain amount of time, it will send the same packet again. Therefore, redundant packets could be bouncing all over the network, not only slowing things down, but clogging things up. Save yourself and everyone else some trouble and keep the total number of repeaters on your LAN under five.

Bridges

A step up in sophistication from a repeater, a *bridge* in its simplest form is a physical device that enables two or more networks to exchange information, regardless of their specific topologies. These box-type devices also play the role of a repeater between different segments on the same LAN or between two or more LANs. For example, a bridge can connect an Ethernet network to a Token Ring network, thus creating one big LAN. Or it can act as a partition used to break a single network into two smaller network segments.

Additionally, a bridge can distinguish good packets from bad. It prevents bad packets from getting any further down the LAN, thereby keeping bad data from cluttering the system. In its capacity as a data traffic regulator, a bridge dividing two segments on the same LAN memorizes all of the addresses for each node on both segments to which it is connected. If the bridge receives a data packet containing an address it does not recognize, the bridge will not allow it to go any further.

Like repeaters, bridges can accept data packets being sent across the network and boost their signal strength to offset the signal-carrying limits of the cable, then send the packets on their way. The advantage a bridge has over a repeater is that it can read the header information of a packet, called the *Media Access Control* (MAC) address, and determine the packet's intended destination. Then the bridge acts as traffic cop and waves the data on its way.

The MAC address is the unique number assigned to each NIC within each node on the LAN. Since the bridge knows the addresses for all NICs on the segments it is attached to, it can easily ascertain where the packet is going and allow it to cross over. Simply put, a bridge acts like a postal carrier. A bridge delivers packets specifically to the address on the packet. Also like a postal carrier, some packets are intended for all addresses, sort of like those "Dear Resident" letters you get, so the bridge broadcasts the packet to all segments.

BRIDGES USED BETWEEN SEGMENTS

A bridge keeps tabs on packets transmitted between nodes on both of the LAN segments to which it's attached. However, bridges don't let any old data pack cross over. For example, there's a bridge installed to separate a LAN into two segments, with one segment designated for Sally and one for Sam. If the bridge receives a data packet from Sam's network going to Sally's, the bridge recognizes it as needing to cross over and allows it to pass. However, if Sam sends a message to someone else on the Sam segment, the bridge recognizes that the signal doesn't need to cross over and thus allows it to continue on the Sam segment.

BRIDGES USED BETWEEN LANS

We've told you how bridges are used to connect segments of the same LAN. Now let's discuss how bridges are used to connect multiple LANs.

Imagine a company housed in one or several buildings, with each floor of each building represented by its own independent LAN network. Now, imagine the need to connect all of those LANs together to create a WAN or CAN. Bridges provide this ability. For example, if Sally's LAN is on the fourth floor of XYZ Corporation and Sam's LAN is located on the sixth floor, and XYZ wants to connect the two, a bridge can be used to make the connection.

CASCADING BRIDGE CONFIGURATION

To perform the function of connecting segments or LANs, bridges are typically used in one of two configurations. The first and least efficient is called *cascading*. In the cascading theme, a single bridge links one segment to another or one LAN to another in a daisy chain format, as seen in Figure 7.2.

A network connected to others via cascading bridges

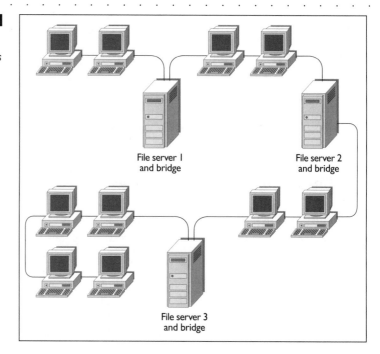

The problem with this arrangement is that for a signal to pass from segment C to segment A, it must traverse through all three segments and both bridges. Remember, a segment can be thought of as a length of network cable with more than two computers on it. For instance, think of the floors in the XYZ building used in our previous example — each floor represents one segment. The cascading configuration is the least popular because it requires data packets to go through several devices before reaching their intended destinations. This in turn provides a lot of opportunity for the data packet to be garbled from line noise or some other interference.

BACKBONE BRIDGE CONFIGURATION

The more popular and efficient manner of bridging networks is called a *backbone*. We discuss backbones in more depth in our internetworking chapter. Briefly stated, however, in a backbone configuration, each bridge for each segment is directly linked to the others, as seen in Figure 7.3.

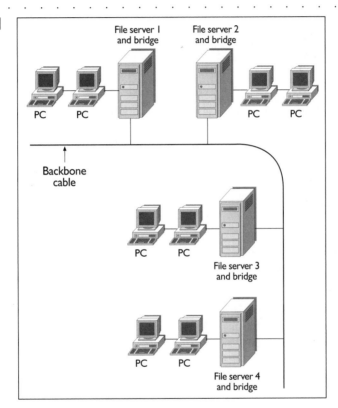

FIGURE 7.3

Networks connected via a backbone

In a backbone configuration the bridges share the responsibility of passing packets around. Each bridge is linked not only to each other but also to each segment — as you can see from the figure. These schemes are also referred to as *switching*.

With regard to price, the backbone plan is more expensive because of the higher number of bridges required. However, for budgetary justification purposes, the speed and efficiency of the network packets is greatly enhanced.

An added benefit of bridges is the capability to also filter out packets based on preconfigured criteria in addition to the maladaptive ones. For example, if a computer research department is testing a new type of signaling scheme on an active network but doesn't want the new signals to interfere with the mainstay of the network, the bridge can be configured to "segment off" their area. This will allow the test to occur without interfering with the rest of the network.

As is the trend with computers, smarter and more robust bridges exists for even more complicated scenarios. For the purposes of this book, however, let's stick to the basics.

Again, bridges, like the other devices we've discussed, are not all created equal. Some are very basic in design and task, while others are complex and hard to distinguish from routers. This creates a perfect segue to the our next device in this stroll through networking gear — routers.

Routers

Routers take us to another level of sophistication because they operate on the data transport layer of the OSI model (see Chapter 2). Offering significant capabilities beyond that of a bridge, routers are not beholden to any specific topology or protocol. Unlike bridges, routers don't care what MAC address is attached to a data packet making its way across the network. Routers only pay attention to the destination addresses attached to packets as a set of four decimal numbers separated by periods. This address describes the interface as a node within the network.

Routers come in several shapes, sizes, and capabilities. Some routers are external devices, some are internal, and some are nothing more than sophisticated software on a server.

Some sophisticated routers consist of two distinct devices rolled into one neat box. Designed to work in tandem within the router, these devices can receive, send, and process multiple protocols. A bridge decides when to forward each packet, but it cannot see other bridges or routers. Likewise, bridges are invisible to routers; hubs are invisible to bridges; and routers only know about other routers. Special additions to certain protocols allow routers to know about end nodes, but that is very rarely used. Generally, routers only know about other routers and network segments. Think of a router as a professional makeup artist. It receives data packets masked in one type of protocol, wipes the mask off, puts on a completely different protocol face, gives it the best directions to the stage, and sends it packing (excuse the pun).

How do routers do it? Through the use of routing protocols, which come in the form of sophisticated software designed to make specific decisions regarding the distribution of data packets over a given network. Routing protocols determine what information other routers need to know and keep all the routing decisions current in case the system administrator needs to see the information. Here are just three of the more common routing protocols used today:

▶ *OSPF* stands for *Open Shortest Path First,* one of the most widely used routing protocols for LANs running *Internet Protocol* (IP). OSPF tracks external routing information by using the IP multicasting transmission method. It can talk to all types of other routers, both internal and external, authenticate packets, and avoid routes that may cause transmission problems.

▶ *IGRP* stands for *Interior Gateway Routing Protocol* and offers the capability of managing a wide variety of bandwidths and delays. IGRP gives the user the option of configuring operating characteristics such as internetworking and bandwidth. This protocol manages internal, external, and other system routes.

▶ *RIP* stands for *Routing Information Protocol* and is used in TCP/IP and NetWare to identify all attached networks, as well as the number of router hops required to reach them. The responses are used to update a router's routing table.

Keep in mind, as we mentioned earlier, routers take several forms. Your network may not require an actual physical routing device. You may be able to conduct routing completely through the use of routing software.

ROUTERS AT WORK

To better illustrate the role both physical routers and software-based routing protocols play, let's look at how Novell's NetWare Multi-Protocol Router manages the routing process.

The NetWare operating system provides built-in support for the LAN protocols associated with each type of workstation that NetWare supports. Routing services can be made a part of a NetWare server that provides other services (such as file and print sharing), or they can be dedicated to their routing functions. Both integrated and stand-alone routers function the same way, but performance differences can be considerable. Stand-alone routers almost always offer better routing performance; however, they are more costly to set up and manage.

Internal routers reside within a NetWare server and consist simply of one or more network interface cards (NICs) and protocol NetWare Loadable Modules (NLMs) to provide routing segments (each serviced by a separate NIC in the file server) that are managed by the NetWare operating system. Using internal routing, NetWare can interlink as many LANs as there are distinct NICs in the server. The practical limit, based on cable and common machine constraints, is six to eight distinct network segments. This simple and effective approach to creating an expanded network is illustrated in Figure 7.4.

The principal external routing solution from Novell is called the *Novell Multi-Protocol Router* (MPR). It is a single-user or run-time NetWare operating system, combined with a number of NLMs to support routing for various networking protocols. If you want to think of it as an internal router, you're partially correct. Although the MPR runs on top of a NetWare OS (either 3.x or 4.x), it only provides file services for one user. In other words, an MPR is a NetWare server with more than one NIC.

NOTE Here we get into a discussion that mandates a shift in attitude or perception. In the past, NetWare and the NetWare file server were, for all intents and purposes, the same thing. When Novell introduced NetWare 3.0 and the NLM architecture, that changed in theory, but it was still true enough in practice. Only after NetWare 3.11 and the release of a number of NLM-based applications did the user community begin to see that one could take advantage of the NLM architecture in and of itself. They began to design networks with run-time NetWare servers that were dedicated to supporting the NLM applications (while maintaining file services). We call these *NetWare Core Protocol* (NCP) servers, since the operating system itself is NCP, but there are no file services present. We tend to call a NetWare file server an NCP server with file services (but only when we're being really nit-picky).

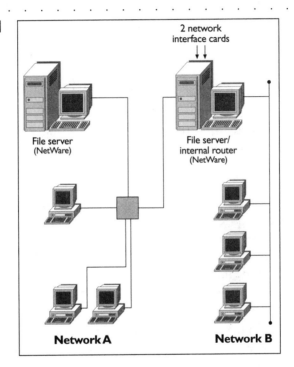

Network with server containing internal router

The NetWare MPR can be loaded on a full-blown NetWare file services server (which makes it an internal router), or it can be loaded on run-time NetWare (which makes it an external router). If you think of the difference between the two as simply the presence or absence of file services, you'll have an easier time with the concept of the product. Since the MPR is, in all other respects, a NetWare 3.x or 4.x file server, it has the same requirements as a file server: 386 or better Intel-compatible CPU, 4MB of RAM (preferably 8MB or more for reasonable performance, depending on disk storage size), at least 25MB of disk space in addition to a DOS partition, and so on.

When would you choose the MPR instead of allowing your server to act as an internal router? There are various practical reasons, some having to do with overcoming physical limitations. A short list of common reasons follows:

▸ The file server has no remaining expansion bus slots for additional NICs.

▸ The file server is already laden with activity, and performance is crucial.

▸ The file server is not conveniently located for interconnection of the dispersed networks.

▸ The applications in use are critical to the business, and all non-critical functions have to be off-loaded from the file server for *fault tolerance*. (Fault tolerance is the ability to avoid system failure due to problems with a single component or subsystem, whether hardware or software.)

▸ The routing functions are critical to the business and must be isolated from any possible causes of performance reduction, conflict, disruption, or failure.

▸ One of the links is a heavy-duty, high-traffic network segment that acts as a highway among multiple network segments, known as a *backbone*. (A backbone typically carries heavy traffic that might take up too much of a multipurpose server's processing capacity. Using a stand-alone router guarantees that the router will do its job properly and that local servers will not be bogged down by routing traffic on and off the backbone.)

▸ A special-purpose link must be integrated. Sometimes cable segments require 32-bit interfaces to be worthwhile; for instance, to get the best use out of a 100Mbps technology like the FDDI.

Figure 7.5 shows a multiprotocol internetwork using a Novell MPR. The MPR in the illustration routes IPX/SPX (NetWare's native protocol), TCP/IP (the native protocol of UNIX systems), and AppleTalk (the native protocol of Apple

Macintosh networks). Each of the separate networks can access each of the others by using the routing function of the MPR.

FIGURE 7.5

Multiprotocol internetwork using a Novell Multi-Protocol Router

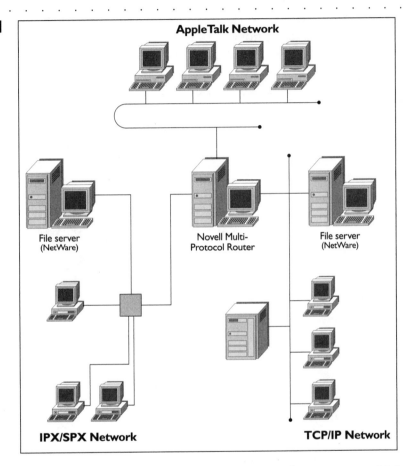

AppleTalk Network

File server
(NetWare)

Novell Multi-
Protocol Router

File server
(NetWare)

IPX/SPX Network

TCP/IP Network

Of course, Novell isn't the only vendor producing routers that support multiple protocols. There are others who provide dedicated devices that support many protocols. These products tend to offer higher performance at a higher cost than the Novell MPR. One advantage of the Novell MPR is that many system administrators feel less intimidated by the it than by other dedicated devices. MPR is based on the familiar architecture of the NetWare operating system and uses hardware that is as easily available as a personal computer.

Remote links can be configured when the distance between networks makes it impractical (or impossible) to physically connect them with standard network cables. In this case, telephone lines or *public data networks* (PDNs) are used to provide an intermediate transmission medium. You can connect networks that are located far apart from one another by configuring a router on each network with modems, as shown in Figure 7.6.

F I G U R E   7.6

Use routers for remote linking to other networks.

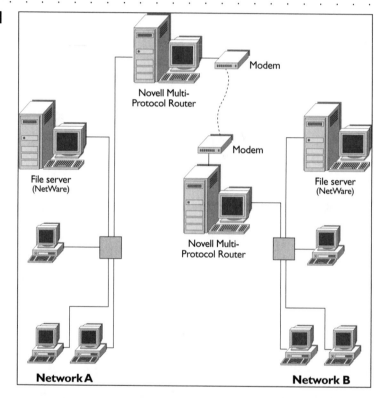

One last note regarding routers: Consider their role carefully when planning your network. Understand the difference between an external, internal and software router and what types of service you expect them to provide. Also, consider at what level you expect them to perform these services. By understanding the benefits routers can provide when used in conjunction with the right protocol, you avoid a lot of transmission problems and enjoy the performance properly placed routers provide.

Switches

We close this chapter discussing switches because they have a lot in common with the device we opened this chapter with — hubs. If you recall, we said that today's more sophisticated hubs are difficult to distinguish from switches. (In fact, many of the latest generation hubs are so sophisticated that they are better characterized as switches because they incorporate per-port switching capability.) Switches automate network reconfiguration, and therefore, increase network availability and capability. For example, Sally's LAN cables all come together at the central location device known as a switch (much like a hub). Once Sally completes all of the physical connections for the servers, printers, nodes, and modems, she then uses network management software to program the switch's memory module with information about each cable connected to each of it's ports. She tells the switch that port 1 contains a node segment, on port 2 there's a network printer, and on port 3 there's a modem. From that point on, when the switch receives a data packet destined for the printer on port 2, it turns port 2 on and allows the data packet to travel down that cable segment only. A typical hub is not capable of turning the individual ports on and off. Additionally, if Sally installs another printer somewhere on the cable connected to port 2, she simply updates the switch's memory module electronically with the new configuration information.

Another important feature that some switches provide is disaster recovery. These switches provide LAN managers the ability to build and store alternate configurations in preparation for a potential disaster. If a disaster strikes, the switch can turn on ports connected to specific stations designed to back up the data, or the switch turns off specific ports in order to isolate those segments experiencing problems. This capability provides some security features in that it enables the network administrator to switch off certain ports during certain days of the week or hours of the day, thereby denying access to some users.

Last but certainly not least, switches provide some degree of fault tolerance. For instance, imagine that in place of the sophisticated switch, Sally uses a typical hub as a central connection point for all of her network cables. If the hub malfunctions or experiences a *fault*, Sally's entire network will go down. Not a good scenario, is it? A sophisticated switch can sometimes isolate the problem while still allowing the unaffected portion of the network to operate, thereby providing a certain degree of fault tolerance.

Summary

That about wraps up this chapter on networking gear. Remember, there's a lot to learn about the gear involved in setting up a LAN, and you might find it difficult at times to determine the best gear to use on yours. But hang in there; you're not alone. Even the most experienced network administrators who spend many hours of their lives knee-deep in the networking industry, sometimes have a hard time distinguishing the difference between a bridge and a router.

CHAPTER 8

Internetworking

Some day philosophers will no doubt look back at the close of the twentieth century and marvel over our sudden rush to get connected. People these days don't just want to connect to devices like printers, or applications like databases, they want to connect to everything and everyone.

Years ago, when Cheryl Currid was designing and building one of the first large scale corporate LANs, a technician came up to her and said, "When are we going to stop hooking up these computers. Every day, we receive new requests for people to hook up." Cheryl looked at him, smiled, and replied, "When we run out of desktops, branch offices, manufacturing plants, homes, hotel rooms, suppliers, customers, and consumers. That's when."

The point: The quest for connectivity doesn't end until everything (and everyone) gets connected. And that quest for connectivity takes us to the topic of this chapter, *internetworking*.

The notion of networking doesn't stop at the workgroup or department level. Nor is it bound to the physical constraints of a single building, enterprise, or location. Moreover, in business, the desire to connect spans beyond organizational boundaries to the industry and beyond. New business models dictate that companies work efficiently with suppliers and customers. Further, electronic commerce is already here for many industries, and it brings with it special new requirements for connectivity to outside organizations.

Still another opportunity exists. As PCs have become almost as pervasive as the telephone, they may someday replace it. New network switching components and new architectures are beginning to make people question, "Why do I have a separate telephone system for voice and a network system for data. Can't both voice and data run over the same lines?" The answer is yes and no. The capability is possible, the technology is here, it just takes time and motivation to convert.

In this chapter, we turn our focus to the first step beyond the local LAN or work group. We lay the groundwork and map out the likely connections that almost any network will ultimately need. Then we discuss the various technologies that you might apply as you extend the physical and logical reach of your network. Even if you are sure that your network will never extend beyond the five people in your workgroup, read this chapter anyway. You never know when you'll want to connect up to external services like the Internet or CompuServe. Likewise, new voice processing technology may turn into a compelling opportunity for you.

The purpose of this chapter is to give you an introduction to internetworking and WAN technology. We don't expect to make you an overnight expert on internetwork design or installation, but we believe it's valuable for everyone to understand the options and choices to expand the network.

What Is Internetworking?

Let's start with a simple three-word definition of the term internetworking: tying together LANs.

The union of networks should operate invisibly or seamlessly, as if they were one. Network users should not know from response time lags that Sue sits in sunny Florida while Sam stays in Syracuse. It shouldn't matter if all the data and devices are on the network. An easy concept, right?

Networks can be tied together by very simple means. Two LANs connected by a cable represents the simplest form of an internetwork. So does a single cable running vertically through the telephone closets of a high rise building. Just as long as it stops at each floor to connect to the local LAN, every network can be easily connected to each other. As shown in Figure 8.1, internetworking can start out with an extremely uncomplicated design.

Realistically, however, internetworking doesn't start and stop by just tying together a few nearby workgroup LANs. Invariably, your organization's connectivity needs will go far beyond a few local sites. As different technologies are deployed, the simplistic picture of a lone cable connecting LANs disappears, replaced by a complex set of technologies and considerations.

Sometimes people confuse the terms internetworking and WAN. As we described in Chapter 1, a WAN connects LANs that are housed at different physical locations. Most WANs require special long-distance or leased phone lines to make that connection.

By contrast, an internetwork can connect multiple LANs in one single location. For example, several buildings of a campus environment or several floors of a high-rise office building would make up an internetwork. In short, a WAN always involves internetworking but an internetwork doesn't always require a WAN.

We make this distinction to help you think about the technology you'll need when selecting your internetwork. Because you are probably buying your own cable for a local internetwork, you have slightly more control than you would with a WAN. Building a WAN almost always dictates that you work with a long distance carrier, such as AT&T, Sprint, MCI, and so on.

Internetworking can be as simple as merely tying together two or more LANs.

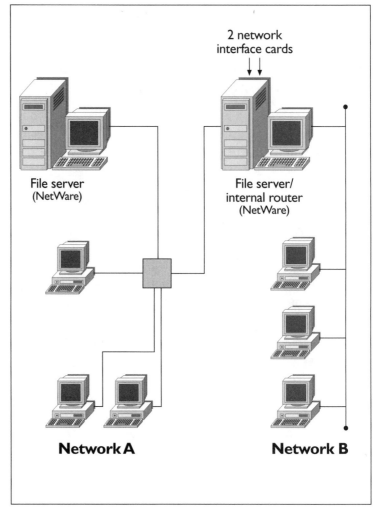

Network Connection Devices

On each end of the communications line, you need a device to make the connection to the local LAN. Depending on the type of wire or line you use, you have a choice of devices, from a simple modem all the way up to a complex multiprotocol router.

Bridges often maintain the semblance of a single logical LAN by simply forwarding packets of data from one segment to the next. For example, a two-port bridge splits a logical network into two physical segments. Then it transmits packets across the bridge only if its destination lies on the other side. By forwarding packets only when necessary, it helps to reduce network congestion. This approach works fine for local interconnections or high long-distance bandwidth lines, but isn't as efficient as other means. Newer bridge models combine some of the functions of a router (described next) to manage the packet traffic between networks more efficiently.

Routers select which data packets to route between multiple LAN segments. They make intelligent decisions about the path that packets should take around the backbone and they know where the final destination is located. In so doing, routers are much more efficient. Until the advent of multiprotocol routers, however, routers would only handle one protocol, such as Novell's IPX. Therefore, PCs on a routed internetwork that connected Novell's IPX along with an IBM mainframe running IBM's *Systems Network Architecture* (SNA) might not see the mainframe. The SNA packets wouldn't have gotten over the router.

Hubs, or concentrators, handle the cabling requirements of linking up internetworks, connecting the ring or bus topology of each LAN to the network backbone. Traditional Ethernet LANs run at 10Mbps over a common bus-type design, even when they are physically attached to a hub, repeater, or concentrator. Every station is capable of receiving all transmissions from all stations, or sending to all stations, although not simultaneously. They can either talk or listen. See Chapter 7 for more information about these devices.

Switches also handle the cabling requirements of linking up networks and internetworks, but they're much faster than hubs and concentrators.

Consider the reality of what bandwidth is really available on your network. Most LANs run at either 10Mbps or 16Mbps. If you have thirty nodes on a segment or ring, that bandwidth is shared among all thirty nodes. Each node only gets $\frac{1}{30}$ of 10Mbps, or to be more technically accurate, $\frac{1}{30}$ of 25 percent of 10Mbps, which is the maximum traffic for an Ethernet segment. That computes to 83Kbps per node, which is faster than a modem but slower than an ISDN line.

Now you know why switches challenge hubs. Great speed advances come with switched rather than shared media. Replace the hub with a switch, and each node gets a full 10Mbps. Replace the 10Mbps cards with 100Mbps cards and each node gets a full 100Mbps. Giving full bandwidth to each user on a LAN ought to speed up those difficult sessions where packets are flowing but not fast.

Switches do more than simply direct packets to one side or the other of a network. They identify the target and send traffic directly to its destination without waiting.

Also, just to tweak up speeds a little higher, there are two types of switching architectures: *cut-through* and *store-and-forward*. The cut-through approach reads the destination address of a packet and immediately sends it on its way, without waiting for the entire packet to arrive at the switching device. The store-and-forward technique buffers incoming packets in memory until it runs a *cyclic redundancy check* (CRC) looking for errors. This approach adds a little time to the process, but avoids problems associated with bad packets going out unchecked and collisions that can slow down the overall performance of the network segment.

Which mode is best? According to Harvard University networking expert Scott Bradner, if you have a noisy network, you might think twice before enabling a cut-through mode; the decrease in network slowdowns might be outweighed by the increase in LAN traffic because of corrupted packets.

Communications Lines

To make the connection, there must be something between the devices, namely a communication line. In a local environment, the communication line might be as simple as a single cable. Generally speaking, internetwork designers use high quality cable that can support the fast traffic, and lots of it.

As described in Chapter 6, most cable choices are made from coaxial, twisted-pair, or fiber-optic cabling. Your specific decision may rest on what's already available in your building or what can be most easily installed.

WIRELESS LINKS FOR INTERNETWORKING

Before we talk about the various types of phone lines and transmission options, we must also consider connecting without wires. Depending on your physical environment, you may find the most cost effective connection is the one you make through thin air.

Two primary wireless technologies are available for internetworking: *microwave* and *spread spectrum*. Either can make a cost effective option, especially when the only other choice might be to lay your network cable and conduit by digging up a parking lot. Day-to-day operating costs of wireless technologies are low too. Because no one owns the air, you don't pay fees for air time, as long as you control both sending and receiving units. Of course, that also means if your wireless link goes down, you can't call the telephone company. You'll have no one but yourself to fix it.

A microwave signal can travel several hundreds of miles, as long as the transmitters have line of sight with each other. They must be pointed directly at each other without obstructions from other buildings or trees. Speeds of 2Mbps to 34Mbps are available from this technology.

Regulatory issues may affect your ability to use microwave systems. Licenses from national authorities are required for all microwave transmission schemes, some may be restricted altogether. Construction activity may also affect your ability to use microwave technology. If someone decides to build a high rise and disrupts your transmission, you may have to find an alternative technology, or rent roof space on the newly constructed obstruction.

Spread spectrum is a wireless radio technology originally developed by the military for secure and interference-immune communications. Spread spectrum has been available to commercial users since 1985. There are actually two types of spread spectrum in use today, both developed for the military: *frequency hopping* and *code division multiple access* (CDMA). Frequency hopping is an analog technique, whereas CDMA is digital.

Frequency hopping is based on the fact that transmissions are hard to intercept. Using short transmissions on many frequencies spreads the message out, making it hard to intercept the whole message. CDMA is far more useful, but much more complex.

Spread spectrum technology also promises some help to interconnect certain nearby LANs. For example, the Proxim RangeLINK family of high-speed, wireless data bridges connects LANs in buildings up to three miles apart. This technology is faster than long distance phone lines, but slower than LAN speeds. Most spread spectrum LANs operate at about 2Mbps or less, compared to a standard Ethernet, which is 10Mbps. However, Proxim's 1.6Mbps radio data rate delivers a throughput that rivals most leased line connections, such as 56/64Kbps, Frame Relay, and T-1.

RangeLINK supports a transparent bridge architecture that works with any protocol or network operating system that supports Ethernet, including Novell NetWare, TCP/IP, Banyan Vines, DECNet, IBM LAN Server, AppleTalk, and others.

TELEPHONE AND LEASED LINES

When data traffic must travel beyond the immediate building or campus, you have two options for connections. You may choose from dial-up or leased lines to make the connection from one LAN to another. The speed of the connection will vary too, depending on what type of line you order.

If the concept of internetworking is new to you and your organization, we suggest that you first take a look at the types of applications likely to be used. If workers merely run PC applications and electronic mail from the network, you probably won't need high speed lines. If, however, there's a chance that you'll be installing distributed databases, groupware, or desktop video conferencing, beware of their hefty bandwidth requirements.

Today, with the right equipment and lines, you have options for almost any type of demand. From dial-up networking with regular modems at speeds of 28.8Kbps to super sonic ATM speeds of over 600Mpbs, you can buy bandwidth. Table 8.1 lists some popular connection technologies and their maximum speed ratings. Table 8.2 shows the same considerations for LANs.

TABLE 8.1	WIDE AREA TECHNOLOGY	SPEED	COMMENTS
Popular Connection Technologies and Maximum Speed Ratings	POTS	33.6Kbps	Nearing theoretical limitations as we currently know them.
	ISDN	128 Kbps or two 64Kbps	Can be divided into two lines. One line can be analog, for use as a normal phone line.
	T1	1.544 Mbps	Can be split into numerous channels or divided up into sixty four 256Kbps lines (called fractional T1).
	ADSL	8Mbps receive 640Kbps send	Other than differences in send/ receive, this works like other digital lines.
	STS-1 SONET	51.84Mbps	Not used.
	ATM	25Mbps, 155Mbps, 622Mbps	Gaining popularity.

TABLE 8.2	LOCAL AREA TECHNOLOGY	SPEED	COMMENTS
Popular LAN Connection Technologies and Maximum Speed Ratings	ARCnet	2Mbps and 20Mbps	An all but extinct technology.
	Token Ring	4Mbps and 16Mbps	Once the preferred companion to mostly IBM shops; more expensive and less popular than Ethernet.
	Ethernet	10Mbps and 100Mpbs, Gigabit	The most popular choice.
	FDDI	100Mbps	Token passing.

These options vary dramatically in cost. Generally speaking, you get extra speed, reliability, and convenience for extra dollars. Don't let that stop you from comparison pricing. Each year, new technology developments tend to change the rules. Your day-to-day operating expenses could quickly change depending on new types of technology introduced.

Watch out about trusting theoretical limitations. Often you'll find today's technical limitations become tomorrow's history. It wasn't too many years ago that no one thought you could transmit data faster than 9.6Kbps over unconditioned phone lines. Today, that figure looks foolish when compared to the low-cost 14.4Kpbs, 28.8Kbps, and 33.6Kbps modems available today.

Another consideration is dial-up versus continuous connection. Unless your budget is very tight, let us suggest that you dedicate the line to interconnecting your LANs. While it is possible to share some of the phone line technologies with other applications during the day, it isn't recommended.

People will not learn to use the internetworked resources efficiently when the connection isn't persistent. Imagine Sue trying to set up a weekly report to print for Sam in Syracuse. Say that Sue knows how to print the report to a printer near Sam's office. If she prints the report every Thursday without problems, then both she and Sam will be happy, but if the network connection is up and down sporadically, then she's unlikely to trust the system. Chances are Sue doesn't care that you are trying to save a few dollars on phone lines. In fact, she'll spend so much extra time and effort express mailing the report to Sam that it will more than make up for the savings.

Now for the communication options. For connecting LANs together, consider some of the tried and true options. These alternatives include *plain old telephone system* (POTS), ISDN, T1, frame relay-based internetworking, and ATM.

Using POTS and dialing out with the PC's modem or a modem server on the LAN, the maximum speed is slow (only 28.8Kbps or slightly higher with newer modems that use advanced compression). POTS lines can be dial-up or dedicated. POTS requires a modem for each line on the service.

The bad news about POTS is reliability. Regular phone lines were configured for voice traffic and not data. Line noise during data transmissions can slow down or disconnect a communications session. The good news about POTS is cost. It requires only one extra business telephone line per location.

ISDN lines are available from most telecommunications providers that serve a local area. Maximum speed is 128Kbps if you use the full capability of these lines. Many, however, split the lines into two 64Kbpschannels, one for data and one for voice. With certain types of software overhead, the true throughput speed may actually turn into 56Kpbs. This is still a lot faster than POTS, but not as fast as the advertised rate.

ISDN lines can be dial-up or dedicated. To complete the connection, ISDN requires a terminal adapter device to connect the LAN to the ISDN lines much the same way as a router works. Alternatively, the device can be directly connected to an individual PC to service that unit only. These devices are not modems but are starting to look and act much like regular modems. Some makers even call them *ISDN modems*.

T1 lines are specially purchased or leased lines that let data travel up to 1.544Mpbs. These, like ISDN, can be split up into channels to accommodate other simultaneous traffic, such as voice or slower data traffic. To complete a T1 connection requires a special device. Like ISDN, it is available to multiple users on the LAN, but you also need a router.

Frame relay-based internetworks are strong, fast, and somewhat unsophisticated. Coming from an older technology, called *X.25*, frame relay is similar, travels over faster lines, and is unencumbered with X.25's error control. Frame relay can be implemented up to T1 speed, which is 24 times faster than X.25. Some phone carriers push it even faster, up to T3 rates, which makes it 672 times faster than X.25.

ATM is an even faster communications technology, with speeds ranging from 25Mbps to 655Mbps. These lines, like other high performance lines, can be divided up to accommodate other types of voice and data traffic. An ATM adapter is required to complete the connection to the line.

Of these choices, you have many options for line speed, as shown in Figure 8.2. It's almost as if you are choosing different sized plumbing pipes for your home.

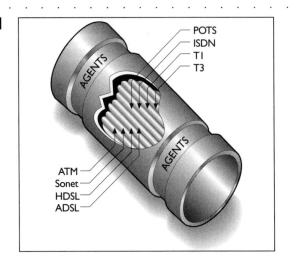

FIGURE 8.2

Different communications technologies provide you with virtual pipes for data to pass through. It's helpful to imagine them as plumbing pipes of different widths and capacities.

Connecting LANs to Host Environments

While internetworking LANs is a popular activity, it frequently isn't the only one network managers must face. Organizations that have mainframe computers or minicomputers want those attached to the network, too.

Many minicomputers attach to the network easily through standard Ethernet connections and the TCP/IP protocol.

Many companies still have large data stores in their mainframes to which end users need to have access. Even as companies migrate to more network-centric client-server computing, data still needs to be shared between mainframes and servers.

Connecting LANs to IBM Hosts

IBM brand computers use a different network protocol, SNA. It requires a little special handling when it comes to making a connection.

Gateway servers are used by some organizations to communicate and translate data stream into a format understood by SNA. The data is then sent to the mainframe over a token ring, Ethernet, or other line. Then, on the mainframe side, a network processing application runs called *Virtual Telecommunications Access*

Method (VTAM), which is responsible for taking the data stream and passing it to the application on the mainframe.

Depending on the exact product, the gateway PC and software sits between your PC and the mainframe and performs protocol conversion. It enables your PC to emulate a dumb 3270 terminal, so you can run any standard mainframe application. The solution also provides software that runs on the individual's PC to provide a shell for the terminal screens that are returned.

On Novell LANs, you can install NetWare for SAA to give you a simple but powerful connection. Using standard IPX/SPX and TCP/IP protocol stacks, the desktop PC and server communicate without the need for SNA and NDIS drivers at each workstation. The network administrator is freed from the time-consuming chore of installing and configuring each PC with special LAN support and NDIS drivers.

NetWare for SAA 2.0 can support up to two thousand concurrent sessions with any *logical unit* (LU) type, such as display, printer, file transfer, and applications. It is sold by the number of host sessions, in packages of 16, 64, 128, 254, 508, or 1,016. You can increase the number of sessions by combining packages.

For the AS/400, the number of independent sessions available can be a little difficult to determine. It varies depending on different AS/400 models, disk space, the type and number of processors, the data link types, data link speed, the specific software applications running, total system usage by users, system memory, and system jobs/applications at any given time.

Summary

As we said at the opening of this chapter, the quest for connectivity is insatiable. That's one of the few indisputable facts of running a network. Your own network design should always keep growth and extra connectivity in mind, even if no one asks for it today.

Even if your company is no longer growing, and the number of computers in the office remains stable, don't count out connectivity. It seems that someone always wants that link that you haven't planned.

As we watch business trends and their effects on technology needs, we see continued changes ahead. So, if you are planning your company's network, remember the advice given to that inquisitive LAN technician so many years ago: We'll stop growing networks "when we run out of desktops, branch offices, manufacturing plants, homes, hotel rooms, suppliers, customers, and consumers. That's when."

CHAPTER 9

Choosing a Network Operating System

So far we've talked a lot about the choices you make when planning a LAN. Among the most basic of all the choices is deciding on the type of *network operating system* (NOS) as the central platform upon which to start. This chapter focuses on the advantages of the major systems from which to choose: Novell NetWare, Microsoft Windows NT, Banyan System VINES, IBM OS/2, and Macintosh. In addition, we review some non-network operating systems designed specifically for the PC or client: Microsoft DOS, Microsoft Windows, Windows for Workgroups, and Microsoft Windows 95.

We suggest that you read our description to start, pick two or three platforms you want to know more about, then surf the Internet or visit a good bookstore and pick up detailed guides for each of your choices. Table 9.1 lists Internet URLs and books that we recommend you take a look at if you want to learn more about these network operating systems.

TABLE 9.1	NETWORK OS	URL	REFERENCE BOOK
Reference Information for Common Network Operating Systems	NetWare	www.novell.com	Novell's Guide to NetWare 4.1 Networks (Novell Press, IDG Books)
	Windows NT	www.microsoft.com	Microsoft Windows NT Server One Step at a Time (Microsoft Press)
			Networking Essentials (Microsoft Press)
	Banyan VINES	www.banyan.com	Banyan VINES: The Professional Reference (New Rider Pub.)
	OS/2	www.ibm.com	OS/2 Warp for the SoHo Environment: Making the Most of the Small Office Home Office PC (McGraw-Hill)
	System 7	www.macintosh.com	Networking the Macintosh: A Step-by-Step Guide to Using AppleTalk in Business Environments (McGraw-Hill)
	Windows 3.1 & Windows for Workgroups 3.11	www.microsoft.com	Networking with Windows for Workgroups (Sybex)
	Windows 95	www.microsoft.com	Microsoft Windows 95 Step by Step; Running Microsoft Windows (Microsoft Press)

Learn as much as you can about the different NOS platforms and what options they offer, before you buy. It's time well spent.

The first choice outlined, Novell NetWare, is covered in more detail than the rest because it shares similarities with most NOSs.

Novell NetWare

Positioned as the number one network operating system used today, Novell NetWare has become the NOS of choice for both large and small organizations, not only in the United States, but around the world.

Unlike many peer-to-peer setups, NetWare does not use MS DOS as an operating language. Instead, NetWare runs its own OS, and is compatible with any number of workstations running dissimilar systems. Therefore, NetWare servers can support DOS, UNIX, and OS/2 workstations or Macintosh clients.

NetWare is currently offered in four versions: 3.12, 4.1, 4.11, and IntranetWare. For the purpose of this discussion, we concentrate on NetWare 4.1 and 4.11. From this point forward we'll refer to these versions as 4.x.

Probably the biggest advantage offered by Novell NetWare 4.x is its *NetWare Directory Services* (NDS) capability. NDS provides a powerful scheme for arranging your entire organization's network into a unified structure, so careful planning is crucial. In addition, NDS enables you to organize network resources, gain easy access to those resources, and centralize the administration of your network.

Imagine a network with thousands of objects, hundreds of servers, and dozens of network administrators in various departments. With Novell NDS, all of these objects and servers exist in one network database. NDS provides consistency and logical organization so large networks can streamline the work of all network administrators. Without this capability, the network is very confusing and cumbersome.

When planning to use NDS, consider the following issues:

▶ What organizational structure of the directory tree makes the most sense for your network resources?

▶ How are you going to name objects?

> ▸ How do you want the directory database to be partitioned, and where do you want to store replicas of those partitions?

> ▸ How should time be kept and synchronized among the servers on the network?

We tackle each of these issues one by one in the following sections.

PLANNING YOUR ORGANIZATION'S DIRECTORY TREE

To begin planning your directory tree, look first at your organization's structure, functions, and needs. NDS is designed to reflect a hierarchical structure. Generally, this means that your directory tree will be patterned according to the structure of your organization, whether or not that structure is formal.

For example, if your organization is formally divided into departments, you may decide to structure your directory tree by departments as well. On the other hand, if people in several departments work together on long-term projects and need access to common resources, it may make more sense to divide your tree by project teams instead of departments. Also consider the location. If users exist at more than one site, you will want to reflect that in the tree.

When planning your directory tree, also consider who will be running the network. With NetWare 4.x, you can centralize network administration so that a single person or small group of people controls the entire directory database, or you can distribute administration so that many network administrators throughout the enterprise control their own portions of the directory database.

If network administration will be distributed among several people, it is crucial that those people be involved in planning the network. They must also be kept informed of all decisions and rules made about creating and naming objects, assigning security, and so on. Otherwise, there is no way to ensure the consistency that makes NDS so powerful. Designing by committee always has its downfalls, but in this case, designing in a vacuum could be even worse. Making massive, fundamental changes to a directory tree once it has been established can be difficult.

Designing the directory tree so that every network administrator is happy could become a political issue, but in most cases, a smooth outcome is in everyone's best interest. Therefore, try to concentrate on simplifying the hierarchy as much as possible. Then publish a description of all rules and guidelines for naming objects and defining information about those objects. Published guidelines make it much easier for network administrators to create new users with correct e-mail names, consistent addresses and phone numbers, and so on.

At some point in the directory-tree planning stage, someone may suggest that different portions of the organization could have separate directory trees. Resist this temptation. There are several problems with having multiple trees. The point of NDS is to unify the organization's network resources. Having separate trees defeats this. Also, it is difficult to get from one tree to another. If you are in one tree, the only way you can access another tree is to log in to its server using bindery emulation — but only with 16-bit clients; 32-bit clients can log in to as many as fifty trees. This makes it impossible to use the second tree in NDS mode, which eliminates many of the useful features of NetWare 4.x. (Bindery emulation is explained later in this chapter.) Finally, though it is possible to merge two trees after they've been created, it is much easier to set up a single tree in the beginning.

If the reason people want two or more trees is because different people or groups want to "own" their own portions of the network, it is easy to set up a single tree so that administration is distributed to different people. A single person does not have to have control of the entire directory. You can set it up so that several people each have ultimate control over their own portion of the tree.

NDS is designed in large part around the international communications specification X.500. This specification is an attempt to standardize worldwide telecommunications. Before the X.500 specification was even complete, Novell attempted to comply with as much of the specification as possible, while at the same time simplifying some of the characteristics that are not even directly related to computer networking.

The following sections explain more about planning your directory tree.

The Hierarchy of Objects

In its most basic form, your organization can probably be broken down into a beautifully simple pattern. This simple pattern is what NDSs uses to organize objects in the directory tree.

There is a top-level, all-encompassing entity to which everything else belongs. This entity may be a company, an organization, an association, a government agency, a school district, or the like. In NDS, this level is called *an organization object*. Your directory tree must have at least one organization object.

Within the top-level entity, there may be subgroups, each of which have their particular responsibilities. These subgroups may be divisions, departments, subsidiaries, workgroup units, schools, offices, project teams, and so on. In NDS, these subgroups are called organizational unit objects. Organizational unit objects can contain other organizational unit objects as well. For example, the sales department of a company may contain sales teams called Inside Sales, Outside Sales, and Sales Support. If your organization is very small, you may not need any organizational unit objects. If your company is very large, you will probably have many levels of organizational unit objects.

Finally, within any organizational unit, you find all the individual resources of which it is comprised: people, computers, printers, and similar single entities. Each of these entities has its own object in NDS. There are server objects, user objects, printer objects, print queue objects, computer objects, and so on.

These three elements — organization objects, organizational unit objects, and single-entity objects — are what you will use to set up the hierarchy of your network.

There is a fourth level of objects that you can use if you wish, but it is less useful. The country object is an optional object that is even higher than the organization object. If your organizations span countries, you can use the country object to designate in which country each is located. However, it is better to divide a multinational organization into organizational units than into countries. We recommend against using the country object because it will make it more difficult for users to navigate the directory tree. This is explained more fully in the section on naming objects, later in this chapter. Country objects are not necessary for complying with X.500 directory services guidelines, so there really are few reasons to use the country object.

The last type of object you need to know about is the root object. The root object is the very first object in the directory tree, and it cannot be deleted or modified. All other objects, including organizations, are contained within the root object.

Container Objects Versus Leaf Objects

All of the different types of objects fall into two categories: *container objects* and *leaf objects*. Container objects can contain other objects. Country, organization, and organizational unit objects are all container objects.

Single-entity objects are leaf objects, because they cannot contain any other objects, just as a leaf on a tree cannot contain other leaves or branches. For further reading on this subject, refer to *Novell's Guide to NetWare 4.1*.

Considering Object Security in the Directory Tree

Another aspect of objects you may need to consider when planning your directory tree is object security, known as *trustee rights*. Just as there are NetWare trustee rights that control what users can do with directories and files, NetWare 4.x includes an additional set of trustee rights that affect objects and their properties. These object rights and property rights control how objects can work with one another. For example, a user object might have rights to read the telephone-number property of another user object. The same user might also have the rights necessary to change the postal address property of another user object.

Like trustee rights in the file system, trustee rights for objects and properties can be inherited. If you have certain rights to a container object, you can inherit those rights and exercise them in the objects within that container. However, each object has an *inherited rights filter* (IRF) that can block some or all of the rights a user inherits on that object. If an IRF is applied at the container level, then inherited rights are blocked for the container object and the entire subtree below.

This concept of inherited object rights is one that may help you plan your directory tree. Grouping users with similar security needs within the same container object may simplify some network administration tasks.

Files and Directories Are Not Objects

It is important to make a distinction between the directory database and the file system. The directory database contains information about all the resources on the network, including volumes. However, the directory database does not include files and directories. The files and directories on a network are components of the file system instead.

In some ways, the distinction between the directory database and the file system is quite clear. In others, the line is blurred, if not erased.

The two different sets of NetWare trustee rights are a good example of the clear separation between the two. One set of trustee rights in NetWare 4.x is the traditional set that controls what users can do with directories and files. Previous versions of NetWare have included these file-system trustee rights as an integral part of NetWare. In NetWare 4.x, file-system trustee rights still exist and operate just as they first did in NetWare 3.11.

In addition to these trustee rights, NetWare 4.x introduces an entirely different set that affects objects and their properties. Object and property rights are separate from file-system rights. They do not affect each other.

Another example of the separation between the file system and the directory database is in directory partitions. Replicas of the directory database partitions are stored on several servers on the network so that there is no potential single point of failure. This means that if one server disk crashes, the database is not lost — replicas on other servers continue to provide the database information. However, the file system is not part of the directory partition, so the files and directories stored on the crashed disk will not be available to the network. (This is a good reason for ensuring that you have established disk mirroring or disk duplexing on all of your critical servers. See Chapter 11.)

These examples illustrate how the file system and the directory database are separate. To smooth the transition between the two systems, NetWare 4.x has integrated them so that you can easily work with both from within the same utilities. This is where the line blurs between the two.

For example, with the NetWare Administrator utility, which is a graphical user-interface utility that runs under Windows or OS/2's Presentation Manager, you can browse through the directory tree to see the objects on your network. As you open each container object, a list of the objects within that container appears. When you reach a leaf object, you cannot open it because there are no objects within it.

However, when you open a volume object, which is a leaf object, it does appear to open and list the files and directories within it. This is the point where NetWare seamlessly melds the directory database with the file system.

Also, although object rights and file-system rights are separate, they again overlap at the volume object. The ADMIN user is granted the supervisor object right to the volume object when the volume object is created. That assignment automatically grants the ADMIN user the supervisor file-system right to the files and directories within that volume.

PUTTING YOURSELF IN THE RIGHT CONTEXT

Finding your way around the directory tree requires that you understand how objects are named and what their context is in the tree. The following sections explain these concepts.

What Is an Object's Complete Name?

Each object in the directory tree has a name, such as Fred, Anne, Queue2, or Sales_Server. Each object also has a complete name. An object's complete name in NDS is actually more of an address that indicates the object's position in the tree. An object's complete name includes the name of each container object that precedes it, all the way to the root object.

For example, to find Mary at her home, you have to know the country she lives in, the state or province, her city, her street, and finally her house number. In essence, you could say that this address actually defines Mary's complete name. "Mary Whitmore, 1200 Pennsylvania Avenue, Washington, DC, 20044-7566, USA" is a more complete definition than simply "Mary." Without all that information about Mary, you might never reach her.

Similarly, to find Mary on the network, you need to know the organization object and any organizational unit objects that contain her. If Mary is located in an organizational unit object called Sales, which is in an organizational unit called LabProducts, which is in an organization called HighTech, Mary's complete name is Mary.Sales.LabProducts.HighTech. Periods are used to separate the object names. They act much as backslashes do in a DOS directory.

Depending on the tasks you wish to perform, you may need to specify an object's complete name when you work with it in the directory tree.

Using Name Types

Another element of an object's name, called a name type, can complicate the picture slightly. In some cases, you may need to specify not only the complete name but also the type of object each portion of the complete name indicates. For example, Sales is an organizational unit object. To show what type of object Sales is, you use the abbreviation OU, and you would enter OU=Sales.

Each container object has its own abbreviation to indicate its name type:

C	Country
O	Organization
OU	Organizational Unit

Leaf objects all have the same name type: CN (for *Common Name*). Therefore, regardless of whether the leaf object is a NetWare server object, a user object, a printer object, an alias object, or any other object, its name type is CN.

Therefore, if you have to indicate Mary's complete name with name types, you must use the following syntax:

CN=Mary.OU=Sales.OU=Lab_Products.O=HighTech

This is obviously a cumbersome method of indicating an object's complete name, and it is another good reason for avoiding the use of the country object. If you use the country object, you will always have to use name types in object names. This is because with the country object, there are four possible object types, and it is more difficult for the system to know which object type you are indicating.

The Name Context

Fortunately, it is not always necessary to use an object's complete name if you are in the same name context as the object you are referring to. An object's name context is its position in the directory tree. If two objects are located in the same container object, they have the same context.

For example, suppose you are trying to tell someone else where Mary lives. If you are both already standing in the city where Mary lives, you can skip the country, state, and city in your explanation. All you need to specify is her street and house number, because all three of you are in the same context — the same city.

Similarly, in the directory tree, Mary's context is Sales.Lab_Products.HighTech. If a printer called FastPrinter is also in the organizational unit object Sales, Mary probably would not have to indicate the printer's complete name when she wants to access it, because the printer is in the same context as she is. Instead, Mary could just select the printer's partial name: FastPrinter. When Mary selects FastPrinter, NetWare will look in Mary's context (meaning within the organizational unit object Sales) for the printer.

Now suppose Mary wants to use a wide-carriage dot-matrix printer that is located in another organizational unit called Accounting. The printer's complete name is WIDE_DOTM.Accounting.Lab_Products.HighTech. Mary could enter the printer's complete name, or she could enter only the part of the printer's name that is different from Mary's own context. Mary and the WIDE-DOTM printer are both located in the Lab_products.HighTech context, so Mary would have to enter only the partial name WIDE_DOTM.Accounting in order for the system to find the printer.

Hints for Planning Contexts and Names

Because names and contexts can become confusing for users, you may want to consider the following hints:

▶ Seriously consider limiting the levels of container objects you have in your tree. Because it is difficult for users to remember long, complete names with multiple layers of organization units, try to avoid having more than two or three levels of organizational units, and keep the names as brief as possible. For instance, using the name Lab instead of Lab_Products would eliminate some typing on Mary's part.

▶ You can have up to one thousand objects in a container object.

▶ If users frequently need to access an object that is not in their context, use alias objects to simplify your user's work. For example, you could create an alias object for Accounting's WIDE_DOTM printer and put the alias object in Mary's context. Then Mary could find the printer in her own context, and she wouldn't have to remember the longer "real" name of the printer.

▶ Avoid using spaces in names when naming objects. You can use them, but they will appear as underscores in some utilities. In other utilities, you may have to enclose the name in quotations marks to avoid having the utilities treat the two-word name as two separate commands or objects.

MIXED NETWORKS: UNDERSTANDING BINDERY EMULATION

In many cases, large enterprises may upgrade their NetWare networks to NetWare 4.x over an extended period of time. Therefore, they may be running some servers with NetWare 3.11 or 2.x, and other servers with NetWare 4.x. However, they still need all of their servers to be able to function together on the same network, regardless of which versions they're running.

To address this common situation, NetWare 4.x has included a feature called *bindery emulation*. Bindery emulation is a way for NDS objects to appear like bindery objects to bindery-based servers.

The bindery is a flat database, meaning that there are no container objects and there is no hierarchy, unlike the directory database.

By default, bindery emulation is installed automatically whenever a new NetWare server is added to the tree. The container object that contains the new server is established as the context for bindery emulation. This means that whenever a bindery-based client logs in to a server in that container object, the user at that client will see all the objects in that container as being bindery objects. Whenever NetWare 4.x clients log in to the network at that container object's context, those users will see all objects as being directory services objects. This way, both groups of users can function. The NetWare 4.x users can use NetWare 4.x utilities and work with the directory tree normally, and NetWare 3.11 or 2.x users can use their bindery-based utilities and still accomplish their tasks.

When you install NetWare 4.x on a server, the INSTALL utility will ask you for the context for bindery emulation. If you decide you do not need bindery emulation, you can turn it off after installation by using either the SET server utility or SERVMAN.NLM. You can also use SET (or SERVMAN) to change the bindery emulation context to a different container object.

 Up to sixteen containers may be set in the BINDERY CONTEXT, meaning that sixteen containers can be lumped together to be the bindery of this server.

NOTE

PLANNING DIRECTORY PARTITIONS AND REPLICAS

The key to NDS is its single, unified database of network information. This directory database makes it possible for an entire networked enterprise to function smoothly as a whole. However, it's also easy to see how a single, huge directory database could become unwieldy and difficult to manage, especially if portions of the database are separated by WAN links.

There is also, of course, the issue of where to store the directory database. If you store it on a single server and that server fails, it would be a catastrophe for the whole enterprise. Clearly, it is critical to establish a way to divide the database into manageable pieces and then to ensure that those pieces survive even if one or more servers fail. The solution: *partitions* and *replicas*.

Using Directory Partitions

Directory partitions are portions of the overall directory database. You can also create new directory partitions after you've installed a server by using the NetWare Administrator graphical utility or PARTMGR text utility. The root object is included in the directory partition that is created for the first organization object or organizational unit object you install. To make it easier for users to use the directory tree, users do not see directory partitions. To users, all of the directory database appears as a whole.

Using Replicas to Protect the Directory Database

Even with the directory database divided into partitions, if a partition is stored on a single server and that server goes down, all the information in that partition will be unavailable. Users won't be able to log in and won't be authenticated to use network resources. To prevent this from happening, NetWare 4.x makes copies of the directory partitions, called *replicas*.

There are three types of replicas:

- ▸ Master

- ▸ Read/Write

- ▸ Read Only

You can store these different types of replicas on servers throughout the network so that there is no single point of failure for that partition. Make sure you have at least two replicas of every partition on your network. If you have only one partition and the server that contains it is damaged, you may not be able to recover the partition. By default, every server you install in a partition — but no more than three — must automatically have a replica stored on it. This will ensure that there are at least two replicas of that container's partition. You can also use the master replica to create new partitions.

A Read/Write replica lets you make changes to objects within the partition, but you cannot use a Read/Write replica to create new partitions or change the partition's relationship with the rest of the database. A Read/Write replica of a container object's partition is placed on the server that contains the parent container's master replica. (Read/Write replicas are required on every server that will be providing bindery emulation.)

Read Only replicas are not installed on servers by default, but you can create them and install them on additional servers. Read Only replicas only provide information about the partition. You cannot use them to change objects in the partition. We don't recommend Read Only replicas, however, because you cannot authenticate or log in using them.

Replicas are useful for two reasons:

▸ They prevent the partition from being lost if one server goes down.

▸ They allow users in different partitions to have local access to each other's objects, which is especially useful across WAN links.

Servers can contain several replicas of different partitions. In general, 486-based servers can contain more replicas than 386-based servers, because the 486-based servers' increased speed allows them to handle more updates to the various replicas.

If your enterprise covers a large geographical distance, you may want to consider placing replicas of your partition on a server in another area. This accomplishes two things: It allows users in that area to see your partition, and it protects the existence of your partition if a disaster, such as a fire, destroys your own servers and replicas. (Of course, this does not protect your files, so be sure to mirror your file server disks and keep up-to-date backups of your data in a secure location.)

Storing a Read/Write replica on servers that are across a WAN link can be helpful because it cuts down on the traffic that has to cross the link when users try to access the other partition's information. With a replica of a distant partition stored locally, users have immediate access to the objects they need. The only time that information needs to cross the link is when the replicas are being updated.

To change replicas after you've installed them, you can use either the NetWare Administrator utility or the PARTMGR utility.

KEEPING TIME SYNCHRONIZED

Because you can have more than one replica of a directory partition from which changes can be made, it is very important that all the servers in your network are running on the same, synchronized time. Otherwise, changes made to the partitions from different places could get out of order, and an earlier change could overwrite a later one. *Time synchronization* is a method of specifying how servers keep time consistently with one another.

With time synchronization in NetWare 4.x, you can specify which servers actually set the time and which servers simply set themselves to the other servers' time. There are two ways to set up your network's time synchronization scheme:

> ▸ If you have a small network, you can select the default configuration. In the default setup, the first server is designated as the only timekeeper and all other servers are set so they get their time from the first server.

> ▸ If you have a larger network, you can customize your time synchronization setup by specifying which servers set the time and how they synchronize with each other.

Using Default Time Synchronization

When you install a server, the INSTALL utility will prompt you for the type of time server you want that server to be. If this is the first server you are installing in your network, the default type of time server offered by the INSTALL utility is called *single reference*. A single reference server is the only server on the network that sets time for the other servers. All other servers on the network will be installed as *secondary* time servers, which means they get their time from the single reference server. Workstations can get the network time from either single reference or secondary servers. All secondary servers must be able to contact the single reference server with as few links as possible, so that they can be synchronized without undue delays. If you have a relatively small network, the default setup is a good choice.

Customizing Time Synchronization

If you have a large network, you may not want to let a single server distribute time to the entire network, because too many links will cause delays. In this case, you can use three different types of time servers that work together to keep network time (workstations can synchronize with any of the following types of time servers).

A *reference time server* serves as the central point of time-keeping on the network. On a large network, this reference server can be synchronized to an external time source, such as the server's own internal hardware clock or a radio clock. There are third-party NLMs available that allow you to set your server's time to a radio clock or other national time service. Ideally, there should be only one reference server on a network. However, it is possible to have more than one, which might be desirable if the servers are far apart, such as on opposite sides of a WAN link. If you have more than one reference server, they should each be connected to an external time source.

A *primary time server* polls other primary or reference servers to establish an average "correct" time and provides that time to secondary servers. Place at least one primary server in each geographic location so that secondary servers don't have to cross WAN links to synchronize themselves. One primary server can provide time for up to 150 secondary servers.

A *secondary time server* gets its time from a primary or reference server. Secondary servers do not participate in establishing the network time. This means that no other time server will use a secondary time server as a synchronization source.

When you install a server, you can specify which type of time server you want it to be, or you can accept the default time-server types that the INSTALL utility offers you.

SAP Versus Custom Configuration

By default, time synchronization uses a method called *Service Advertising Protocol* (SAP) to allow the different types of servers to find each other and share time information. Secondary servers use the SAP information that primary and reference servers send out to locate a time server to follow. In networks that are fairly stable (in which servers aren't constantly being added and removed), SAP is recommended. It generates a small amount of traffic on the network when servers are advertising themselves to each other, but it is generally not enough to be a problem.

In larger networks where servers are frequently added and removed or where the extra SAP traffic is undesirable, you can use several parameters in the SET or SERVMAN server utility to turn off SAP and set up time synchronization in a custom configuration. You add these SET commands to the TIMESYNC.CFG file, located in SYS:SYSTEM. When you reboot the server, this file executes and specifies which time servers should be contacted by secondary servers.

Custom configuration of your time servers gives you more control over time synchronization and requires more planning so that servers are synchronized efficiently.

As you can see, Novell NetWare 4.x Network Directory Service is just one very appealing feature of this very popular network operating system. *Novell's Guide to NetWare 4.1* offers much more information about NDS and all other features offered by NetWare 4.x. We suggest you take the time to check it out.

As a direct competitor to Novell and its NetWare network operating systems, Microsoft offers several options. Chief among them is Windows NT.

Windows NT

Microsoft Windows NT offers a comparable alternative to NetWare, with some distinct differences. Windows NT offers the advantage of keeping your entire network operating on Microsoft. Known more commonly as simply *NT*, this operating system is an easy to use interface that offers good network security features and is easy to install.

Windows NT is a good choice for anyone who is looking for a networking environment that easily interacts with other NOSs, like Novell NetWare. NT's ability to support several different transfer protocols, such as TCP/IP and IPX/SPX, enhances its appeal.

Not only does it hit a home run in compatibility, Windows NT provides major league growth opportunity. For example, you can establish a domain for all the nodes and servers used by the accountants in your organization, and you can establish a domain for all of the nodes and servers used by engineers. Simply put, a *domain* is a logical group of servers organized by user-defined criteria. How domains are grouped depends totally on you. The important thing to note about domains is that grouping means users don't have to log in to individual servers. Each user logs in to a domain and therefore has access to all servers in that domain as long as they're permitted security access.

Anyone comfortably using Windows 3.1 or Windows 95 on their desktop can very easily manage NT as their NOS in small environments. Because Windows NT is built on the same easy to use point-and-click concept as other Windows products, there's no need to memorize hot-key combinations or complex syntax.

Developed as one member of an entire family of products, NT is part of Microsoft's BackOffice suite. BackOffice also includes a database program, two electronic mail programs, Internet and mainframe access software, and a system management program for managing large networks.

Banyan Systems VINES

Coming in a close third in the race for the most-used network operating system is Banyan Systems VINES. Most commonly known as *Banyan VINES,* this network system supports UNIX, DOS, Windows, OS/2 and Macintosh users. VINES, much like NetWare and Windows NT, provides basic file and printer services.

Similar to Novell NDS, VINES StreetTalk enables every resource on a Banyan VINES network to be addressed by name with the addresses stored in a distributed database, making objects easy to access and manage. StreetTalk doesn't offer as complex an architecture as NDS; however, it does offer some interesting attributes that make objects easier to qualify and locate.

For example, if Sam has a Hewlett-Packard 5M network printer in his office and Sally has the exact same kind of printer in her office two floors up, and both are running off the same network server, StreetTalk's attribute indicator will show whose office each printer is located in. In other words, StreetTalk takes some of the confusion out of selecting the right object for the right job.

Macintosh

Though many attempts have been made by Macintosh to gain a competitive edge in the computer networking market, to date they've been, by and large, unsuccessful. That's not to say that they're out of the race.

With the latest estimates putting Mac users at somewhere between ten and fifteen million, Macintosh still commands a large and loyal customer base, both end-user and industry alike. In business and industry, however, users are primarily in specific departmental areas.

Mac's network operating system, AppleTalk, is used by some very large corporate customers, and Macintosh perfected the icon-based graphical user interface concept.

AppleTalk networks are fairly simple to set up and offer many of the same advantages as other, more common operating systems, including the ability to accommodate IBM PC-compatible computers. As an added advantage, all Macintosh computers come configured with a ready-to-use AppleTalk networking port installed.

However, Macintosh has been slow to catch up to the increasing demands of growing LANs and WANs. AppleTalk networks are slow compared to high speed network systems like Ethernet. As a result, Macintosh is usually not considered a viable choice in the minds of many computer pundits.

IBM OS/2

With such a big name in computing, it should come as no surprise to discover that IBM has a network operating system. It's called *OS/2 Warp Server*. Originally developed through an ill-fated joint effort between IBM and Microsoft, this *Operating System/2* (OS/2) was to be the IBM PC-compatible answer to the 640K RAM barrier, provide high-level simultaneous security programs, and allow dynamic exchange of information between different applications.

In spite of this highly publicized venture between the two biggest players in the computer business at the time, IBM and Microsoft's new breed of operating system had no real future.

While OS/2 was poorly running the few software programs developed for it, Microsoft was vigorously developing the MS-DOS graphical user interface we now know as Windows. By the time Windows 3.0 hit the streets, industry support for OS/2 began to wither in the shadow of the Microsoft Windows craze.

Today, after several major overhauls, OS/2 primarily provides storage protection and preemptive multitasking services for server platforms, and is used as a back end for such applications as distributed databases. However, there are only two NOSs directly supported by OS/2: LAN Manager and LAN Server.

LAN Manager uses sophisticated, dedicated servers to run the OS/2 operating system, but hasn't commanded much of a following. OS/2 LAN Server, however, is available in a couple of versions, depending on the size of the network to be served.

Although OS/2 has sustained only a small niche market, it's important to know that this particular NOS is available. We recommend, however, that if you consider using one of the less popular NOSs like OS/2 or Macintosh, make sure you're using it for what it can offer in flexibility, compatibility, expandability, and most importantly, survivability.

As you can see, your options for networking software are many. Let us assure you, we've just scratched the surface on a few of the most popular available. Please take the information we've given you and seek out more specific information on the NOSs you feel are best-suited to meet your networking needs.

Non-network Operating Systems

The following OSs are designed to run on the node or client-side of a network or stand-alone desktop computer. We begin this section with a brief description of the most popular OS, MS-DOS.

MS-DOS

Since its introduction in 1981, MS-DOS (better known more simply as *DOS*) has been the industry standard as a command-line operating system. It requires users to memorize a fairly simple language, or syntax, that brings a high degree of control over the system's capabilities. Seasoned DOS users write automatic executable batch files, create directories, set up file attributes, and manipulate system settings easily.

However, DOS has just about seen its end in Microsoft's release of Windows 95, because Windows doesn't rely on DOS in order to operate. Microsoft has so tightly integrated its newest DOS 7 into Windows 95, that the two are virtually indistinguishable from one another.

WINDOWS 95

Now that you know Windows 95 has all but replaced DOS, we're going to tell you the networking capability it provides both as a workstation running on a server-based LAN and as a peer-to-peer OS. But first, what is Windows 95?

Windows 95 is Microsoft's newest generation in Windows computing. Since its release in 1995 (hence the name), Windows 95 has been cheered and reviled in both industry and public press. From its ease in installation and excellent error recovery systems to its short-comings with compatibility and vivacious appetite for RAM, Windows 95 is today's number one choice in the highly competitive personal PC (end-user) market.

Chief among its end-user appeals is that it requires fewer mouse or key-strokes than its nearest relative, Windows 3.1. Windows 95 also makes file and menu handling less complicated through easy-to-use pop-up menus and a highly praised task bar.

Windows 95 is available in three packages. The first two are Update Windows 95 for CD-ROM and 3.5 inch floppy disk. These are purchased as upgrades for those who already have a previous version of Windows installed. The other, Windows 95, is the more expensive, first-time user version, and is intended for those who don't have at least DOS 3.2 installed on their PC. The majority of PCs available today come with the full version of Windows 95 pre-installed on the hard drive.

On the industry or business side, Windows 95 does offer great local area networking and peer-to-peer networking options for the business user.

Windows 95 is a good choice for any workstation running on the types of server-based networks we've discussed throughout this book and an ideal choice for peer-to-peer networking.

In Chapter 6, we told you about the LAN concept that doesn't require a central file server, known as peer-to-peer. In a peer-to-peer network, all of the workstations are linked together via cables instead of through a central server, and can access one another to share files, disk drives, printers, CD-ROM drives, and even modems — a reasonable choice for the small or home office. Windows 95 can provide limited networking capability without the cost associated with server-based setups.

Windows 95 is a popular choice for clients running on a Novell NetWare network, as well as being compatible with virtually every NOS used today. This software was designed with networking in mind. Shipped with a 32-bit protected-mode client for Novell NetWare, Windows 95 blends well with the demands put upon it when used as a networked workstation.

MICROSOFT WINDOWS 3.1 AND WINDOWS FOR WORKGROUPS 3.11

Microsoft introduced Windows 3.1 in 1992 as a major overhaul of its initial Windows 3 release. With the new and improved Windows 3.1 came better file and program management, TrueType font software, multimedia extensions, drag and drop capabilities, and improved network support. However, until the release of Windows for Workgroups 3.11, Windows wasn't the preferred choice of networked client software.

Although in very limited use today due to advances in OSs like Windows 95, Windows for Workgroups 3.11 offers features in networking a workgroup that Windows 3.1 does not. It closely incorporates the user-friendly Windows environment into an NOS. It also offers integrated electronic mail, electronic scheduling, calendars for individuals and groups, and network document management, which allows groups to work on one common document.

Windows for Workgroups runs simultaneously with traditional server-based network operating systems, such as Novell NetWare or Microsoft LAN Manager.

Easy to use, easy to setup, Windows for Workgroups has low administrative requirements and works as smoothly with the OS as other peer-to-peer networks, making it feel to the user as if network capability were part of the computer.

Summary

As you can see, shopping for an OS is a lot like shopping for a new car. Each make of automobile offers slightly different comforts and levels of sophistication. But when you get right down to it, they're still cars. The question is, do you want to ride in a Cadillac or a VW Beetle? Should you buy a utility vehicle or something economical? These questions are similar to the ones you should ask yourself when considering the operating system that's just right for you. Select the one that will provide the types of services and capabilities specifically associated with the type of LAN you build. After all, a carpenter can't haul much lumber in a Miata. In the next chapter, we discuss choosing the right hardware.

CHAPTER 10

Choosing Hardware

Many people begin networking by choosing the hardware. But this chapter appears near the end of this book because hardware choices should be made only after you understand topology, cable, networking gear, and software choices. In the following pages, we consider such hardware as file servers, workstations, and print servers. Hardware must be matched to the task it is expected to perform. Unless we begin with an empty office, we don't always have the luxury of starting from scratch. Most companies accumulate an assortment of PCs and printers of various makes and configurations prior to tying them all together as a LAN.

Sometimes equipment can be upgraded to handle any increase in load the network places on hardware, but often it's more cost effective either to keep only that hardware that fits squarely into the planned architecture or just start completely from scratch. Today, with the price of new equipment lower than ever, costs associated with upgrading existing equipment often exceed the cost of buying all new components. The hardware market is very competitive, and hardware technology has a short life span.

If your network were a person, the server would be the heart; the software the brain; the cables the arteries, veins, and nervous system; and the workstations the hands, feet, and smaller organs. If the heart stops beating, the entire body dies. If the brain stops working, the body continues living but cannot work. If we lose a hand or a foot, the body continues living but is disabled. This analogy will be used throughout the chapter and helps us understand how to budget appropriately for hardware.

Always purchase the highest quality hardware you can afford. When cutting corners on network hardware, use the analogy of the body. The heart (server) needs to be the strongest part of the network. The circulatory system (cables) is next in importance. You don't want them to get clogged. The workstation is the only place that corners can be cut. If a single workstation is down, or not operating, the rest of the company continues. If the server is down, so is the entire company.

When you are considering less expensive workstations, calculate what any lost productivity will cost the organization. What does it cost to have an employee sitting around waiting for repairs or a replacement computer? The price difference between clones and name brands has drawn closer. Name brands usually offer longer warranties, help desks, and even on-site service. Do the math and make the best decision for your organization.

Workstations

Workstations are the last link in the network, often referred to as *network nodes*. Workstations are configured according to the job they are expected to do. A data entry clerk who enters accounting data into the database does not need the power of an engineer using a 3-D modeling program or the chief financial officer running company-wide sales projections in a spreadsheet.

Workstations access the server, run local software programs, handle network traffic and communicate with attached peripherals such as tape drive backups, CD-ROM drives, modems, printers, and scanners. Diskless workstations, PCs without a hard drive and/or floppy drive (more commonly known as dumb terminals), can be utilized if the user does not need local programs or data and can run all the applications needed from the server. Dumb terminals are generally less expensive than hard drives, but as the difference narrows, fewer businesses use dumb terminals.

Most workstations today are IBM-compatible microcomputers or PCs. A minority of workstations are Macintosh. Compatibles are not all created equal. Name brands cost a few dollars more than clones, but they typically use better components, have longer warranties, and have better support options.

It's hard to retire working equipment that shows no signs of failing anytime soon, but the increase in productivity can justify the cost for a better workstation. The general rule of thumb in the computer industry is to expect to get four years from equipment. This time can be stretched if the state-of-the-art or the fastest and largest workstation available is purchased.

A workstation is composed of a motherboard, CPU, accessory cards, keyboard, monitor, mouse, and other attached peripherals. The motherboard is the main board on the computer that memory and accessory cards are plugged into. A CPU is the processor and determines the speed of the computer, the most common speeds being Pentium, 486, and 386. Accessory cards add functions to the computer such as modems, sound cards, and other peripheral-controlling cards.

Next, we discuss the components that affect our selection of workstations for the network.

MEMORY

Random access memory (RAM) is the component of the computer that executes programs and stores data before it is written to the disk. Most PCs come with four to eight memory slots on the motherboard that receive 1MB, 2MB, 4MB, 8MB, 16MB, 32MB, or 64MB *single in-line memory modules* (SIMMS). Select the largest SIMM the motherboard can handle. This leaves room for expansion later as the need arises for additional memory. If the motherboard has four memory slots and all slots are filled with 4MB SIMMs the only way to upgrade memory is to remove some or all of the memory and buy all new memory. If one slot is populated with a single 4MB SIMM, three slots are left for future expansion. Memory must be added in pairs on Pentium processors. A Pentium with 64MB RAM will have two 32MB SIMMs installed.

Originally SIMMs were 3.5 inches long and had 30 pins. Newer SIMMs are 4.5 inches long and have 72 pins, as illustrated in Figure 10.1. To further complicate matters, SIMMs can use either 9-bit memory (8 bits plus a parity bit) or 8-bit memory without parity. SIMMs also differ in the number of memory chips soldered to the SIMM board that make up the total memory. Some computers can mix SIMM types and others cannot. When upgrading your PC, if you're not sure what chips your PC takes, make sure whatever you buy is returnable, or have a PC technician do the upgrade. Technicians have most varieties on hand and will find the one that works on your system.

F I G U R E   10.1

72-pin SIMM

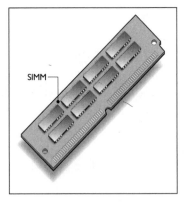

SIMM

Memory requirements are dictated by the programs to be run, type of internal OS, and network OS. Software and network vendors will provide minimum and optimum memory requirements for their respective programs. Always purchase the most memory you can afford. A slower machine with more memory will often run a program faster than a faster machine with less memory. It is better to have too much memory than not enough. A good rule of thumb is to check the memory requirement on the software box and double or triple it. Windows and graphical interfaces in particular require a lot. Try to budget for the optimum suggested memory instead of the minimum.

Most users today are *multitasking*. Multitasking is the running of two or more programs at the same time on a single computer. Mainframes and minicomputers have always multitasked, but the PC was originally designed to do one thing at a time. The advent of Windows made it possible for PCs to multitask.

Two terms that go with multitasking are *foreground* and *background*. The foreground program is the one the user is currently working on, and the background program is whatever is running behind the scenes, such as a print spooler or spreadsheet recalculation. Priority is given to the process in the foreground, but if the process in the background is disk or CPU intensive, a slowdown of the foreground program occurs. Users sometimes think that they are multitasking when they have multiple programs open in multiple windows, but really they are just suspending and resuming programs when needed. True multitasking is running multiple processes simultaneously; therefore, the maximum memory possible should be installed to reduce slowdowns and increase productivity.

PROCESSING SPEED

Processing speed is the function of the CPU and is measured by the number of instructions that can be performed in a period of time. Pentiums and 486s are the most common CPUs in use today. Each CPU class comes in various speeds measured in megahertz (MHz). To further confuse matters, manufacturers have doubled, tripled, and quadrupled internal clock speeds to increase performance. This does not increase the speed and power incrementally and should only be used as a guide to system performance and power. All components must be matched to provide the best performance. For example, a Pentium 120MHz does not run programs twice as fast as a Pentium 60MHz. The speed of the Pentium is a result of the 64-bit internal bus compared to the 32-bit bus on the 486 CPU. The Pentium PRO, available in 133, 150, 166, and 200MHz speeds, runs 32-bit operating systems better than the Pentium, and actually has a performance drop when running 16-bit operating systems. Processing speed is also a function of the bus, accessory cards, and hard drive interfaces installed in the computer. The processor or CPU can only communicate as fast as the other components in the system. A fast CPU can process data faster than the video, hard drive, or interfaces to other peripherals. We examine these other components in later sections.

The processor plugs into the motherboard, as seen in Figure 10.2. The motherboard affects processor speed because it includes the cache and the bus for the accessory cards. The cache is an additional memory that stores frequently used data and reads and writes the data when the other peripherals are ready for it. The cache acts as a buffer between memory and the CPU. The bigger the cache, the better. The most common sizes are 128K and 256K, but we suggest 256K as a minimum.

▶ · ◀

FIGURE 10.2

A CPU on a motherboard

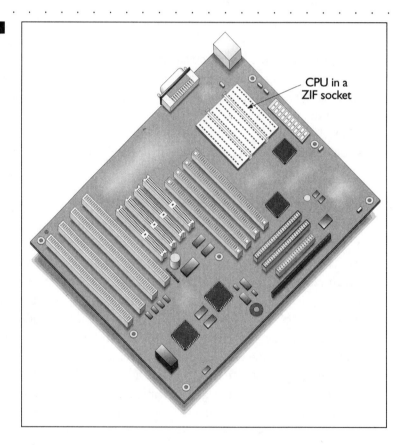

CPU in a
ZIF socket

Pentium computers have come down in price to the point of being a viable choice for workstations. The 386 class machines are no longer being made, and 486s soon will follow, leaving upgrade paths for older workstations limited. Some motherboards have slots for overdrive processors, or the existing CPU can be replaced with a faster CPU. Remember that a faster CPU can only pass data to the hard drive, video, and other peripherals as fast as the device can receive them. If all the components are not replaced, performance gains will not be as great as expected. Again, the costs associated with examining the system, finding appropriate upgrade chips and installing them are often greater than the cost of a new workstation.

BUS PERFORMANCE

The bus is the highway your data travels on. Data travels along this highway between the CPU, monitor, hard drive, and other peripherals. The CPU internal bus, or local bus, operates faster than peripheral buses. The popular bus varieties are *Industry Standard Architecture* (ISA), *Extended Industry Standard Architecture* (EISA), *Video Electronics Standards Association* (VESA), and *Peripheral Component Interconnect* (PCI), and each handles data in a different manner and at different speeds. A highway with six lanes and a 70mph speed limit can handle more cars or data faster than a single lane residential road, so select the fastest and widest bus you can afford. The bus is usually the bottleneck in any computer, so it's important to know the difference between the various types.

ISA, seen in Figure 10.3, is the slowest and oldest of the buses. The vast majority of expansion cards are ISA, and most PCI and VESA computers have a few ISA expansion slots for backward compatibility. ISA cards are either 8-bit (half cards) or 16-bit (full cards). A half card can fit in any ISA slot, but a full card can only be inserted in a full slot. Half and full slots are readily identified by their respective lengths and the number of pins they accept. ISA cards will fit in all EISA slots.

An EISA bus doubles the ISA 16-bit path to 32-bits, but still uses the same 8MHz clock speed as the ISA card to maintain backward compatibility with it. EISA slots accept all ISA cards. For this reason, VESA and PCI cards are faster than EISA.

A 16-bit ISA connector, shown here on an adapter card

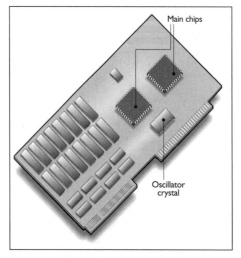

Main chips

Oscillator crystal

Local buses such as the PCI bus and the VESA local bus (also known as *VL-Bus* and *VLB*), pictured in Figure 10.4, talk directly to the CPU's internal bus at the same, or nearly the same speed. They are faster than ISA and EISA because the VLB runs at 40MHz and PCI runs at 33MHz. It is thought that PCI will eventually replace all the other buses.

Bus connectors for a VLB. To the right are the standard 16-bit connectors and to the left are the smaller, local bus connectors.

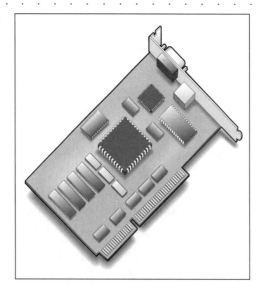

Video and network controllers obtain the greatest benefit from the local buses. Wherever possible, purchase the fastest controller your computer will handle.

Cards

Thousands of expansion cards are available that will add to a workstation's usefulness. Each card is designed to do either a single job or a number of jobs. Cards exist for video, multimedia, modem, voice mail, fax, hard drive controllers, tape drive controllers, CD-ROM controllers . . . the list is endless. Rather than discuss all available cards, we cover the most popular and most frequently used accessory cards.

Motherboards are manufactured with three to seven expansion slots. Make sure your workstation has enough expansion slots to accept all the cards you want to add. As the previous section on bus speed explains, you want to select cards that use the fastest bus available in the motherboard. Some motherboards come with both ISA and VLB or PCI slots, and EISA slots can accept ISA cards. The bus is usually the bottleneck in system performance, so take advantage of the fastest bus available.

VIDEO CARDS

Every workstation must have a *video card*. This card, seen in Figure 10.5, communicates to the monitor and translates computer code to graphics and text on the screen. Video cards have their own memory on board, and the more graphic-intensive a program is, the more memory it needs. Older programs use mostly text screens with very little graphics or pictures.

WYSIWYG (What You See Is What You Get) programs display on the screen exactly what the printer will print. Graphics address the screen by pixels, which are the size of a pin point. It is now possible to display millions of colors in high resolution. Standard VGA monitors are able to display 1024×768 pixels in 0.28 inch pitch. The video card controls the speed at which the screen is refreshed or repainted and the speed of the memory on the card buffers, or it stores video information to help speed screen painting. Each manufacturer claims to have special features such as *Dynamic Random Access Memory* (DRAM), *Enhanced Data Output DRAM* (EDO DRAM), or *EDO Video RAM* (EDO VRAM) that set their cards above the competition. Simple DOS programs can use 256K or 512K video cards, but any workstation running Windows should have at least 1MB of memory on the video card.

A standard video card

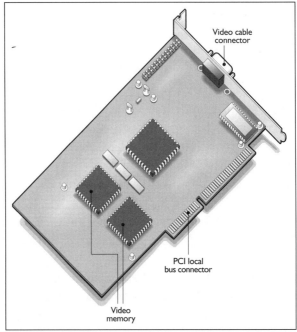

Video cable connector

PCI local bus connector

Video memory

MULTI-I/O CARDS

Another card found in all workstations is the *Multi-Input/Output* (Multi-I/O) card. These cards control the hard drives, floppy drives, and communication ports. Most cards provide two serial ports and one or two parallel ports. Serial ports are used for modems, mice, scanners, and some printers. The parallel ports are used for printers and some special peripherals such as tape drives and external CD-ROM drives. The most common hard drive controllers for workstations are the *integrated drive electronics* (IDE) and the increasingly popular *enhanced IDE* (EIDE). The EIDE permits more and larger drives to be installed in the system in addition to faster access and enhanced features over IDE. An interface gaining popularity is the *small computer system interface* (SCSI), by far the most popular for servers and larger workstations. SCSI devices transfer data to and from the hard drive faster than the IDE and EIDE interfaces and can accept from seven to fifteen devices attached to the same controller. Choose the controller that is most cost effective for your application.

MODEMS AND FAX CARDS

Modem and fax cards, such as the one seen in Figure 10.6, are quickly becoming standard on all workstations. Since most faxes originate on the PC, it makes sense to fax directly from the desktop instead of printing the document and standing by the fax machine while it sends. Fax/modems (all in one) can be installed internally for convenience or externally if desired. Modems also allow access to e-mail, bulletin board services (BBSs), the Internet, and remote offices or home computers. Fax/modems can also be installed and shared on the network. A communication program routes faxes to a single fax/modem or bank of modems and sends the fax when a port becomes available. This eliminates the need for a modem and phone line for each workstation. Modems are now available that also provide voice mail in addition to fax and data transfer.

FIGURE 10.6

A fax/modem card

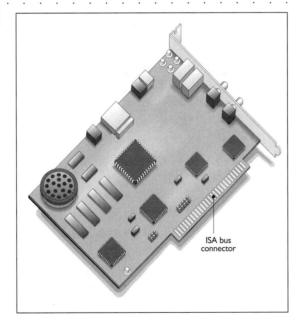

ISA bus
connector

NETWORK INTERFACE CARDS

The last card we discuss is the *network interface card* (NIC), pictured in Figure 10.7. The NIC must be matched to the topology and cables of the network. Cards can be purchased for a single type of network, or combo cards can handle a variety of cable types. Combo cards usually have Thin LAN, Thick LAN, and Ethernet

UTP connections. These cards are useful if workstations are moved or a cabling change is imminent. Again, we cannot emphasize enough the importance of purchasing an NIC that uses the fastest bus available on the motherboard. NICs are not the place to save money on a network. Network cards range in price because of their distinct differences. A good, medium-priced card from a reputable company that specializes in networking equipment is your the best choice.

A network interface card

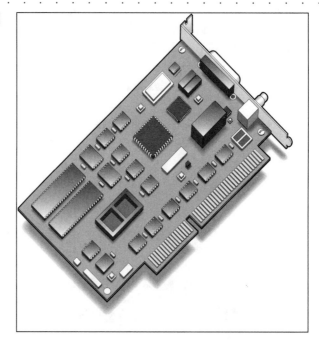

Servers

Everything we discussed about workstations applies to servers. The only difference is the magnitude and scalability of the system. A server is not simply a larger and more powerful workstation, although that was the trend for many years. The server is the heart of your network. It should be the strongest link in your LAN topology. Servers need larger hard drives and more memory to handle all the traffic from users accessing it. You may also want to provide fault tolerance for the hard drives.

Larger networks have multiple servers for applications, databases, engineering, and communications. The term *file server* refers to the most common server that stores applications and files for use across the network. *Database servers* store and retrieve data from a database.

A *print server* handles printing services. A print server can be a microcomputer with printers attached, or it can be a hardware device that handles print spooling or storing output from users and managing when they are sent to the printer. The *communication server* handles modems and fax/modems and is sometimes called a *modem pool*.

Instead of providing each user with a modem and phone line, a few modems attached to a communications server can service an entire network. Faxes are placed in a queue and sent when the fax modem is free. Users can request a modem for dial out purposes and are notified when one becomes available. Modems can also be configured to accept incoming faxes and permit remote access to the network. A single server fulfills all these functions in a small network, but in larger networks it is advantageous to distribute the communication to a separate server.

HARDWARE

Desktop, minitower, full tower, rack mount — what size do I need for my network? The answer lies in the projected use and the peripherals to be attached to the server. The main difference is the number of drive bays and number of expansion slots.

The desktop server is only useful in the smallest of networks because of limited drive bays. The smallest acceptable server should have at least five drive bays. It is amazing how quickly the bays become filled with hard drives, CD-ROM's, and a tape drive. Expansion slots are also filled quickly with network cards, SCSI controllers, video cards, and modems. Top-of-the-line servers have external, hot-swappable drive bays, which can be removed and replaced without downing the server (logging off all users, unloading network software, and turning off the server). This is very desirable in mission-critical applications where downtime is unacceptable.

Some rack mount servers are motherboards that install into a large rack which provides power to all the computers. This saves space in large installations where many servers would clutter the computer room. Switches can be installed that share a single keyboard, mouse, and monitor with all the processors. Internal components are easily accessible by opening a door and sliding the component out, instead of opening a case.

Rack mount servers also support *symmetric multiprocessing* (SMP). A single operating system is loaded in memory and multiple CPUs share the processing. The SMP advantage is scalability. Up to thirty-two processors can be added when needed to handle additional traffic. SMP computers can also be used on the desktop, but are used most often as servers.

CPU selection in a server should be made carefully. The use of the server determines the level of CPU needed. In true client-server applications, the processing is occurring at the client or workstation. The CPU is managing data storage and retrieval, which is less CPU intensive. A mission critical application or database server needs the fastest CPU available. Servers running accounting programs that process large amounts of data need all the horsepower they can get. Servers used for simple file storage can use a slower CPU. Communication servers and print servers often need only 386 or 486 level CPUs and they're a good place for the retired application server. With rapidly growing demands on the server, and CPU prices dropping, it makes little sense to skimp on processing speed.

Another consideration is fault tolerance and diagnostic software. Major manufacturers include diagnostic software that predicts failure, keeps the server running even though a component may fail, and can recover automatically from failures. Predictive software alerts the network manager to potential failures by monitoring system performance and predicting possible problems. Fault-tolerant software can shut down the server in an orderly manner, without losing data, in the event someone accidentally pulls the plug or reboots the computer.

WARRANTIES

The server is the place to buy the best quality you can afford. Servers from the prominent manufacturers come with extended, on-site warranties. Do you want to cease doing business while the server is carried to a service center for repair? Of course not. Let's discuss some warranty terms.

On-site means that the manufacturer comes to your office to repair the unit. *Depot* or *carry-in service* means the server must be carried by the customer to a shipping depot that either has a repair shop or ships the unit to a repair shop. Read the warranty before purchasing, not after.

Extended and *expanded warranties* are offered by most manufacturers. Extended warranties extend the time period equipment is covered. Expanded warranties expand the scope of services. Most on-site warranties provide for service within one business day, meaning a call made on Friday will be answered Monday before 5:00 p.m. This only guarantees the system will be diagnosed. If the technician needs additional parts, the repair takes longer. The maximum coverage available covers equipment twenty-four hours a day, seven days a week, with four-hour or less response time.

Wherever possible, try to use the same manufacturer for all components, such as hard drives and memory. Warranty work is simpler and finger pointing is eliminated. For instance, if generic memory or a different brand hard drive is installed in a name brand server, the repair technician cannot replace the memory or the drive. Using all the same brand components greatly simplifies warranty work.

MEMORY

Server memory should be calculated by a network technician. Factors that affect memory usage are the network OS, number of users, volume size, software to be run, and desired performance. An equation is used, factoring all the variables, to arrive at the optimum memory size. Too little memory on the server can even cause crashes. Use the largest SIMMs to provide room for expansion later. Purchase the best quality memory modules available or memory modules from the server manufacturer. Once again, memory provided by the server manufacturer is tested in the server and makes your life and the technician's life simpler.

DISK SPACE

You can never be rich enough or have too much disk space. Calculate the disk space you think you need and double or triple it. Storage space has steadily dropped in price, so cost shouldn't be a factor. Hard drives are rated for their access rate and spin speed. The faster the spin and the lower the access time, the faster the drive is. SCSI drives are also the best choice for servers, as they provide faster throughput and therefore better response time.

Everyone is always complaining about the lack of disk space. However, disk space is usually not the problem. The problem is typically file management. Users are notorious for saving multiple copies of the same document, and should be encouraged to practice good file maintenance. Network managers make copies of entire directories and then forget to purge them. Programs create temporary files and backup files that never go away until someone manually removes them. Files that haven't been used for a certain period of time should be purged. Disk space must be managed by someone in the organization. Technicians have reported freeing as much as 30 percent of a disk from never-used, seldom-used, not-used-for-years, and duplicate files.

Many drive options are on the market that provide fault tolerance and redundancy. These schemes produce a system that almost never goes down. Each scheme has its benefits and drawbacks. We will discuss duplexing, mirroring, and the various levels of *Redundant Arrays of Inexpensive Disks* (RAID).

Duplexing

Duplexing duplicates hard drives, controllers, and power supplies and writes to both drives at the same time. If a drive system goes down, the other takes over with no change in response time.

Mirroring

Mirroring spreads data across two different drives by duplicating the data on one drive and storing it on another (or by repeating data on two different locations on the same drive). If the mirroring writes to two different drives, the system can continue if a drive goes down.

RAID

No, we're not endorsing a bug spray. We're referring to methods of data redundancy and fault tolerance. RAID uses drive arrays, which are two or more disks working together.

RAID 0 is *data stripping*, or spreading data across more than one disk. This speeds transfer rates but does nothing for fault tolerance. If a disk goes down, the data on that disk is lost. If the data is in the middle of a file, the entire file is often lost.

RAID 1 is the same as *disk mirroring*. The disadvantage is that both drives must match. A server with a large, expensive primary drive must have a second, large, expensive drive.

RAID 2 provides fault tolerance by *interleaving data*, or spreading data across several disks. This system can rebuild a failed disk from error correction data spread across the other disks.

RAID 3 is a popular process that transfers data to many disks and stores parity data on a dedicated parity drive. *Parity* is the ninth bit of either a zero or a one depending on the data in the byte. This is checked for accuracy and notifies the user of an error. One byte is written at a time and the controller only permits a single write at a time.

RAID 4 is almost the same as RAID 3, except it permits *multiple writes* at the same time.

RAID 5 is the most popular method. The data and parity information is spread across all the drives in the array with no dedicated parity drive. Performance is boosted by simultaneous reads and writes. Errors that occur on writes can be corrected from the error correcting data.

The bottom line is, if you are willing to pay for redundancy, a system can be designed that, theoretically, can never go down, barring natural disaster. Natural disaster can also be provided for by spreading redundant servers across a WAN in different cities. The days of chronic network crashes are over.

DRIVE MAPPING

Drive mapping is a way of organizing directories on the disk into logical trees and assigning the paths to drive letters. This enables users to find their data quickly and effortlessly. The directory SALES/CORPORATE/SOUTHERN/DATA can be mapped to a drive letter whereby the user simply needs to type F: to access that directory. The user is shielded from remembering and typing the long path name, and security can be set according to user, to allow only authorized access to the F drive. This is not a physical drive, as in DOS, where a drive letter denotes a specific piece of hardware such as a floppy, hard drive, or CD-ROM. The mapped drive is a logical drive, and the operating system treats it as if it were a physical drive. Drive mapping is simple when you consider the logical place to put data and files, and who is permitted access to that data.

PRINT SERVERS

Print servers control printing to shared network printers by acting as a traffic cop that controls the flow of print jobs. If Sally and Sam both sent a letter to the same printer without the benefit of a print server traffic cop, the document printer might print part of Sam's letter and part of Sally's letter on the same page. The traffic cop permits the output from a program to go to the printer while holding other print requests until that job is completed. When that job is completed, the next print request is sent to the printer. This prevents print output from crashing into each other, confusing the printer and users.

Print servers are workstations or hardware devices specifically designed for the task. A workstation print server can have as many printers attached as there are ports on the PC. Hardware print servers are available with combinations of parallel and serial ports in various numbers. The same distance restrictions apply for network printers as for DOS printers. Parallel printers are suggested to be within 15 feet of the port and serial printers can be up to 50 feet or more away. This distance limitation is important when placing the print server. All printers attached to the print server must be within the suggested distance, unless you use a distance-extending device. Larger networks employ multiple print servers, strategically placed for users' convenience.

Summary

We hope you've gained an understanding of the significance of selecting hardware when planning your network. We suggest that you carefully consider the aspects of LAN computing in the order that we've outlined in this book, because all considerations are uniformly connected.

PART III

Network Management

CHAPTER 11

Network Management Responsibilities and Tools

When is the last time you heard these words: "I'm sorry, I can't help you right now because the server's down. We'll have to wait until the systems people get things back online." A very frustrating experience, isn't it? It's in situations like this when the skills of the network manager are the most crucial. It's also when the LAN architect's principles of design and implementation show their true colors — a well-planned success or an embarrassing failure.

In this chapter, we don't spend a lot of time discussing the intricate details of LAN management, but we do familiarize you with many of the general responsibilities and management tools associated with the subject.

Before a LAN can be properly managed, however, a person must be identified to do the managing. This person is usually referred to as the *LAN administrator, network manager,* or *network engineer.* No matter what title this person holds, the job is very crucial, and though sad but true, many times a thankless one.

What the LAN Manager Does

As a key member of the technology team, you are responsible for installing, maintaining, and troubleshooting the network. Good people skills are essential for your success in this role. Stay in touch with the specific goals and objectives your company has established and create a LAN that will function toward meeting them. Keep abreast of departmental changes, for this will allow for more easy and open discussion with the various department managers. Managers, in turn, gain a better understanding of how the LAN uses their data and can then improve on the uses of the data their department generates. Have you ever known a department manager to refuse ideas that will improve the productivity of the staff? Attend departmental meetings, if possible. This gives users a recurring opportunity to express any specific needs or problems they are experiencing. It also gives you the opportunity to provide instant feedback regarding potential or realized solutions. As LAN manager, it is incumbent upon you to think logically, be impeccably organized, and have the skills to develop methodical, recurring task lists.

As LAN manager, dealing effectively and efficiently with people is a skill you constantly work to improve. After all, computers aren't your customers; people are. Constantly look for opportunities to build your one-on-one and group communication skills. Don't just communicate electronically. When possible, spend the time to meet with users as individuals. Let them see a face on the other end of the LAN. Presentations that provide valuable information, group training, and answers to questions are an excellent forum for developing relationships with your customers.

Keep in mind, however, that your responsibilities go well beyond your people skills. You will provide technical assistance to your customers in the form of technical reports, online and in-person support, and advice to key decision makers regarding the use of technology within the company. Therefore, as LAN manager you must possess technical expertise that covers a broad range of skills. These skills fall into three major categories, each containing categorical tasks:

- **Maintaining and operating the LAN**

    ► Managing files and hardware

    ► Organizing directories, files, and hardware

    ► Setting up users and access control

    ► Allocating disk space

    ► Planning for and performing disaster recovery

    ► Backing up the network

    ► Monitoring performance

    ► Providing LAN security

    ► Providing risk management for networks

    ► Troubleshooting

- **Enhancing the network**

    ► Assessing software and hardware products

- Optimizing LAN performance

- Expanding the network

- Internetworking

• **Administering network operations**

- Creating documentation

- Managing support for users

- Developing training for users

- Managing LAN configuration

- Keeping technology current

Add to this the ability to identify and replace failed or malfunctioning equipment and, in some cases, read complex wiring diagrams or technical manuals.

In today's fast moving world of network computing, sometimes even the most seasoned network engineers have difficulty keeping up with the dynamic changes. It is for this reason that the concept of network management was born.

LAN management is not merely a skill, it's also specially designed management tools in the form of hardware and software. Refer to Chapter 7 to review several network management options designed to assist LAN managers in their role.

Equally important as these electronic tools is *attitude*. The systemic responsibility of managing a LAN is just as important as the know-how. What do we mean by *systemic responsibility?* Perhaps it's best characterized as *good habits*.

Good Habits to Follow

Just as an automobile engine needs proper care and maintenance to operate smoothly, a LAN requires preventive maintenance and some tender loving care as well. If sound management and maintenance habits are formed during the earliest stages of LAN development and implementation, they're more likely to continue as the network grows.

No, we're not talking about washing and waxing your servers and PCs every Saturday. Preventive maintenance for your network consists of:

- ▸ Properly documenting system configurations

- ▸ Installing proper power supplies and power backup systems

- ▸ Maintaining cables

- ▸ Periodic removal of unnecessary data from hard drives

- ▸ Establishing data backup and archiving routines

- ▸ Properly maintaining hardware devices

As the organization's LAN manager, you should not have to spend all of your time maintaining the LAN. Establish daily, weekly, monthly, and yearly routines. Daily routine tasks may include the following:

- ▸ Adding users

- ▸ Cleaning up the file server hard disk drive

- ▸ Installing software upgrades

- ▸ Making backups

- ▸ Restoring damaged or lost files

- ▸ Monitoring traffic

- ▸ Collecting accounting data

- ▸ Generating reports for management

Weekly routine tasks may include:

> ‣ Monitoring and evaluating network performance

> ‣ Managing and documenting the network configuration

> ‣ Exploring and appraising new hardware and software technology

Establishing and continuing good habits like these will pay big dividends when problems do arise, because, as illustrated in the example above, when the system goes down, productivity usually goes with it. While there is no guarantee a well managed LAN will never go down, remember, it's easier to find a pin in a cushion than to find one in a haystack.

Now that we've discussed starting with good habits, let's talk about bringing skill and attitude together to manage the LAN.

What LAN Management Involves

By now you realize all the planning, decision making, and expense involved in developing a well designed networking system. Don't let all of your hard work go to waste by allowing poor management to continue unchallenged. Exert just as much effort into putting solid management practices in place and protect your investment.

Simply put, LAN management is the process of controlling a complex data network to maximize its efficiency and productivity. As we mentioned in Chapter 2, the ISO Network Forum sets standards for computing. Among those standards, network management is divided into five functional areas: *fault management, configuration management, security management, performance management, and accounting management.* Let's quickly get a better understanding of each before going on.

FAULT MANAGEMENT

First of all, a *fault* is a physical condition that causes a device, component, or element to fail to perform in a required manner; for example, a short circuit, a broken wire, or an intermittent connection. Therefore, *fault management* is the process of locating a fault, isolating it, and then fixing it. Locating, isolating, and fixing a fault are all aided by and almost totally dependent on good fault-tolerant systems.

The first aspect of a disaster plan is not really even a disaster plan. It is the design of the system itself. A network can be designed with manageability in mind, so that many problems (faults) can be avoided entirely, or so that in the event of a problem, recovery will be smooth and easy.

To better illustrate how fault tolerance can be designed into a system, the following examples show how Novell NetWare 4.x provides problem solving solutions.

SFT I: Hot Fix Redirection

Over time, hard disks develop defects. NetWare uses a technique called *Read after Write Verification* to ensure the quality of disk writes. It reads back each byte of information after every write. If the data read back does not match the data written to the disk, the process is repeated. If the write fails three times, the area is marked as defective, and the block of data is written to an area of the disk specifically reserved for redirected blocks. This feature is called *Hot Fix Redirection* or *System Fault Tolerance (SFT)* Level I.

SFT II: Disk Mirroring and Duplexing

With *disk mirroring,* all data written to a hard disk is also written to a second disk. If the server's disks are mirrored, the loss of a hard disk is but a minor nuisance instead of a disaster. With disk duplexing, not only are redundant disks installed, but also redundant disk controllers and cables. Then the system can bear the loss of any component in the disk channel itself. Disk mirroring and disk-channel duplexing are termed SFT Level II.

Disk Mirroring Mirrored disks are on the same channel. That is, they are attached to the same hard-disk controller. When you install a NetWare partition using INSTALL.NLM, you have the option of mirroring the disk.

The secondary drive must be at least as large as the primary drive. If the secondary drive is larger (in data capacity), NetWare will only format and use what's needed. The remainder will be inaccessible and therefore wasted.

Disk Duplexing Of course, hard disks are not the only components subject to failure. Disk controllers and cables can also malfunction. *Disk duplexing* is accomplished by installing redundant disks, disk controllers, and cables. All data written to the primary drive is also written to the secondary disk.

One advantage of duplexing over mirroring is that performance is better with duplexed disk controllers. NetWare has the ability to perform *split seeks* and retrieve information from the disk (and controller) that is closest to the read/write head, thereby improving response time for disk reads.

CONFIGURATION MANAGEMENT

The way your network is configured will determine how well it performs. Configuration management put in one word is *documenting*.

This is one of the good habits we talked about earlier. LAN documentation should include the physical layout (floor plans and locations of servers, workstations, printers, cables, bridges, hubs, and so on), the logical structure (login process, scripts, batch files, menus, and so on), and the network infrastructure (a graphical representation of the directory structure of each volume).

You should have a short introduction to the network for new or temporary employees so they can come up to speed as fast as possible, and more importantly, abide by the rules that you set up for system access.

All procedures should be documented. This enables quicker recovery, and it helps technical support personnel give more efficient assistance, whether it's by phone or on-site.

Make a chart of the backup schedule and the location of backup tapes. What is the rotation of tapes that are kept off-site? The list should include names and phone numbers (including pager/mobile phone numbers) of responsible support staff.

Here are the categories we've just discussed in an easy-to-follow bulleted list that you can use as a checklist when documenting your local area network:

- Set up network configuration and operations information.

- Produce network status reports and problem log.

- Create network and user workstation-configuration baseline diagrams and specifications.

- Log configuration change requests.

- Keep daily maintenance documents.

- Document modifications or additions of users and groups.

- Track installed applications.

- Log backups and file server restorations.

▸ Conduct expansion and emergency training.

▸ Create a network expansion plan, including internetworking.

▸ Write test plan for evaluating new products or product upgrades.

▸ Produce network security and risk-management plan.

▸ Formulate disaster recovery plan.

▸ Write user training plans and coarse materials.

Updating Your Documentation

Document every change to the system, problems, and service calls. If you don't keep the documentation current, there's no point in having it at all. It's difficult to be disciplined, but in the long run it is the only way to run any substantial network effectively.

Document Servers

Make a list of the hardware and hardware configuration for each file server. Some network operating systems manuals, *Novell NetWare 4.x,* for instance, come with forms for keeping track of configurations. Copy them (it's legal!) and use them.

Print out the configuration files for each server. The following files are the most important:

▸ CONFIG.SYS

▸ AUTOEXEC.BAT

When running a NetWare 4.x network, also print the STARTUP.NCF and the AUTOEXEC.NCF files for each server. List the contents (and DOS version) of the DOS partition for each NetWare server and services provided (in other words: file, print, communication, database, routing, and so on).

Document PC Nodes (Clients)

Print out the configuration files for each PC node. Ideally, your clients should be somewhat standardized in configuration. If not, this documentation is even more critical. Once again, the two most important files are:

▸ CONFIG.SYS

▸ AUTOEXEC.BAT

If the client is running on a NetWare 4.x network, be sure to print the contents of the NET.CFG file. Also, list services provided, such as remote printing, communications, database, and routing, and make a chart of the standard client directory structure.

Network record-keeping and configuration-management documentation is vital to maintaining and operating a successful network. When the network is being installed initially, collect a set of configuration baseline documents that include the things we've discussed: descriptions of the network components, such as cable diagrams, client computers, and file servers; complete lists of all hardware and software, including the version numbers; lists of users and groups; and lists of directories and files. Change requests should be written to document upgrades and modifications to the network hardware, software, and user information.

All of these suggestions and practices will go along way in assisting the LAN manager in providing the best working LAN for it's users.

SECURITY MANAGEMENT

Security management is the process of identifying and authenticating users and controlling or auditing logical access to network resources. Sound security management ensures the network is protected from unauthorized access, accidental or willful interference with normal operations, and destruction. This includes protection of physical facilities and software, and personal security. For more thorough coverage of this subject, refer to Chapter 12. Security becomes even more important when a network is remotely accessible via the Internet or dial-up networking. Please, take this seriously.

PERFORMANCE MANAGEMENT

Performance management involves tuning the network to increase efficiency and productivity, as well as monitoring performance for overall throughput, percentage of utilization, error rates, and response time; analyzing the data; and optimizing the system to improve identified deficiencies.

ACCOUNTING MANAGEMENT

In addition to services that allow for fault, security, and performance management, most network operating systems offer built-in accounting management capabilities that track network usage by keeping a running account of the following:

- ▸ User logins and logoffs

- ▸ Disk space used by specific users and groups of users

- ▸ Network traffic generated (in packets, bytes, or both)

- ▸ Print jobs sent to network printers

- ▸ Number of pages printed

- ▸ Applications used, including when and for how long

- ▸ Changes made to security restrictions

Many of the accounting components work directly with security features and provide many opportunities for managing and auditing all aspects of network usage.

Network Management Strategy

As we've discussed throughout this book, you must have a strategy for managing your LAN. Implementing and operating a LAN without a well planned strategy is like taking a trip in a foreign country without a road map or translation dictionary: You'll eventually find your destination, but you probably won't enjoy the trip.

In your LAN management strategy, consider what you want your management system to provide, both today and in the future. A comprehensive management system should give you the basic features you need now, plus the capability of being easily upgraded as you need it.

Whatever goals you set in developing an effective LAN management system, make sure that the network management software you choose allows you to set up a management console. For instance, Novell has very good network management systems available for every level of complexity, from simple workgroup management packages to extensive LANs and WANs.

ManageWise is Novell and Intel's flagship management product. Incorporating industry-leading technology from both companies, it provides all the basic management functionality that network managers need, in one convenient package. ManageWise combines the functionality of five products (the first three from Novell, the last two from Intel):

NetWare Management System

NetWare Management Agent

NetWare LANanalyzer Agent

LANDesk Manager

LANDesk Virus Protect

As you can see, Novell ManageWise is a multifaceted, integrated network management software.

Regardless of which LAN management system you choose, most will provide very similar basic features. For example, most management systems implement their capabilities through industry-standard protocols, such as SNMP or CMIP, with the same basic goal in mind — allow the network management console the ability to collect data about the devices it is managing and generate information from that data.

This presents us with a prime opportunity to stop and take a quick look at the key component of effective LAN management — management protocols.

Management Protocols

Management protocols are the language used to communicate with and within a given network. Think of protocol as a set of conventions between communicating processes on the format and content of messages to be exchanged. The simplest protocols define only the hardware configuration. More complex protocols define timings, data formats, error detection and correction techniques, and software structures. The most powerful protocols describe each level of the transfer process as a layer, separate from the rest, so that certain layers, such as the interconnecting hardware, can be changed without affecting the whole. Put very simply, the network management protocol is the method by which your LAN manager exchanges information with your network.

Depending on the platform you choose, you may be able to implement several network management protocols in support of your LAN. Here are two common management protocols:

> **Simple Network Management Protocol (SNMP).** This very popular protocol commonly comes with the purchase of hubs. It runs regular diagnostic tests to keep constant status on devices and notes status of each management information base. In case of a problem, SNMP reviews the information base, locates the problem, and allows system administrators to quickly access and correct system problems, remotely if necessary.

> **Common Management Information Protocol (CMIP).** Although it's not used as often as SNMP, CMIP is more complex because it puts system monitoring decisions in the hands of the LAN Manager. The administrator sets the parameters to be monitored using object-oriented descriptions. This protocol requires much more work and maintenance for administrators, but gives them customized control over all component aspects of the LAN.

The most common methods of monitoring and retrieving information about a LAN at any given time using almost any given network management software are:

> ▶ Protocol analysis

> ▶ Graphical mapping

> ▶ Polling

> ▶ Event logging

> ▶ Device configuration

Let's take a brief look at each of these common activities associated with most LAN management software.

PROTOCOL ANALYSIS

This particular feature is discussed in more detail in Chapter 12 but is worth mentioning here as well. Because clients or nodes are usually more problematic to secure (due to factors such as telecommuting), it's very important to periodically analyze the protocols traversing the network to ensure proper security and system integrity.

Protocol analyzers offer a tremendous amount of information about network performance, and you can use them to analyze networks from the physical-layer through the upper-layer protocols. Generally speaking, however, most troubleshooting analysis happens at the network layer and below. The errors found there are those that a LAN manager can usually handle, such as swapping out a bad network interface card, reloading a LAN driver, or distributing resources or clients to another network or segment.

However, when a problem does occur above the network layer, you can also use analyzers to interpret the communications occurring on the wire. For example, if an application does not load properly from the server, you may wish to use a protocol analyzer to see the downloading process on the wire in order to determine the proper fix.

GRAPHICAL MAPPING

This is where the graphical user interface really plays a valuable role for LAN managers. With this feature as part of the network-management system software, the LAN manager can actually generate a visual characterization of the network and its components. This visual map of the network can be color coded and even use blinking lights or sounds to identify system errors. For instance, a LAN manager may color code all routers green, hubs red, switches yellow, etc., then set the graphical mapping software to blink that color coded component on the map if it is experiencing a problem. Again, Novell ManageWise provides this type of feature.

POLLING

Polling is an important feature of the LAN management system. It should be considered a key component during the strategy and planning phase and definitely be an integral part of any viable network-management system software you consider. It's so important because your LAN manager will rely heavily on the network management system to periodically query all devices on the network and determine their status, thus *polling* them for a response.

Most network management systems allow the LAN manager the ability to configure how often the polling takes place. This ability is important because the larger the network, the more devices and traffic. The more devices and traffic a LAN has, the more polling takes place. This will very easily equate to the network management system keeping track of thousands of polling queries and could, in turn, adversely affect network performance. Finding a happy medium between not enough polling and too much is something of a challenge. Too little polling can delay an alert to a system problem and too much can produce a large amount of traffic. We suggest that you follow the recommendations for poll settings provided by the manufacturer of the particular network management software you choose. This usually provides a good starting point.

As a possible alternative to the polling method we've just discussed, there is another specific process known as *trap-based polling*. With trap-based polling, any given device, upon failure or experiencing a problem, sends the LAN manager's console a message called a *trap*. The trap message identifies the location of the problem, allowing the LAN manager to quickly poll the device in question and determine the nature and extent of the problem.

EVENT LOGGING

Event logging is exactly what it's name implies — the logging of events. With this feature, the results of all polling and trap messages can be captured in a file for statistical analysis, future review or comparison, and as a running record of all network administrative activity taking place at any given time.

DEVICE CONFIGURATION

Device configuration is a feature that all network-management systems should support. Some implement it using industry-standard protocols like SNMP, and some use proprietary agents and protocols. Regardless of the mechanism, a LAN manager should have some way of affecting the configuration of large numbers of devices from the management console. This remote access capability proves itself invaluable in situations where the LAN manager isn't physically located in close proximity to all LAN servers under his or her responsibility.

Summary

This chapter discusses the technical and administrative functions of a LAN manager. The responsibilities for managing a network require both technical and administrative skill, as well as good habits. The success of a LAN manager depends on having the ability to work effectively with other LAN managers and network users alike. An effective LAN manager emphasizes participation in user training, because this better-equips end-users to cope with the frequent, easy-to-fix problems associated with network applications. Training one or more assistants ensures continuity of operations and give the primary LAN manager the time to spend on more complicated tasks.

CHAPTER 12

Maintaining Network Security

Security takes many forms. It's not just passwords for logins or combination safes for storing top-secret disks. Security includes viruses, passwords, protecting dial-in access, file access, hardware protection, and rights to the network. Security is a major concern for large corporations but is usually ignored in small organizations, though it is no less important there. Just ask anyone who loses a single file how important security is.

The Nature of Threats

Many are the evil forces waiting to attack your network. Then there are just stupid mistakes. Do you know which is responsible for more crashed networks and lost files? It's probably stupid mistakes. True, we worry more about viruses, hackers, sabotage, and natural disasters, but the user who types "DEL *.*" at the root directory of their workstation can cause more problems.

In the past, mainframes were fairly secure — locked in an air-conditioned clean room, backed up nightly, given dedicated and clean power, maintained by the hardware vendor, programmed by people with pocket protectors, and managed by an MIS director with a staff of hundreds. The network is different. The server is sometimes under someone's desk, backed up when the mood hits, plugged into the wall, maintained by the person in the office that has had a computer at home the longest, filled with off-the-shelf software (including flying toasters and card games), and managed by the office manager. Larger networks are maintained the way mainframes used to be, because they replaced the mainframe, and the staff and clean room were already in place.

Even the network maintained like a mainframe is more vulnerable than the mainframe was. The mainframe used *dumb terminals* — terminals without memory, disks, or CPUs. They could only do what the mainframe allowed them to do. Exiting a program meant exiting the user from the operating system. Most mainframe users never touched the operating system functions. If the clean room was locked and the security was correct, the only vulnerability on the mainframe was a modem that permitted vendor support and dial-in access for a privileged few. Break-ins and problems were few and far between.

Today's networks are made up of a bunch of computers (many times more powerful than the first mainframes), sitting on employee desks, just inviting someone to do something wrong. A network has many entry points, and some application software uses files in such a way that the rights must be granted to users so they can read, write, copy, and delete files. This gives access to the operating system, and anyone with those rights can cause problems. Users have access to the Internet and bulletin boards, companies are giving laptops to employees, and users with home computers can dial into the network.

Network resources can be protected with carefully designed security built into the NOS, but how do you protect the workstations and all the hard drives on them? You can protect workstations from viruses, but can you protect them from the user installing bad software, changing configurations, failing to back up, or deleting files? The dangerous user is not the one afraid of breaking something. It's the users that think they know something. Such users are unafraid to tweak configuration files, fiddle with the memory, and poke around to see what they can get into. This type of user is usually just trying to speed up their workstation or add some new software program they use at home. A little power in the wrong hands can be dangerous. With power comes responsibility. Anyone with the power to change things should be trained on the effects those changes could have. We discuss this in greater detail later.

And then there are hackers and deliberate saboteurs. These people enjoy breaking in and doing damage. Serious hackers have found a way around every security measure invented. They have dialers that randomly dial phone numbers until they get a modem. They have password generators that try combinations of passwords, unattended, until they get a hit. Once in, they can transfer large sums of money in and out of accounts at will, destroy good credit ratings or fix bad ones, remove or change records, steal secrets and confidential data, introduce viruses, or just erase the entire system. Disgruntled, terminated employees have been known to make their last act with a company one of revenge and destruction. Windows has even introduced another peril into the network's existence, but we discuss this in greater detail later.

With luck you'll never face one of these problems. This chapter alerts you to the possibilities, and you can weigh the cost of prevention against the cost of the cure. Most of the security measures won't cost anything except the time to learn how to protect yourself.

Passwords

Passwords are the most common form of security. Most people feel safe when they password protect their system. How safe are passwords? Passwords are as safe as we make them. Did you know that many passwords are written on a piece of paper taped to the inside of a top drawer on the user's desk? Have you ever seen a password taped to a monitor? Think about your personal passwords. Are they names of a relative or pet, something to do with your hobby, a favorite word, a curse word, something to do with money, or the ever-popular word "password" for the password?

A system manager once challenged an intelligent novice to break the security he had set up on the system. The employee got in by guessing a different user's password (a golf term) and moved some vital files to scattered directories, all in under ten minutes. The novice then promised to tell his boss how he did it, if his boss publicly announced what had happened. The system manager had no other choice than to swallow his pride and make the announcement. Listed below are the top ten rules in using a password system.

1 • Passwords are a secret.

2 • Don't give passwords to anyone.

3 • Don't write down passwords.

4 • Don't pick common or easily guessed passwords.

5 • Don't type passwords while someone is watching.

6 • Don't allow users to log in and walk away from the workstation for extended periods of time. This negates any password protection.

7 • Don't let users place passwords in batch files where they can be read.

8 • Change passwords if you feel your password has been compromised.

9 • Change passwords from time to time, as a safety measure.

10 • Reinforce the previous nine steps when training users about passwords.

Let them know that if they forget their password, you can get them another. This is the main reason users write down their password. They're afraid that they'll lose everything if they forget it. Passwords can be beneficial if managed properly or useless if mismanaged or abused.

Viruses

Viruses get their name from being able to replicate and infect any computer that it comes into contact with. Periodically a virus is so widespread it makes the evening news. Sometimes rumors of a particular virus are themselves a hoax. Where do viruses come from? There are those who claim that the virus-scanning software companies introduce new viruses from time to time to help sell their software, but the truth is that computer hackers are responsible for most viruses. Imagine the feeling of power they get from knowing that something they created is passed all over the world, causes fear in millions of people, and hurts business and establishments. Be forewarned, before you start spending late nights creating your mark on the world. Viruses are illegal, and people developing viruses are being prosecuted whenever possible, with serious consequences.

All of these facts aside, a virus is serious business and should not be taken lightly. A virus can infect a few workstations or completely destroy a network, requiring a complete system regeneration, and causing loss of whatever data was new since the last backup. Does the backup have the virus? If you haven't been affected by a virus yet, you will be sometime.

Viruses take many forms and can enter the network many different ways. A floppy taken from home and copied to the network can contain a virus. Accessing bulletin boards can transfer viruses. A computer technician could be carrying around a virus on one of their utility disks, although there's no excuse for that — they should know better. There have been a few instances of viruses being shipped with very popular commercial software packages. Whether these were introduced on purpose, subversively, or inadvertently is not known, but it emphasizes the importance of not taking anything for granted. Any and all floppies used on a network must be scanned for viruses, without exception.

Viruses come in two main varieties: destructive and non-destructive. Some viruses are fun and simply cause the screen to drop characters or swirl around and disappear. This is just a practical joke. It's funny, until it happens to you when you're in the middle of a project, and the person that instigated the virus isn't around to undo the damage. These type of viruses, while seemingly innocent, have no place in the workplace.

Destructive viruses will either cause intermittent problems or completely destroy the system. Viruses can destroy the boot area of a disk, rendering the disk unbootable and all data untouchable, or they can infect all executable files, causing all programs to abort or give mysterious error messages. Viruses have even been reported to change CMOS settings and reprogram or erase EPROM chips in hardware. Viruses that infect hardware are the most insidious and difficult to correct. Hardware may have to be sent back to the manufacturer. If the hard drive is infected, you can always reinstall the operating system and perform a backup. After all, you do have a good backup, don't you?

Is this meant to scare you? Absolutely! Viruses are mostly preventable. High quality virus scanning software is inexpensive and readily available. It should be installed on every network, workstation, server, and laptop. Updates are available from the software companies to scan for newer varieties as they appear.

Natural Disasters

Natural disasters are often overlooked. Earthquakes, fires, floods, and tornadoes can put you out of business in short order. If you manage a large network that crosses many cities or states, you can install redundant servers around the country. If a server in California is destroyed by earthquake, the redundant server in Chicago can take over without missing a beat. And don't forget those hurricanes on the eastern seaboard or Gulf coast. Small companies do well to have adequate and current backups located in different locations. Two sets of backups in a building that burns down will do little good. Keep one at the office and another in a bank box or the home of an employee; then the odds of both sets being destroyed are slim. Refer to Chapter 13 for more information on creating a network contingency plan in the event of natural disaster.

Dial-in Access

Dial-in access is being added to most networks so employees can work from home or access files and e-mail from the field. Any time a modem is attached to the network, another point of entry has been opened for hackers to gain entry. Passwords can help, but we've already shown that passwords are not foolproof. Be selective in giving access to the system. Make sure the user's rights protect the network. A dial back modem adds another level of security. The user dials the modem, then enters the name and password. The modem checks a table stored in the modem and dials back the user's phone number. This doesn't work for mobile users who are always using different numbers. There's not much you can do about that. Why do you want to secure the dial-in modems? Because you don't want viruses or hackers hurting your network.

Windows

Windows may be the best thing that has happened to the user interface for workstations in years, but unfortunately the Windows operating system circumvents some network security, which poses a serious threat to the network. Some application software requires that user rights be set to read, write, delete, and modify files in the data directory. Directory rights are set so users cannot delete files in the directory from the network operating system. You think you're protected, right? Windows File Manager reads the rights on the files, and a user with access to the accounting data directory can select any or all files in File Manager and delete them with a few mouse strokes. Third-party products are available that cover this hole in security. The low cost of these utilities makes them a very good investment.

▶ · ◀

Hardware

An overlooked area of security is availability of hardware. We discussed mainframes and the care with which they are maintained and secured. PCs are ignored because we are accustomed to seeing them on desktops. Servers, routers, hubs, and workstations all benefit from protection.

The server should be attached to an *uninterrupted power supply* (UPS) that will down the server in an orderly manner in the event that the power is out and the UPS battery supply runs low. Battery backups are needed for mission-critical servers such as airline reservation systems and bank networks.

Is the server console secure and password protected? The console-secure function only permits the console operator to perform certain functions on the server, such as loading software from floppies, changing the date and time, and loading software into memory.

Secure your routers and hubs to protect them from damage, disconnection, and unauthorized access. It doesn't hurt to protect them from lightning either. Routers, hubs, and modems are particularly susceptible to lightning strikes. And beware of laptops, which can be plugged into the network at the hub by disconnecting a cable and plugging in the laptop. The user is then able to run any program on the laptop, with potentially dire results.

Finally, workstations can be protected by requiring passwords to boot the workstation and by removing floppy drives. It is difficult to chain workstations to desks, but they can be protected from theft by commercially produced theft-deterrent devices. Some of these include cables and locks or alarms that are triggered when the device is moved or disconnected from power.

Here again, use common sense when cabling. Use Plenum cables if the building code requires it, and use the best quality cable you can afford. It is important to run the cables in safe areas, such as suspended ceilings, conduit, or channels specially designed to carry cables. Spend a little extra to have the cable terminated in a wall jack instead of run down the wall. Besides being neater, when a workstation is moved, the jumper cable is unplugged from the wall, and there is nothing left hanging out to damage. Cables running across floors are asking for trouble. Refer to Chapter 6 for more information on cables.

Treat your network as if it were a mainframe, as it may very well have been at one time, because it is certainly doing the work of one.

Network Security System

We have discussed the perimeters of network security and the pieces that are outside the network operating system. Now we will examine the security built into the NOS itself. The network security system involves the assigning of various rights to users and administrators. Default settings allow operation of a simple network without an in-depth understanding of all of these features. However, if you are operating a large network, or if you are particular about protecting the data on your network, you will want to take the time to learn all about the security options your network has to offer.

Although rights security is one of the most powerful features of the network, it can be a challenge to learn to use every option effectively. The options include file system rights, object and property rights, trustees and trustee assignments, inheritance, security equivalence, effective rights, and using rights to control access to the directory tree. You can use these security features to define roles in the network to create positions with exactly the authority that you feel is needed to complete assigned tasks.

Another major benefit of network security features is the capability to divide the administration of the network among several individuals, each with authority over only their area of the directory tree. Used correctly, the security system in the NOS can provide you with a highly secure, very structured, and understandable networking environment.

RIGHTS IN THE FILE SYSTEM

Basically, a user is given rights to any file or directory by a *trustee assignment* that is created by a network administrator. Any user who has rights to a file is a trustee of that file. A trustee assignment contains a list of rights that are granted to a certain user for the file where the trustee assignment is created.

Inheritance allows a trustee assignment that is granted at one point to apply to everything below that point in the file structure. Because of inheritance, network administrators do not have to create trustee assignments for every file that every user needs to use. Inheritance is the main reason that rights can be granted to directories. If a trustee assignment grants a user certain rights, that trustee (user) has those same rights to every file and subdirectory in the directory where the trustee assignment was granted.

A distinction must be made here between a trustee who has *explicit* rights to a file and a trustee who has *implicit* rights to a file. Explicit rights are granted to a file when a user has a trustee assignment on that file. Implicit rights are granted when a user does not have a trustee assignment to the file but inherits rights from another trustee assignment. For an example of how inheritance works, see Figure 12.1.

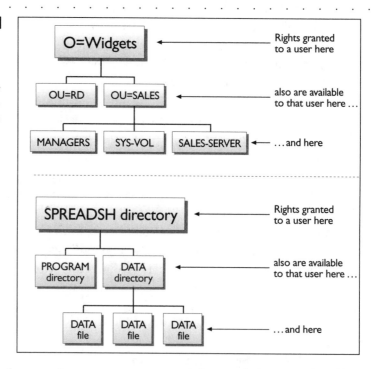

Suppose that you do not want anyone to inherit rights to a certain file. You can *block* all trustees from inheriting rights to it by creating an *inherited rights filter* for that file. An inherited rights filter contains a list of rights, just as a trustee assignment does. But these rights are granted solely to the assigned trustee. The file must be kept in the same folder as the inherited rights filter. If a right that the trustee was granted is not listed in the inherited rights filter, that right is blocked and cannot be used by the trustee to whom it was assigned.

Another key mechanism used to simplify the assignment of rights to files and directories is *security equivalence*. If a network administrator decides that one user should have all of the rights that another user has been granted, the network administrator can make the first user security-equivalent to the second user, and the first user will then have all of the rights that the second user was granted.

The rights that a user can actually use for a file or directory are called that user's *effective rights*. These are a combination of a user's trustee assignments, inheritance, and security-equivalent rights, as shown in Figure 12.2.

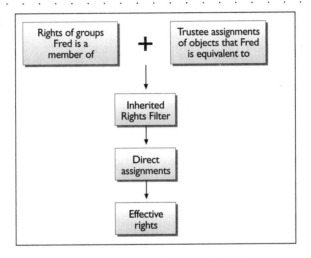

FIGURE 12.2

How effective rights work

All of the trustee assignments for a file, as well as the inherited rights mask, are stored in the Director Entry Table for the file or directory where they are granted. In order to change a file's or a directory's trustee assignments or inherited rights mask, you must have rights to the file, specifically a right called the *access control right*. All of the possible rights to files and directories are discussed below.

We have been talking about how users are able to access files by having trustee assignments. Now we need to expand that idea, because any object in the directory tree can be granted a trustee assignment to a file or directory. (An *object* is an item in a database that represents a real entity on the network, such as a user, group, printer, or server.) For example, a *profile object* can be a trustee of a directory, or an *organizational unit object* can be a trustee of a file. This makes it much easier to assign similar rights to a large group of people. We will see how in the next section.

As we talk about granting rights to users and other objects, a question may come to mind about whether there exists a special user account for a network administrator or supervisor who can always make necessary trustee assignments.

Some NOSs provide a SUPERVISOR account for that purpose. Also, certain regular user objects in the directory tree can be granted the rights to make changes. There is more about this later in the chapter.

DIRECTORY RIGHTS

Table 12.1 lists the rights that a trustee can be granted to work on a directory in the file system. In many situations, you will see only the first character used by itself to indicate the right that has been granted.

OBJECTS: A SIMPLE REVIEW

Objects are entries in a database that hold information about organizational structure or about physical things on the network such as volumes, printers, and users. The objects in the database are organized in a tree structure, which makes some objects higher in the tree than others. We usually imagine the tree as having branches flowing down instead of growing up.

Objects that contain other objects underneath them in this analogy are *container objects*. These include country, organization, and organizational unit objects. Objects that cannot contain other objects are called *leaf objects,* and include things like users, printers, and groups (a group has a list of user objects, but it does not *contain* those user objects). A special case is the *volume object,* which is both a leaf object in the directory tree and the root directory of a physical volume. You must keep in mind the dual nature of this object so that you can recognize where information that is presented in a volume comes from.

Think of an object as a box. Boxes can have other boxes beneath them in the directory tree's hierarchical structure. The boxes are filled with information about the thing that the box represents. The pieces of information inside the box are the object's *properties.* One object can contain a great deal of information in its properties. In particular, a user object holds a lot of information about a user and that user's account, such as the user's password restrictions, login restrictions, station restrictions, group memberships, login script, and so on.

TABLE 12.1	RIGHT	DESCRIPTION
Trustee Rights in the File System	Supervisor	Grants all rights to the directory, its files, and subdirectories. The supervisor right cannot be blocked by an inherited rights mask. Users with this right can grant other users rights to the directory, its files, and subdirectories.
	Read	Grants the right to open files in the directory, read their contents, and run the programs.
	Write	Grants the right to open and change the contents of files in the directory.
	Create	Grants the rights to create new files and subdirectories in the directory. If *create* is the only right granted to a trustee for the directory, and no other rights are granted below the directory, a *drop-box directory* is created. In a drop-box directory, you can create a file and write to it. Once the file is closed, however, only a trustee with more rights than *create* can see or update the file. You can copy files or subdirectories into the directory and assume ownership of them, but other users' rights are revoked.
	Erase	Grants the right to delete the directory, its files, and subdirectories.
	Modify	Grants the right to change the attributes or name of the directory and of its files and subdirectories, but does not grant the right to change their contents. (That requires the write right.)
	File scan	Grants the right to see the directory and its files with the DIR or NDIR directory command.
	Access control	Grants the right to change the trustee assignments and inherited rights of the directory and of its files and subdirectories.

Security allows us to control access to each object (box) individually, and also to each property (piece of information in the box) individually. We can grant access to the box without granting access to see inside the box, or we can grant access to see and change some information in the box, but not grant access to see other information in the same box.

Such finite control allows creative flexibility and power to the rights system. Unfortunately, it can make things enormously complex if good planning and a sound understanding do not precede your actions.

OBJECT AND PROPERTY RIGHTS

Access to the objects and properties of objects in Directory Services is controlled by two sets of rights: *object rights* and *property rights*. Instead of a user just having rights to the file system, a user can also have rights to another user, or more specifically, to see or change the information about that user stored in a user object. Object and property rights are different from the file and directory rights that are used in the file system because different information must be protected.

Next we list the object and property rights that are used to access objects and the information that they contain. Then we talk about how file system concepts like trustees and inheritance apply to objects.

Object Rights

Table 12.2 lists the rights that any trustee can be granted in order to work on any object in the NDS directory tree. Except for the supervisor object right, the object rights do not affect what a trustee can do with the object's properties. In many situations, the first character of the right's name is used to indicate the right has been granted.

Property Rights

Table 12.3 lists the rights that any trustee can be granted in order to work on the properties of an object. These rights can be granted to a trustee for all of an object's properties, or for just one of an object's properties. In many situations, you will see only the first character used by itself in the trustee lists (and in some DOS utilities like NETADMIN, RIGHTS, FILER, and so on) to indicate the right that has been granted.

TABLE 12.2	RIGHT	DESCRIPTION
Object Rights	Browse	Grants the right to see the object in the directory tree. The name of the object is returned when a search is made and matches the object.
	Create	Grants the right to create a new object below this object in the directory tree. Rights are not defined for the new object. This right is available only on container objects, because noncontainer objects cannot have subordinates.
	Delete	Grants the right to delete the object from the directory tree. Objects that have subordinates cannot be deleted (the subordinates must be deleted first).
	Rename	Grants the right to change the name of the object, in effect changing the naming property. This changes what the object is called in complete names.
	Supervisor	Grants all access privileges. A trustee with the supervisor object right also has unrestricted access to all properties. The supervisor object right can be blocked by the inherited rights filter below the object where the supervisor right is granted.

TABLE 12.3	RIGHT	DESCRIPTION
Property Rights	Compare	Grants the right to compare any value to a value of the property. With the compare right, an operation can return true or false, but you cannot see the value of the property. The read right includes the compare right.
	Read	Grants the right to read the values of the property. Compare is a subset of read. If the read right is given, compare operations are also allowed.
	Write	Grants the right to add, change, or remove any values of the property. The write right includes the add or delete self right.
	Add or delete self	Grants a trustee the right to add or remove itself as a value of the property. The trustee cannot affect any other values of the property. This right is only meaningful for properties that contain object names as values, such as group membership lists or mailing lists. The write right includes the add or delete self right.
	Supervisor	Grants all rights to the property. The supervisor property right can be blocked by an object's inherited rights filter.

Rights are granted to objects and their properties in the same way that rights are granted to files and directories — through trustee assignments. As we described for the file system, however, any object can be a trustee of any other object. All of the rights in the tables above are used to grant one object access to another object and its properties.

Inheritance is still an important concept when granting object rights to trustees. If I grant a trustee assignment to a container object, the trustee has the same rights to all leaf objects in that container unless an inherited rights filter blocks some or all of those rights, as illustrated in Figure 12.3. (The figure shows object rights, but it could include property rights as well.) As in the file system, if a trustee has a trustee assignment on the container object, and a trustee assignment on a leaf object within that container, only the trustee assignment to the leaf object is valid; the rights that would have been inherited are not added to the explicit trustee assignment on the leaf object.

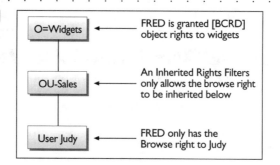

FIGURE 12.3

A user can have object rights to a container, but those rights can be blocked by an inherited rights filter.

A trustee assignment to an object can include rights to the properties of that object as well. Such property rights can be assigned in two ways. A trustee may have either the *all properties right,* which applies to every property of the object, or the *specific property right,* which applies to individual properties of an object. If a trustee has specific property rights to one or several properties, then only access to those properties is defined, and that access overrides what would have been the default property rights from the all properties right assignment.

Using the all properties and specific property methods together to grant property rights to a trustee is useful when you want to control access to particularly sensitive properties in an object. For example, if you want a user to be able to read all of the properties of a printer object but not change any of them, you grant read all property rights. If you want a user to be able to change all properties of a profile object except the login script property, which the user should only be able to read, then you grant both write all-properties rights and read specific-property rights to the login script property. The all property assignment applies to every property of the profile except login script, which has a specific property assignment.

In Directory Services, it is important to know where trustee assignments to an object and an object's inherited rights filter are stored. All are stored as entries in the object trustees *access control list* (ACL) property of each object.

To change trustee rights or the inherited rights filter of a file or directory, you must have the access control right to that file or directory. To change rights to an object or its properties, or an object's inherited rights filter, you must have the write property right to the ACL property of that object. If you do, then you manage that object.

Inheritance with Object and Property Rights

Inheritance is even more important when working with objects than it is when working with files and directories. The reason is that objects must have both rights to other objects and rights to the file system in order for work to be done. A user must have rights to its own object, to the profile script that it uses, to printing objects that it uses, and to all areas of the file system that it will access in order to complete assigned tasks. If we did not have inheritance to assist in granting everyone rights to necessary areas, it might be impossible to keep up with the security needs of the users on a large network. Inheritance makes it easy to make assignments to a large number of users with one trustee assignment. Inheritance in the NOS is just like the inheritance that one uses in the file system. If I grant user KIM a trustee assignment to a container object, such as an organization, then KIM has those same rights to every leaf object within that organization, as shown in Figure 12.4. (For simplicity, only object rights are shown in the figure.) If there are any organizational unit container objects in the organization, then KIM's rights continue to flow down into that container. This continues to every object that is underneath the organization where the original trustee assignment was made, unless an inherited rights filter blocks the inheritance of the original trustee assignment at a lower level. If the inherited rights filter is on a container object, then the rights are blocked for everything below that container, not just for that container object.

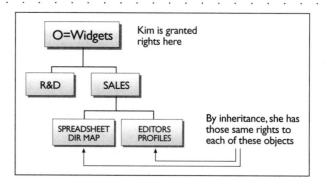

KIM inherits object rights to lower objects in the directory tree because she has a trustee assignment above.

Suppose that all or several directory map objects pointing to all of your main application software packages are located under one of three organizational units in your directory tree. User Megan needs to access all of these applications by having rights to each of the directory map objects that contain paths to applications that she uses. You could grant a trustee assignment to Megan for each of the directory map objects that she needs, but that could take hours and would be difficult to update later when changes occurred. Instead, you grant Megan rights to the organizational unit named APPLICATIONS, which holds all of the directory map objects. By inheritance, Megan now has the same rights to each of the directory map objects within the APPLICATIONS organizational unit.

Remember this, however: Only object rights and all properties rights are inherited, or flow down the tree. Because specific property rights might grant rights to a property that does not exist on the object below, only the all properties right is inherited and then applies to all properties of the object below. For example, if you grant a trustee rights to the login script property of an organizational unit, the trustee cannot inherit rights to the login script property of a directory map object in that organizational unit, because directory maps don't have login scripts. The trustee's all properties assignment to the organizational unit would be inherited for the directory map.

In the previous example, we assume that no inherited rights filters on the directory map objects are blocking Megan from inheriting the rights that are granted on the container APPLICATIONS. Objects also use inherited rights filters to control the flow of inheritance, but the inherited rights filter for objects must be more powerful than the one used for a file or directory in order to deal with the increased number of rights used with objects and properties.

We mentioned that only object and all properties rights are inherited. The inherited rights filter, however, can contain entries for each specific property of an object. Why is this so? First of all, the inherited rights filter is not inherited itself, but is a part of each object, so the properties that it must apply to never change. Second, this allows the all properties rights that are inherited from above to be selectively blocked for each property.

For example, suppose that you create an inherited rights filter for a group object named AUDITORS. You don't care if others read the identification information about this object, but you don't want anyone who does not have an explicit trustee assignment to that object to see who is a member of the auditing team. You create an inherited rights filter for the object that includes:

- ► the browse object right, so that others can see the object,

- ► the read all–properties right, so that the identification information about this object can be seen but not changed by those with rights above this point,

- ► and a specific entry in the inherited rights filter for the members property, which includes no rights, so that no one who is not granted rights explicitly to this property can read that membership list. Of course, if a trustee had the supervisor object right, the trustee would also have access to all properties of the object, regardless of which property rights are inherited or blocked.

Figure 12.5 shows the details of this example, including both object and property rights.

An important concept worth repeating about the inherited rights filter for an object is that *it can block the supervisor object or property right.* This can only be done under certain conditions; namely, that a trustee with the supervisor object right already exists on the object where you want to block the supervisor right from being inherited. The trustee with the supervisor object right at that point is a manager of that branch of the tree. You cannot remove the supervisor object right from that trustee's trustee assignment until the supervisor right is added to the inherited rights filter so it can be inherited again. This prevents cutting off supervisor-level access to a branch of the directory tree.

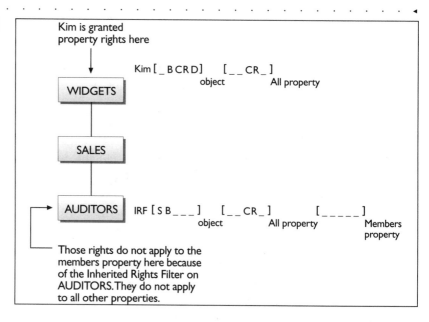

KIM cannot see the Members property of the AUDITORS group because an inherited rights filter blocks KIM's rights.

At least it tries to. If you had a trustee who was the supervisor of a branch of the directory tree, and some other supervisor deleted that user's object (not the trustee assignment, but the user object itself), then the trustee assignment would be invalid and there would be no supervisor of that area of the tree. If that part of the tree included a server and volumes, then supervisor-level access to the file systems on those volumes might also be cut off.

Be careful when blocking the supervisor object. You must keep track of which users are branch supervisors and take care not to delete their user objects. NetWare utilities will not stop you from deleting a user, even though the user is the only trustee with supervisor rights to a part of the directory tree.

Let's talk more about access to the file system through the directory tree. Access to the file system is not automatic for any user. Access comes through the NetWare server object representing the NetWare server to which a volume is physically attached. Any user that has supervisor rights to a NetWare server object will automatically have the supervisor directory right to the root directory of every volume attached to that server.

Because the utilities have safeguards to prevent cutting off supervisor-level access to part of the directory tree, every object should always have a supervisor (or several supervisors), including every NetWare server object. This attempts to ensure that every volume has at least one trustee with supervisor-level access at the root directory. A trustee with this access could then grant explicit trustee assignments to the root directory, granting someone rights that did not come through the server object. This might provide a safeguard if you are concerned about cutting off access. Of course, it is also less secure to have more supervisors.

SECURITY EQUIVALENCE

The concept of security equivalence that we talked about for the file system is based on the idea that one object can be equivalent in rights to another object. That idea is used even more for rights to other objects in the NDS directory tree. A user object can be security-equivalent to any other object. Each user object has a property that lists all of the objects to which the user is security-equivalent. The user has all of the rights granted to itself, plus all of the rights granted to each of the objects listed in its security equivalence property. Other objects do not have a security equivalence property

Besides the objects listed in a user's security equivalence property, every object has three other security equivalencies that are not shown anywhere and cannot be changed. These three extra security equivalencies apply to every object, not just to user objects:

- ▸ **Every object is security-equivalent to the [Public] trustee.** The [Public] trustee is used mainly to grant rights to users who have not even logged in to Directory Services, such as the \LOGIN directory on a SYS volume. You probably won't use the [Public] trustee much anyway.

- ▸ **Every object is security-equivalent to the [Root] object.** This allows you to grant a [Root] trustee assignment to a file, directory, or other object, and every object in the directory tree will have those rights by security equivalence to [Root]. For example, you could make [Root] a trustee of your electronic mail directory so that everyone in the directory tree would have rights to that directory. This odd arrangement prevents you from adding to a security equivalence list people who have more rights than you do, and then using that security equivalence to gain supervisor-level rights to a part of the directory tree or file system.

▸ **Every object is security-equivalent to all of the container objects that are part of its complete name.** For example, in Figure 12.6, user FRED is security-equivalent to organizational unit SALES, organizational unit WEST, and Organization WIDGETS-INC. This security equivalence is not listed anywhere, but you can always see what an object is security-equivalent to by looking at its complete name. You also cannot change this security equivalence. Every object is always security-equivalent to the containers above it.

FIGURE 12.6

FRED is security-equivalent to all of the container objects above him in the directory tree.

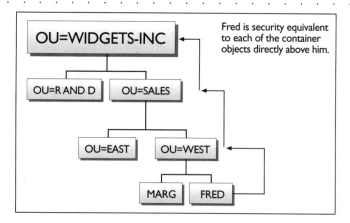

Fred is security equivalent to each of the container objects directly above him.

The third special security equivalence above provides one of the most powerful security features. You can grant every user in a container rights to a file simply by granting the organizational unit a trustee right to the file. This operates like a group object, but with several advantages. First, the membership of the group is automatic. You don't have to list member users, and when a user is no longer in the organizational unit, you don't have to change any trustee assignments; the user is automatically not security-equivalent to the organizational unit, and all of the rights granted to the organizational unit are not applied to that user.

Group objects should be used in place containers as trustees when the users that are part of the group are a subset of the users in a group, or a combination of a few users from each of several containers. See Figure 12.7.

Group objects should be used when the users that you want in the group are a subset of the users within one container or are not all in the same container.

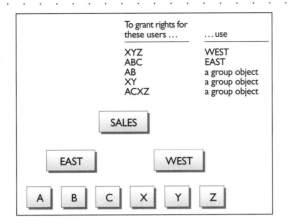

To grant rights for these users …	…use
XYZ	WEST
ABC	EAST
AB	a group object
XY	a group object
ACXZ	a group object

SALES

EAST   WEST

A   B   C   X   Y   Z

You must remember three important points about security equivalence to use it effectively:

- **Security equivalence is not transitive.** That is, if KIM is security-equivalent to FRED, and FRED is security-equivalent to MARIA, KIM is *not* security-equivalent to MARIA through FRED. This also applies to the security equivalence that each object has to every container above it. You cannot make FRED security-equivalent to organizational unit SALES by making him security-equivalent to JUDY, who is in SALES, because the only additional rights that FRED will have are those granted by explicit trustee assignment to JUDY.

- **Security equivalence applies to the file system as well as objects.** That is, if KIM is granted a trustee assignment to a file, and FRED is security-equivalent to KIM, then FRED can access all the files that KIM has rights to, and not just all the *objects* that KIM has rights to.

- **Special rights are needed to make a user security-equivalent to another object.** The rights are special because they are different than the rights needed to perform any other action. In order to make BILL security-equivalent to MEGAN, you must list MEGAN in the security equivalence property of BILL. But to do this, you do not need any rights to the security-equivalence property of BILL. Instead, you must manage user MEGAN, which means that you must have at least the write property right to the ACL property of MEGAN. You do not need any rights at all to BILL. This odd arrangement prevents you from adding to a security equivalence list people who have more rights than you do, and then using that security equivalence to gain supervisor-level rights to a part of the directory tree or file system.

What is security equivalence used for? We suggest three areas where it is useful. The first is when rights are granted to a group or organizational role object. Any user listed as a member or occupant of the group or organizational role is automatically listed as security-equivalent to that object, so that any rights granted to the group are also granted to every user in the group.

Second, use security equivalence to temporarily grant one person all access to another person's data while that person is away on vacation or business. Remember, however, that this also grants all rights to the user's home directory and personal data.

Third, use security equivalence to provide backup supervisors for areas of your directory tree. For example, KIM is granted supervisor right to an area of the tree and manages it from day to day. FRED is made security-equivalent to KIM so that if she is unavailable, FRED has the same rights to complete her tasks. By using security equivalence, FRED always has the same rights as KIM, even though KIM's rights change over time.

[PUBLIC] TRUSTEE

A special case of granting rights is the [Public] trustee. [Public] is similar to the GUEST or EVERYONE in some NOSs, but operates a little differently. [Public] is used to grant rights to anyone who does not have other rights granted. Even users who are not logged in to the network have all rights that are granted to [Public]. Nevertheless, [Public] is not a real object of any kind, and no one can log in as [Public]. It simply says "If other rights are not granted to the person requesting access, grant these rights."

[Public] can always be entered as a trustee when creating a new trustee assignment, but should be used sparingly if at all because it grants rights to users who are not even logged in. It can be blocked by an inherited rights filter, like any other trustee assignment. Do not confuse the [Public] trustee, used to grant rights, with the \PUBLIC directory on every SYS volume, which holds utility programs that all users access.

We have talked about many different ways that rights are assigned in Directory Services. Let's regroup by examining how to create effective rights to a file or to an object and its properties.

Look at Figure 12.8 to see an example of how FRED's effective rights to a file are determined by the NOS each time FRED requests access to the file. FRED's effective file rights can come from any of the following:

▸ FRED's trustee assignments to the file, if there are any

▸ Inherited rights from FRED's trustee assignments to parent directories of the file, if nothing exists from the point above

▸ Trustee assignments to objects that FRED is security-equivalent to, such as group objects, or the containers above FRED

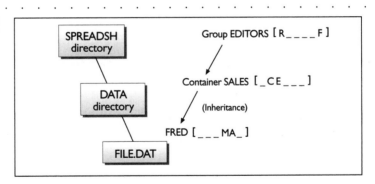

FIGURE 12.8

Group EDITORS and Container SALES are trustee assignments for objects that are security-equivalent to FRED.

If a user has a trustee assignment to a directory on a given level in the directory structure, and also one on a higher level, the current trustee assignment overrides the previous one. Trustee assignments to security-equivalent objects, such as groups, however, are added to individual user trustee assignments.

RIGHTS GRANTED DURING INSTALLATION

Now that you know how rights work in the NOS, let's look at what rights are assigned during the installation process to get you started.

When you install your first server, a directory tree is created with several objects in place. An organization object, an organizational unit object, a server object, a volume object for each volume attached to the server, and a user object named ADMIN are all created under the [Root] of the directory tree.

During installation, user ADMIN is granted the supervisor object right to the root object of the directory tree. This allows ADMIN, the first user on the network, to perform any action on any object, because the trustee assignment on the [Root] object is inherited for all objects.

Similarly, the [Public] trustee is granted a trustee assignment to the [Root] object with the browse object right. This allows all users on the network to see all objects in the directory tree. You will probably want to remove this assignment if your network is large or your security demands are anything but simplistic. However, this provides a starting point so that everyone can work without the need to first create many trustee assignments. Some time may be needed before all of your users understand the idea of the directory tree and of locating their user object in the tree to log in.

Another important trustee assignment is created when you create a SYS volume object. This trustee assignment allows users to begin using the network and network utilities without first creating many trustee assignments. The container of the SYS volume is granted read and file scan directory rights to the \PUBLIC directory of the SYS volume. By security equivalence, this means that all users in the same container as the SYS volume can access the utilities and information stored in the \PUBLIC directory.

When you create a new user in the directory tree, you are prompted to create a home directory for the new user at the same time by simply specifying a path and directory name.

If you choose to create the home directory while creating the new user, the new user is granted all rights to the newly-created home directory. The new user can then log in to the network and have access to both the \PUBLIC directory for networking utilities and to a home directory on the network for personal work, all without special trustee assignments being made by the network administrator. If your user objects are created in the same container as the SYS volume, and you create a home directory for each user when it is created, you will not have to create any additional trustee assignments for your users to be able to log in and work with the directory. The only catch is that a little additional work will be required to be able to access printing services.

SETTING RIGHTS WITH THE NETWARE UTILITIES

The default trustee assignments that are created when you install the network allow users to begin working almost immediately. But how do you make other trustee assignments to serve other needs?

Two administrative utilities are provided with which you can make trustee assignments. One is the text-menu utility NETADMIN. The other is the graphical utility NetWare Administrator, which can be run from OS/2, Windows, Windows NT, and Windows 95.

If you are using the NETADMIN text utility, you can view or change the trustees and inherited rights filters of a selected object by choosing "View or Edit the Trustee Assignments to this Object." You can also view or change the selected object's rights to files and directories on a volume by choosing "View or Edit this Object's Rights to Files and Directories."

The NETADMIN utility does not allow you to work directly with files and directories. You should use the FILER menu utility or the RIGHTS command-line utility to grant rights or change the inherited rights filter of files and directories.

If you prefer to use the graphical Administrator, there are more options available. You can use the Object menu to view or change the trustees and inherited rights filter of a selected object with "Trustees of this Object," or view or change the trustee assignments that the selected object has to other objects with "Rights to Other Objects."

The NetWare Administrator also includes the ability to work directly with files and directories. If you select a file or directory, you can choose "Details" from the Object menu and then view or change the trustees and inherited rights filter of the selected file or directory with the "Trustees of this..." page. If you select an object and then open an object dialog with "Details," you can view or change the selected object's rights to files and directories on a volume with the "Rights to the File System" page.

You need to be careful when working with volumes in the NetWare Administrator, however, because a volume object displays both object properties and information about the root directory of the file system on that volume. Keep your eyes on which rights are listed in the dialog box to keep track of which type of rights you are working on.

Summary

Security is a constantly moving target. As new security measures are implemented or designed, ways around them are also created. Don't assume that you have all the bases covered, and don't assume that what was safe last year is safe this year. Any change in your network means a change in security. Don't ignore security, or you'll be left saying "would've, could've, should've" when (not if) something happens.

CHAPTER 13

Backing Up Your Network

The idea of planning for disasters gives some people a queasy feeling in the pit of their stomachs. Nonetheless, it is advisable to plan for them.

No matter how hard we try, there are some events that are out of our control, and others that it just isn't reasonable to try to control. For instance, despite years of painstaking research, development, and investment, we still haven't learned to predict earthquakes, deflect hurricanes, prevent fires, or even completely control destructive human behavior such as vandalism, terrorism, and sabotage. Maybe you've never experienced any of those things, but all it takes is one event to make all your hard work go up in smoke. Literally.

Disaster Planning

If the term "big disaster" sounds redundant, stop for a moment and think about what constitutes a disaster. Sure, everyone agrees that an earthquake is a disaster, but suppose you open your departmental budget worksheet file the evening before it is due to be turned in, and your computer casually tells you something like, "Unable to open file: #se)%%x.?x^." You try all those fancy utilities that are supposed to recover corrupted or damaged files, and nothing helps. Your pulse is racing. Your blood pressure is skyrocketing. Go ahead, tell yourself it's not a disaster.

The point is this: Disasters can come in all sizes. So how do you know what to consider when you begin planning? The best answer is to work backwards. Begin by thinking about potential disasters and the magnitude of their consequences . Then consider what options you have for avoiding the consequences (you don't necessarily try to avoid the disaster, although that may well be one of the approaches for minimizing the consequences), and what each approach will cost. Compare the cost of avoiding the consequences with the potential cost of not avoiding the consequences, and factor in the probability of experiencing a particular loss. For instance, it is much more reasonable to prepare for an earthquake if you're on the West Coast of the United States than if you're in the Midwest. That doesn't mean you can't have an earthquake in Chicago, but you may not want to spend the money to cover that risk in Chicago.

So, what are the potential consequences of a disaster? They include loss of physical assets such as computers, loss of revenue due to lost time, and loss or theft of data.

Generally speaking, the kinds of disasters that can reasonably be planned for and recovered from fall into a few basic categories: hardware failure, network failure, and lost data. Lost revenue or lost business is really something that results from one of these other categories, and is the sort of loss that can be indemnified with insurance. To recover lost business means to reestablish a business relationship with former customers. It will require human intervention. However, a rapid recovery from lost hardware, lost communications, or lost data can preserve a business relationship.

Redundancy Strategies

Most people think of *backing up* as referring to an operations process, usually run nightly, that makes copies of important data and stores it where it can be retrieved if necessary. They don't typically think of backing up hardware. But it's a common and very useful procedure. The simplest form of "catastrophic" hardware failure is probably the loss of a disk drive. This can be catastrophic, especially in a file or database server, not just in terms of lost data, but also in terms of downtime. It can take hours, or even days, to replace a disk drive in a server, format it correctly, restore the appropriate data, mount the drive, and put it back into service. Although the cost of the disk itself, even including service charges for physical replacement of the disk, may be relatively small, the potential loss of revenue, customers, and goodwill as a result of the downtime may be significant. Indeed, if any of the lost data is time-sensitive, the loss may represent a permanently lost business opportunity.

To avoid the potential consequences of such a loss, there are several hardware redundancy strategies from which to choose. These include using alternate servers, keeping hot spares, using mirroring, and the use of hot-swappable drive arrays. Don't worry if it sounds confusing. The basic principle here is *redundancy*. Table 13.1 describes five different means of making sure you are protected against hardware failure.

TABLE 13.1	BACKUP TYPE	DESCRIPTION
Redundancy Strategies	Alternate servers	Backing up one server with another, so if one machine goes down, the other can assume the processing responsibilities. An alternate server is not the same as a hot spare (see the following); the alternate is normally a machine that is already in use, but has the excess capacity to handle an increased load under emergency circumstances. Access to disk drives shared with the other server facilitates this approach.
	Hot spares	An inventory of machines preconfigured to be used in place of another machine in the event of a failure.
	Mirroring and duplexing	The process of simultaneously maintaining duplicate copies of data on separate physical disks, so if one disk fails, the operation can continue uninterrupted. This is done primarily with software, but does require multiple disk drives. Duplexing also requires an additional SCSI.
	Hot-swappable	This means that in the event a failed disk is mirrored, the replacement can be installed without bringing down the host computer. Because of the invasive nature of installing a disk, this is normally done in external storage units or a RAID (see below).
	RAID	RAID is an acronym meaning Redundant Array of Inexpensive Disks. It is a standard technology for implementing mirroring across a number of disk drives. RAID technologies also allow performance enhancement by use of other software technologies such as stripping, which are not discussed here.

Hard drives (fixed disks, hard files, disk drives) are the most vulnerable part of any computer for one very easily understood reason: They spin constantly and are read from and written to with movable magnetic heads; therefore, they sustain the kind of wear and tear associated with friction. The rest of the computer is also vulnerable to heat and humidity, as are all electronic devices, but the disk is definitely the most vulnerable. Of course, it also happens to be where the data resides, so it is the most valuable in terms of a potential loss.

Likewise, the principle of redundancy is applied to vulnerable devices other than disk drives. If a primary server fails, an application may be restored to a secondary server in order to make it available, or an alternate server may be able to accept logins from the other's users. A good example of this might be using what is normally a "development" or "test" server to run a mission-critical application if the production server normally assigned to it should fail.

Another approach to implementing this kind of redundancy is to use *hot spares,* or idle machines preconfigured with all the necessary bells and whistles to fit a particular purpose. This amounts to keeping excess inventory on hand in case of emergency. Depending on the criticality of a specific purpose, this may be the best approach to take, but it does have financial consequences. Hot spares may prove particularly useful in highly distributed environments; that is, in environments in which the computing resources are located in a variety of distant geographical areas. By maintaining a centralized stock of hot spares, a machine can be pulled from inventory, the configuration tweaked as necessary, and then shipped to the end location, where it only needs to be installed. This approach also allows for the down machine to be shipped to a maintenance center, rather than requiring on-site maintenance, which is generally more expensive.

Remote installation can be a trickier proposition than it sounds, however. Usually, it is not possible to restore a configuration with 100 percent fidelity to the original at the time of the equipment failure. What usually happens is that the machine is preconfigured as much as possible, shipped to the remote site, installed, and then "polished" until the configuration is right. With a good network design and the proper tools, much of this work can be done remotely once the replacement machine is installed.

When designing the network, it's also a good idea to consider how to build in alternate paths in case a circuit fails. This is actually a kind of hardware redundancy all its own. When a circuit fails, it may be because a router failed somewhere in the network (and if you're using a public network, the router may not be your own), or it may be because someone cut a cable somewhere. In essence, when a circuit fails, the locations at either end of the circuit may be isolated from one another. If that happens, it's wise to have a backup path for communications. When you deal with major telecommunications vendors, and especially if you purchase public data network services, make sure there's more than one way to get from point A to point B.

Even in a private network, it's not a bad idea to build in some redundancy. After all, you never know when a backhoe operator somewhere is going to accidentally sever a cable. There is more than one approach to this situation. One of the more popular (and relatively less expensive) options is *dial back up*. This means that if a circuit goes down, the router servicing that circuit can use a serial connection to a modem to dial over conventional telephone lines to reestablish connectivity.

While this is a serviceable and fairly inexpensive way to provide circuit redundancy, it has major performance consequences. Most digital circuits are able to communicate at higher speeds than are normally accomplished via modem, even with high-speed modems and data compression technology. Modem data transmission tends to be more error-prone as well, meaning retransmission of data is more likely.

Modems also add a certain amount of overhead to the data transmission, since they must perform the modulation/demodulation process. Finally, many routers are connected to their CSU/DSU units (the digital equivalent of a modem) with v.35 cables, which are able to move data faster than the more common RS-232 serial technology used to communicate with a modem.

But despite these drawbacks and all the various cost implications of redundancy, the idea is to avoid the cost of lost revenue, downtime, and loss of goodwill. In short, it's usually better to tell the customer, "I'm sorry this is taking a little longer, but we've had a system failure and we're doing our best to keep things going" than it is to say, "I'm sorry, our systems are down; can we call you back on that later?"

MIRRORING AND RAID TECHNOLOGY

A particular approach to redundancy as it relates to the security of data is to use a technique called *mirroring,* which was first introduced in Chapter 10. This is a technique that does pretty much what the name suggests: Specific areas of a disk or a file system are duplicated, byte by byte, on another physical device (that is, a disk). Yes, this requires more disk space and disk drives, but provides very good protection against the loss of data in the event of a hard disk crash. Anyone who has suffered from a hard disk crash on his or her own workstation knows how difficult the situation can be, and might be willing to spend a little extra money to avoid the experience in the future.

If a mirrored disk fails, the host system simply uses the mirror image until the failed disk can be replaced. In fact, when a volume is being mirrored, the host system actually uses both of them all the time. While the system administrators may find that the disk crash provides a bit of excitement in an otherwise routine day, most of the system's end users will hardly notice any difference. At least, that's how it's supposed to work.

In reality, mirroring is a strategy that requires a good bit of forethought and planning. Some kinds of data are obvious candidates for mirroring, such as system areas. Other areas matter less, such as temporary storage areas or areas reserved for individual users' home directories. Data which is not particularly dynamic in nature, such as executable code that can be reinstalled from the original source, may not be a good candidate for mirroring. On the other hand, if the code is critical to daily business operations and short down times are not acceptable, then it may be advisable to mirror even relatively static code. These are decisions that have to be made on a case-by-case basis, given the demands of the organization and the structure of the systems environment.

Different operating systems may implement mirroring technologies differently, so it is important to consider which file areas are to be mirrored before setting up the systems. Once a file system is implemented on a host system, it can be very difficult and time consuming to change it. Of course, the system must be able to respond to the needs of the organization, and those needs may change, so the system must be able to adapt as well. Careful planning can help to minimize the cost of those changes.

The tendency of data to grow over time is also an important consideration. The system manager who says, "Gee, I really don't need all this disk space" is a rare individual indeed, and the end user who says to the system manager, "Here, please, take some of this storage off my hands" is even rarer. The pack rat syndrome runs rampant among users of networked computer systems, especially when their own local hard disks become crowded with data. The natural inclination is to move data off of the personal workstation to the server, where resources appear infinite. Unfortunately, those resources are neither infinite nor without cost, but the system exists to serve the users; Therefore, the tendency is to allow the amount of disk space to grow. This in itself is not a bad thing, but again, it means that the system managers must carefully consider what data and how much data they intend to mirror — *before* they set up the system.

Mirroring is accomplished by software, provided there are two destination volumes (that is, disks) available, but there is an increasingly popular (and affordable) technology known as *RAID* that is used in conjunction with mirroring. RAID (introduced in Chapter 10) is an acronym meaning Redundant Array of Inexpensive Disks. Essentially, this is a series of relatively inexpensive disk drives and controllers (the hardware that allows the computer to read from and write to the disks) configured so as to facilitate mirroring. The RAID array may be internal, that is, mounted within the computer cabinet itself, external, housed in its own cabinet, or rack-mounted (meaning it is treated as a separate component, but is mounted in a rack that may contain any number of other components — including the computer, for instance).

RAID technology provides data security through mirroring, and also improved performance and security through the use of multiple controllers. The controllers provide a channel through which the computer communicates with the disks. Think of the controller as a bridge. If only one bridge exists between the processor and the data, then all the traffic going to or from the disks, no matter which disk the data is destined for, must travel across the same bridge. Sound like a formula for a traffic jam? Well, it might be, depending on how much data needs to travel over that bridge. At some point it may be a good idea to build a second bridge. That is basically what multiple controllers provide. Instead of making all the data go over a single channel to the disk drives, multiple controllers allow the computer to use a path that is less congested.

This strategy can be very helpful with respect to mirroring, because when particular volumes are mirrored, the amount of read/write operations associated with that data are increased. That is, if you are keeping a mirror image of all the data on a given volume, then every time you access that volume, you must consider two separate physical locations.

Many RAID arrays also include hot-swappable drives, which aid the recovery from disk failure in a mirrored environment. *Hot-swappable* means that the disks can be changed without shutting down the computer. This leads to some very dramatic presentations by vendors, as one might imagine; however, the real advantage is in the replacement of a failed drive.

Finally, it's worth noting that RAID has performance advantages that are not necessarily related to the security of data. There are clear advantages to setting up host file systems so that read/write operations that are normally executed in tandem (such as executing and logging transactions in a database system) can be executed on separate physical structures. This means using different disks and controllers. Stripping (building logical file system structures across multiple physical resources) is another way of enhancing performance in sophisticated environments, and RAID technology can be very useful in implementing stripping as well.

Backup Strategies

Is there anyone left who hasn't lost an important file at one time or another? We've all had nightmares about that file that just blew up for no apparent reason. System managers may have more nightmares of that kind than most people, since they're in charge of files that don't even belong to them.

There's something comforting to the rest of us in thinking, "Oh, it's all right if something happens to that file. I saved it on the server, so it gets backed up every night." That thought isn't so comforting to the system manager. Somehow, the restored file is never exactly the same file you lost, and it's always the system manager's fault, of course. The litany is endless: "Please back up anything you can't afford to lose. Don't assume someone else will take care of it for you, even if we intend to. Accidents can happen to anyone."

We've all heard it. And we've all taken heed and make our own frequent backups . . . in theory. Until you've been burned yourself, you never quite believe that it can happen to you. After you've lost a file, or even a disk, you tend to be more careful, but even then most people, even systems professionals, are not very structured or methodical about it. It tends to be an afterthought, not something that's considered critical.

Well, for the system manager, it is *absolutely* critical, and it better not be an afterthought. Computers are, after all, machines, and all machines are eventually fallible. When someone is driving a car with over one hundred thousand miles on it, we tend to be impressed. Most of us expect our cars to fail before we get that far. For some reason, we don't ever expect our computers to fail. But they will. Eventually, all machines wear out. And when a computer fails and data is lost, someone is expected to restore the data. That is the reason we do backups. Not for peace of mind, not simply to keep generations of data for historical purposes — although both of those things may enter into it — but because one day we will be called upon to restore data, and we must be prepared to do it. In order to restore data, we have to have a backup.

What is a backup? Essentially, it's just a copy of important data, but that copy may come in a variety of forms. Saving a copy of a file to an alternate disk is the simplest form of a backup. Likewise, there are various utilities to create archives of files, and other backup and restore applications create backup sets (basically a set of files stored — perhaps on multiple disks or tapes — in a single volume). There are various advantages and disadvantages to each approach.

Using DOS or Windows 95 to copy a file, for instance, has the advantage of creating a file that can be used as-is, in whatever application was used to create it originally. A .ZIP archive file must be unzipped using a utility program. And a backup set usually has to be used with the program that created it (although not necessarily on the same machine). Backup utilities also create a log file in addition to the backup data itself. The purpose of the log file is to provide a record of the backup and restore application of the files that were originally backed up and included in the set.

The log file enables a user, when executing a restore operation, to use the application to select a particular file, a group of files, an entire directory, or even an entire disk drive's contents for restoration. As a result, there is considerable flexibility. In other words, the backup can be used to restore a copy of a single file, or to reconstruct an entire disk, whereas a single file copy can only be used to replace that single file. Most backup and restore applications also include a convenient user interface that makes performing the backup and restore operations easier and more intuitive.

WHAT TO BACK UP?

It's tempting to make the assumption that anything that's important enough to put on your disk in the first place is important enough to back up, but the truth is, some data really matters and some really doesn't. For instance, if you're a user of any of the versions of Microsoft Windows, you probably make use of a "swap file," which may be permanent or may be temporary. If you use a permanent swap file, then there is a specific file created on your disk for Windows to use. When you exit Windows, the file definition remains (and the file is usually relatively large). This is not a file that needs to be backed up, because it has no purpose after you exit Windows in any case.

Likewise, there may be other files on your hard disk that, in the event of a total loss, would be best restored from an original source medium (disks or CD-ROM, for instance), rather than from a backup set. In fact, in some cases, such as your operating system or your backup and restore application, you may have to reinstall the software in order to be able to use the restore function. So, not all files are necessarily good candidates for backing up.

There are other files and directories that, although it may be wise to have a backup copy, don't change very often. A good example of this is most application software. Your word processing software isn't likely to change very often (although your document files probably are), so it's probably not necessary to back it up every week. One copy of the original is enough. This kind of backup, a one-time-only thing, is referred to as *archiving*. In fact, most software license agreements prohibit the end user from copying the original disks, *except for archival purposes*. In other words, even the vendors expect you to make a copy of the original disks, just in case something happens to them.

There are certainly some files that are subject to frequent change. These files, dynamic in nature, are usually the ones that are the most difficult to replace if something happens to them. For example, if a printer driver file used by Windows becomes corrupt, it's usually fairly simple to re-install the printer. As long as you have the original disks (or an archive copy), Windows will recreate the printer driver and put everything back in order. But if you lose your budget model, the one you've been working on for six weeks, the one that's due to be turned in tomorrow morning, you can bet your last dollar it's going to be next to impossible to recover. This, of course, is more than a matter of inadequate backup planning, it's Murphy's Law in action. But that's why we make backups, right?

Finally, some data files are actually extracts from other sources. Many decision support systems (*ad hoc* query and reporting systems), for example, are built using databases that actually consist of copies of data maintained in other systems. It's worth asking yourself just how important it is to make a backup of that data. If the extract is fairly complicated in nature — for instance, if the data is organized differently in the decision support system versus how it is kept in the originating system, or if the extract takes a long time to run and impacts performance of the originating system — then it may be a good idea to back it up.

Another reason to backup secondary data sources (data extracted from other original sources) is to preserve the integrity of historical perspective. Many times production systems are oriented toward the current status of the records. Historical data may not be maintained in the production environment. However, historical data can be critical to decision support environments. Marketing analysis, for instance, makes frequent use of historical data to identify trends or pinpoint problem areas.

What about e-mail? The whole issue of whose mail it is remains fairly controversial, although it is now generally understood that e-mail does not possess the same assumption of personal privacy that postal mail has always had. E-mail is, after all, an electronic communication, and the messages end up stored in files on disks. Should that data be backed up? If you think this question is perhaps carrying the debate a little far, think again. Suppose those backed-up e-mail messages constitute evidence of criminal activity — conspiracy, for example. Or perhaps they contain internal communications on the status of sensitive business negotiations or new product developments. Maybe you want to keep copies of those files, maybe not.

There is, of course, a huge difference between losing data and destroying it. Destroying evidence of criminal activity is a crime, and that's obviously unethical. However, that doesn't mean that you have to keep backup copies of sensitive business documents — strategy memos, trade secrets, investment negotiations, and so forth. That's an individual business decision, but then, that's the point of this entire discussion. There are many factors that affect the business decision regarding what data to back up. Table 13.2 gives some guidelines and criteria on strategies for your choice in what to back up.

NOTE

There is another form of backup known as *image backup*. Image backups are fast and easy and work quite well as long as you're willing to restore the entire disk at once. Because you're really just making an image of the physical storage device (that is, the disk) at a point in time, you cannot selectively restore a single file or a group of files. You have to restore the entire disk or nothing at all. That's why they are useful for complex configurations (mostly desktop operating systems). Overall, image backups are not very practical for most circumstances.

HOW OFTEN SHOULD I BACK UP?

It is essential for the organization to plan its backup strategy, and a part of that planning process is deciding what to back up, what kind of backups to do, when to do it (as in what time of day or night), how often, and where to keep them. All of these issues enter into the decision. So far we've discussed what data needs to be backed up. But how often should you do it?

TABLE 13.2	DECISION FACTOR	WHY IS IT IMPORTANT?
Backup Strategy Decision Criteria	Nature of the files	Do you care if this gets lost? If not, why bother to back it up? Good examples include swap files, temporary space, lab environments which can be easily recreated, and so on.
	Frequency of change	Determine how often you may need to back up this data. Sometimes it may not make sense to back it up at all, as in the case of application executable files, which you may be able to restore from original media just as easily and efficiently as from backups.
	Data sources and use	Secondary data sources do not need to be backed up if it is just as easy to recreate the data by going to the original source and rerunning the jobs that create the files. On the other hand, if some of the data is historical in nature, you may not be able to recreate it from the original sources anymore.
	Security and privacy	Do you have a document shredder in your office? Do you keep electronic files that you might like to put through "the shredder" under some circumstances? Then don't back them up.
	Legal issues	There may be legal or regulatory reasons why an organization is required to keep historical data or to maintain data for a specific period of time before destroying it (tax returns, environmental compliance reports, and so on).

Well, to offer a reasonable answer to that question, it's necessary to consider two others:

► How often does your critical data change?

► How important is it to capture every nuance of every change in the data?

The first question addresses the dynamic nature of the data; the second, the consequences of losing it.

We've already discussed the importance of backing up data that almost never changes, and we decided that archival was a reasonable approach. But even data that is not suitable for archival doesn't necessarily have to be backed up every time you run a backup. For instance, a file may change daily but only be used at month-end. Is it important to back up that file on a nightly basis, or is it enough to back it up at month-end? Although this example may make it sound as if the decision is a simple one, in reality it involves a detailed understanding of the databases, the way the applications use the databases, and the way the organization uses its applications.

This last issue, the way the organization uses its applications, goes to the heart of the second question we asked a moment ago: How important is it to capture every nuance of every change in the data? Another way of thinking about this question is to consider what might happen if you failed to capture every nuance of every change in the data. What are the consequences?

If the consequences of losing data, even just a particular iteration of some important data, are more than the organization can stand, then obviously it's important to make sure that all the necessary files are covered. The budget model we have mentioned before is a good example of this at the individual level.

If you've ever gone through the budgeting process, you know how many times you may make seemingly minor changes to account for different scenarios. And even though the changes seemed minor at the time you made them — after all, you were just experimenting with several possibilities, right? — it invariably turns out that, say, the third variation you did on the staff plan came out with the numbers you need now. But you've already moved past that particular version of the model, and you can't quite remember what your assumptions were. "Now, how did I get the salary and bonuses to work out that way?" you ask yourself. Did you save a copy?

The budget model really relates to how hard it is for *you* to recreate your work, not how much the organization suffers if you have to stay up late. But the principle is the same: If it's going to hurt to lose it, back it up often. Again, this may sound like a simple decision, but in reality it involves forethought and planning, just as the choices about redundancy involved careful planning.

BACKUP MEDIA

Once you've got a plan for what files to back up and how often to back them up, you'll probably end up with some kind of a schedule. For instance, you may decide that you'll make a *full-system backup* (meaning a backup of all the files worth backing up, regardless of whether they've changed since the last time you backed them up) every Sunday morning beginning at 2:00 a.m., and a *modified-files backup* (a backup of all the files that have changed since the last time you backed them up) every morning, Tuesday through Saturday, beginning at 2:00 a.m.

You may notice a couple of things about this schedule. First, this process is set to begin at 2:00 in the morning, not an hour that many of us wish to be found in the office. There is the occasional hearty soul, but unless your organization runs a late shift, 2:00 a.m. is likely to be a difficult time to find someone to put disks in the drive every couple of minutes.

Second, this schedule runs from Tuesday through Sunday . . . shouldn't that be Monday through Saturday? Well, not if you begin at 2:00 in the morning, it shouldn't. But the fact is, you may have reasons to make backups every day, even Monday morning (Sunday night, if you prefer). The point is, this is something that needs to be done on a regular basis, and because you cannot usually back up open files, it needs to be done at an hour when most of the files are not in use. Remember, in many production environments, batch processes run from the close of business into the night. If those processes result in updated data files that need to be backed up, the backup can't start until late.

So, backups need to be automated. Let's face it, the graveyard shift is a lonely place. Fortunately, it is possible in most cases to schedule backups for late hours and to run them unattended. That is, they can be run unattended unless the destination medium (tape is the most common) fills up and needs to be changed. At that point, the backup will usually stop and wait for someone to change the tape. And if you started at 2:00 a.m., it's likely that no one will change the tape until people start arriving for work in the morning, at which time they will want to start using their systems and the data files that go with them. That presents a problem, because open files can't usually be backed up. Either the people wait for the backup to finish, or the backup isn't done that night.

It's important to consider the backup target medium. That is, what kind of device do you back up to? Most of us have done back ups to disks at some point. Think about how many disks it takes to back up as little as 20 or 30MB of data. Now ask yourself how practical it is to use that medium to back up 5 or 6GB of data stored on various servers. Obviously, it isn't practical at all. Fortunately, there are other media available.

Sometimes the easiest thing to do is to back up data to other online disk storage devices. If you need to back up, let's say, 5GB, and you just happen to have an extra 5GB of available disk storage online, it's easily the fastest and simplest target medium to use. It's also easily the most expensive.

Optical storage devices (writeable CD drives) are sometimes used for backing up. These are very reliable, have a relatively high storage capacity per CD, and last for a very long time. They're also not subject to contamination by magnetic fields, and they're difficult to write over. For these reasons they make a pretty good target medium for archival backups. However, this technology is still fairly expensive and ultimately destructive, because data is stored on a CD by a laser burning its surface. It is not intended to be erased and written over multiple times, so it's best used as an archival medium.

Tape drives are the most common form of backup media. Tapes come in all size formats (quarter-inch cartridge or QIC, 8mm DAT, and others), and a wide variety of storage capacities. As drives and software evolve, compression algorithms have become more and more efficient, resulting in tape formats that hold ever increasing amounts of data. Today it is possible to store gigabytes of data on a single cartridge.

In high-volume backup situations, even that may not be enough to avoid having to change tapes. There are two basic approaches to this problem. The first is to use a device that can change tapes automatically, ejecting one and automatically loading the next from a stack or a carousel. Tape arrays are also available, which are similar in theory to RAID arrays for disk drives.

The second approach is to use more than one machine and more than one backup device to manage the process. Although this may require the purchase of more than one copy of your preferred backup software and more than one target device, it enables you to run backups of different file areas, simultaneously, to different target devices. This has the obvious advantage of reducing the time required to complete the backup. It also may be wise to make sure your backup system is behind locked doors in the event of a break-in.

So now you have a backup strategy, a schedule, and the necessary hardware, software, and backup media to perform your backups. Finished? Well, not quite. There's one other issue to consider: What do you do with your tapes and how many do you need? Although tape backup is less destructive than optical backup, it isn't indestructible. The tapes will eventually wear out. If you've gone to all the trouble to carefully plan your strategy, the last thing you want is to find yourself in the position of needing to restore a file from backup, and discovering the tape is no good. The solution is to develop, in addition to a backup strategy and schedule, a tape rotation strategy.

Consider how many times you can use the tape before it wears out, and how important it is to keep specific versions of your backups. For instance, if you are making a full-system backup once a week and modified-files backups every other night (except Sunday night/Monday morning), and you want to keep each nightly tape for a week before you write over it, you need six tapes. If you're willing to overwrite each tape once a week, that's all you need. If, on the other hand, you want to save each week's full-system backup for a month, then you will typically need an additional three tapes. If you want to do a special month-end backup once a month and save that tape for a year, you will need an additional twelve tapes. This can be simple, or it can be very complicated.

Perhaps the simplest approach is to do a full-system backup every night and keep each day's tape for a month. In that case, you need 31 tapes, and each night you would pull the tape with that day's date on it, insert it in the tape drive, and trust the backup software to kick off the job that night. As long as you can get a full-system backup on one tape and you don't mind having some extra tapes each month, this system will work quite well, and no tape will be used more than twelve times in a year. If that seems like too many uses, you can replace the supply of tapes after six months and no single tape will be used more than six times. However, it does require a lot of tapes, and therefore costs a bit more than a more conservative strategy. (But tape is cheap, so don't be too conservative.)

Finally, you may want to consider periodically sending at least one of your tapes to a safe location away from the office. Why? For the same reason you might send sensitive documents off-site. You spread the risk of loss that way. And to the extent that the off-site storage location is fire-proof and maintains tight security, you not only spread the risk, you spread it to a low-risk site as well. For instance, you may want to store your month-end tapes in a safe-deposit box at a bank.

RESTORING DATA

Thankfully, most of the planning and organization required for the backup strategy is not required for the restore step. On the other hand, the reason it's not as difficult to plan and execute is that you hope you never have to do it at all; and if you do have to do it, there isn't a lot to think about. Usually you aren't asked to restore a file until every other avenue has been exhausted, and by that time, everyone just wants the file back, regardless of what it takes. That makes things simpler, but there are still some things to think about.

For instance, it is important to manage people's expectations, particularly with regard to how long it will take to complete the restoration, and how complete the restoration will be. Generally, when someone asks to have a file restored, they are already frustrated and nervous, so they want it back immediately. They also expect to have everything they need in place as soon as the restoration is done. Occasionally, there is more than one file required to put things back the way they were, which the end user may not realize.

How long should it take to restore a file? That depends primarily on the size of the file and the medium it's on. Bigger files take longer to restore, which isn't usually a problem unless the file begins on one tape and ends on another. Also, the tape medium is sequential, whereas disks are random access devices. To get to a particular place on the tape you have to roll the tape forward to that point. With a disk, the read/write heads can simply move to the correct location. As a result, it may take a few minutes to advance the tape to the point where the file begins. If you have a multiple tape backup set, it may be necessary to load the first tape, read the header to determine which tape contains the affected file(s), load the correct tape, advance to the right location, and begin the restoration.

As for the completeness of the restoration, modified-files backups can make things complicated. If, for instance, a particular file was changed daily for an entire week, then there will be six different copies of the file (based on our previous example of one full-system backup and five modified-files backups). Which version is the correct one? Remember that if the user wants the version with which he or she was working on Wednesday afternoon, then the tape made Thursday morning will have that file If the user is actually looking for the version he or she saved at 3:30 p.m., but later modified and saved again at 5:15 p.m., the 3:30 version wasn't backed up anywhere.

Occasionally it's not enough to simply restore a particular file. There may be other files associated with the data file that need to be restored also. For example, there may be both a document file and an associated graphic that was imbedded in the document. If the graphic file was not stored in the document (that is, a link to the graphic file was stored, but not the graphic file itself), then it may be necessary to restore the graphic file also. Obviously, it's advantageous to know everything that has to be restored before beginning the process, because it can take a long time to find the right files on the tape.

Finally, it may be wise to perform a verification of the restored file before reporting its restoration to the user. Sometimes the process of restoring a file to disk from tape doesn't succeed for some reason. Most backup and restore software is able to verify that the restored file is identical to what is on the tape. (By the way, this can be done in the other direction when the backup is made, but verifying a backup can add a substantial amount of time to the process.) Whether to verify your backup or not is a question of how much risk you are willing to assume.

Disaster Recovery

Back at the beginning of this chapter we defined a disaster, and we said it can be something as apparently trivial as a lost file, or something as major as an earthquake. Most of this chapter has been devoted to the discussion of backup and restoration because, frankly, if you've had a fire or an earthquake, you probably have a lot of problems to deal with, and recovering your data and systems is only one of them. After all, in a real disaster there may be loss of life, people may have lost their homes — the scale of trouble can easily exceed the kind of issues related to protecting the organization's data.

That is not to suggest that the organization should just cross its fingers and hope for the best. Ultimately, even in a major disaster involving real human tragedy, the resumption of the business that provides people their livelihood is still an important issue. And it is not enough to simply hope it doesn't happen here. You must ask the question, "What do I do if it does happen to me?"

Insurance is very important but it's not enough. Its purpose is to indemnify you against the potential financial losses of a catastrophic event. It doesn't help you get back in business, though. Fortunately, there are some viable strategies for planning the resumption of business.

Most major systems vendors and many management and systems consulting firms provide expertise in the area of creating a business continuation plan or a disaster recovery plan. It is a complicated process, and may well be worth hiring professional advisors to help develop the plan. Even if you don't hire help to create the plan, it's probably worthwhile to consider hiring for other services.

For instance, begin by considering the worst possible scenario. Assume a disaster has resulted in the complete destruction of your place of business. (By complete destruction, understand that we mean your building is simply gone. If this sounds extreme, well, perhaps it is, but it is not excessive — the destruction that Hurricane Andrew brought to South Florida was clearly of that scale.) Where do you begin? Logically, the first thing you need to look for (after checking on your *people*, of course) is a place to set up shop. Next you need some replacement machines. You have to reroute communications circuits to the new location (if wide-area data communications are an issue, that's one thing, but at the very least you need your voice telephones moved), and you need to reestablish your own operating environment — not just computers and software, but all the various combinations of machines and people that are the real nuts and bolts of any modern business enterprise.

If the disaster was localized to your particular building, then you probably have a chance at finding some space in the same general vicinity where you can begin to restore all your operations. But let's say there's been a hurricane, and the devastation is complete for a radius of fifty miles. Where do you go? How do your people get there?

Even once you've found a place, how fast can you replace the machines? If all you need are PCs, you stand a reasonable chance of finding a good number of the size and type of equipment you need, and can probably have it shipped to your new location quickly. But what if you need some special equipment? Say, a high-performance minicomputer, superserver, or even a mainframe? Those machines usually have a lead time associated with delivery. If you have to wait eight weeks to get your database server, are you going to be able to get back in business at all? Maybe you should just take the insurance settlement and start a new business.

Even if you are able to locate a site, and you miraculously find all the machines you need, do you have sufficient staff to set it all up again? And once you get it all set up, do you have your backup tapes, or were they destroyed with the building?

OK, this is hypothetical and very depressing. But take heart; no matter how bad things look, if you've planned carefully, you've already thought of all this. And if you've signed deals with the right people, you may even have rehearsed for just this sort of situation. Yes, there are vendors who can provide services to address some or even all of these issues. Let's take them one at a time.

Office space — where are you going to find it? Many of the vendors will promise to make space available to you at an alternate site within a specific period of time. It may not be in your general area, especially if the disaster has been widespread, but under the circumstances, will you care? They will also negotiate to provide transportation and housing for your staff at whatever location they have. Of course, the more you want, the more it will cost, but consider the consequences. The vendors we're talking about aren't office space companies, by and large. They are systems vendors and consulting organizations who specialize in disaster recovery planning.

How quickly can you get replacement machines? Remember the hot spares concept? It applies here, too, except you don't necessarily have to buy a spare machine and keep it idle. Most manufacturers will offer some kind of agreement to give you priority access to new machines in case of an emergency, or to temporarily provide you with surplus or reconditioned equipment until you can take delivery of replacement equipment. They even provide the staff to install and configure the equipment at the new location. You will likely have to provide supervision and direction to ensure that things are done according to your standards, but you can get that help on an emergency basis.

As for getting your data back, remember that discussion of off-site storage? If you took care to make sure your data was protected in a fail-safe environment, you should be able to get it all back in relatively short order. In the end, you can negotiate agreements for all the services you need to get your business back up and on-line quickly. But how do you know it will work? You rehearse. Once a year or so you have a rehearsal. You pretend the hurricane just hit and everything's gone. You take a few days and put your vendors and your agreements to the test. If you get your business back in business within tolerable time limits (you have to decide what that is), then you can have confidence that it will be done under real conditions.

Summary

The question isn't *whether* disaster planning is worth it, but *how much* is it worth? Like all other business decisions, this one boils down to how much risk you are willing to assume. What's a reasonable risk, and what's not?

Realistically, you can't prevent earthquakes. You can do a lot to prevent fires, but they still happen. In the end, Mother Nature is still bigger than we are. Even the things we do to ourselves aren't completely preventable. As with security, it's not possible to build a completely foolproof disaster prevention system, and if it were, it probably wouldn't be financially responsible to do it. So we try to anticipate the things we can do something to prevent, and we prepare to recover from the things we can't.

The basic lessons are simple. To the extent that you can afford redundancy, practice it. Machines fail; it's just part of the nature of machines. They may last a long time, they may prove to be more reliable than you have a right to expect, but they're still machines and eventually they fail. Rarely do two of the same machine fail at the same time, however, so redundancy is a very effective strategy.

If you can't afford complete redundancy, at least make backups on a regular basis. Make sure to back up the things you really need, and don't waste time on what you don't need. Be careful and methodical. Take care of your tapes and store them in a safe place. If you have to use them, make sure everyone understands the limitations, and make sure you've done everything you can to minimize the impact of those limitations.

And for those things you can't prevent, plan what to do if they happen. Consider what risks you can afford to assume, cover the ones you can't assume, and rehearse so everyone knows what to do when the time comes. Also, remember to keep things in perspective. Real disasters cause real problems for real people. Machines can be replaced, data can be restored, but people are the heart of any organization.

If you plan carefully, implement your plans, test your assumptions, and finally, rehearse, you should be prepared if a disaster comes to pass. Then you can concentrate on the things that really matter, knowing your business will recover.

CHAPTER 14

Training Users

In this chapter we discuss the importance of training everyone in your organization who uses the LAN. You have worked so hard to plan, develop, and install your network, make sure everyone is ready to enjoy it. Just as you wouldn't dare buy an expensive automobile for someone without a driver's license, don't attempt to manage a network or allow users to access your LAN without first preparing yourself and them with the necessary skills.

LAN Manager Training

In keeping with our use of Novell NetWare 4.x as an example . . . Novell provides a host of NetWare-related courses, including those dealing with teaching technical subjects. Attend the training course yourself. Then you can assist novice users by conducting in-house courses yourself, or you can arrange training to be conducted by hardware and software vendors. By explaining how to use the network and teaching the users how to use their applications, you save hours responding to unnecessary phone calls and repeatedly answering hundreds of routine questions. Many users' questions are nontechnical and concern their applications, such as "I can't log in," "The printer isn't working," or "Why won't my spreadsheet sort properly?"

Although you need some fundamental training, you can support the organization best with a broad knowledge of the ways the network can improve users' productivity. Of course, you will have to deal with crises from time to time. You may need to have an outside support group help you with the hardware failures, but you should be able to do basic troubleshooting to identify the causes of failures.

If you choose NetWare 4.x as your network operating system, you should have the following technical skills as LAN manager:

- A good working knowledge of the major NOSs (Novell NetWare, Microsoft Windows NT, Banyan Systems VINES, and IBM OS/2)

- A good working knowledge of the particular NOS software currently used on the LAN you are managing

- An understanding of the NOS's security rights

- An understanding of network hardware and software components

- The ability to create a workable directory structure, construct login scripts, create new users and directories, and provide a working environment for users

- The ability to load applications, perform system backups, and define and control print queues

- The ability to create and maintain a database of network component and workstation configuration information

If you are an aspiring LAN manager, you will need to receive some training to carry out advanced maintenance and operations of your LAN. Some of the subjects with which you need to be familiar include:

Hardware and software basics	Console utilities
Directory structure	Printing
Mapping	Login scripts
Security	Menu creation
Command line and menu utilities	Loading application software
Supervisor utilities	Backup and restore

With the above knowledge and skills, you are well prepared for developing procedures to conduct routine network maintenance and operations tasks.

Training someone to be a comfortable user of applications residing on a LAN isn't complicated and can be conducted in many different ways over a period of time. Let's discuss some of your options, beginning with the basics.

User Training

As a thoroughly trained LAN manager, it's important that you participate in the process of developing user training programs. The more knowledge the users have, the less time you will spend supporting them. Beginners should first learn about basic computer operations and networks, followed by training in the applications and procedures they use in their jobs and how the network supports their work. Although self-paced instruction is the least expensive, we have found that classroom instruction is the most effective. Users can return to their desktop PCs and immediately begin to apply what they have learned and then take advanced courses to build on their knowledge. However, always start with the basics.

COVERING THE BASICS

If you ever learned to ride a bicycle as a child, you probably remember the first time you sat on the seat. Perched high, with one foot on a pedal and one firmly on the ground, you looked back to verify that indeed the training wheels had been removed, took a deep breath, then launched yourself on a wing and a prayer. Much to your amazement and exhilaration, you rode. Why? Because you started with the basics.

As a new user riding a PC on a LAN, you probably won't feel anything near the emotions characterized in the above situation, but you should be no less prepared before pedaling yourself onto the local "information bike path."

The basics of network computing can be presented by simply having users take advantage of the tutorials that come with various desktop applications. Another effective basic training method is to require all first-time users to read the user manuals that come as part of the various application software packages loaded on your network nodes.

Formal training can be either conducted in-house or out-sourced, depending on the level of complexity and the resources you have available. We recommend, again, that you start with the basics. The basics include one-day familiarization classes for those members who will typically use Windows 3.1, Windows 95, Windows NT, etc., as a normal part of their job.

It's very easy to set up introductory-level classes designed to familiarize new users with these products, as long as you have the resources available and someone willing to develop the course outline.

DEVELOPING A BASIC IN-HOUSE COMPUTER TRAINING COURSE

A typical course plan will consist of the following general areas:

- ▶ Course title (to include number of hours or days required)

- ▶ Course description

- ▶ Prerequisites

- ▶ List of objectives

- ▶ Topical outline

- ▶ Class agenda

If you use the above list when developing a computer training strategy for your organization, we feel your courses will be a comprehensive and constructive learning experience. For a better idea of what a typical computer applications course plan looks like, take a look at the sample shown in Figure 14.1.

If you, as the network manager, also end up being the basic computer training course instructor, use this time with your "captive audience" to share your management philosophy and general network rules and procedures. Also, consider issuing user network access and passwords to each trainee upon their completion of the basic computer training course.

TRAINING ENVIRONMENT

Ideally, if you have the facilities, your training classroom should meet some or all of the following criteria in order to provide the best possible environment for effective, hands-on computer-related instruction:

- ▶ Convenient location

- ▶ Room to accommodate ten to fifteen students (any more becomes too impersonal)

Sample plan for computer training course

Introduction to Microsoft Office 95

One Day Course

Course Description

This class is designed for students who want to learn to use the Microsoft Office Shortcut Bar; start, open, and save Office documents; and use Binders. In addition, students will learn to use the new features of Word 95, Excel 95, and PowerPoint 95.

Prerequisites

Microsoft Windows 95 or Microsoft Word 6.0 for Windows, Excel 5.0 for Windows, and PowerPoint 4.0 for Windows

Objectives

- ▶ Use the Microsoft Office Shortcut Bar
- ▶ Start, open, and save Office documents
- ▶ Use Binders

Topical Outline

1. Using the Microsoft Office Shortcut Bar
2. Introduction to Office 95
3. Starting the Office Shortcut Bar
4. The Office toolbar
5. Changing toolbars
6. Switching between toolbars
7. Hiding the Office Shortcut Bar
8. Moving the Office Shortcut Bar
9. Fitting the Office Shortcut Bar in the title bar
10. Customizing the Office Shortcut Bar view options
11. Creating new toolbars
12. Adding and removing buttons
13. Starting a new Office 95 document
14. Opening an Office 95 document
15. Saving documents in Office 95
16. Using the Answer Wizard
17. Introduction to Binders
18. Creating a Binder
19. Adding sections to a Binder
20. Saving a Binder
21. Working with sections
22. Printing a Binder

Class Agenda

7:30 a.m.–8:00 a.m.	Instructor introduction & facilities familiarization
8:00 a.m.–9:00 a.m.	Instruction on topical items 1–5
9:00 a.m.–9:15 a.m.	Break
9:15 a.m.–11:30 a.m.	Instruction on topical items 6–12
11:30 a.m.–1:00 p.m.	Lunch break
1:00 p.m.–2:00 p.m.	Instruction on topical items 13–18
2:00 p.m.–2:15 p.m.	Break
2:15 p.m.–3:15 p.m.	Instruction on topical items 19–23
3:15 p.m.	Formal training ends
3:15 p.m.–4:30 p.m.	Instructor available to provide additional assistance

▸ Good environmental controls (The ideal training class temperature is 68–76 degrees.)

▸ Comfortable seating and training stations

▸ One computer training station per student

▸ Large computer monitor or LCD (to project instructors own computer screen)

▸ Proper lighting

▸ Easy access to rest rooms and break rooms

PURSUING OTHER OPTIONS

Not all computer-related training has to take place in front of a computer terminal. Many subjects can be taught in a more traditional classroom or conference room setting. The following subjects could be taught or reviewed without the use of a computer:

▸ Network security features

▸ Desktop (node) security practices

▸ Company network policies and procedures

▸ How a network operates

Network Library

In Chapter 11 we outlined the importance of the extensive documentation that you need to maintain as references for the various aspects of your local area network. These documents don't have to be in paper form; however, until your users become familiar with accessing these read-only files, we suggest they take what we like to call "the temporary form of information" — paper.

We certainly encourage you to use electronic documenting methods wherever and whenever possible, but regardless of what medium you choose to keep your documentation on, make sure it's available to your LAN users and administrators alike.

The following is a basic list of library items you can start with and add to as time goes on:

▶ Binders containing all network documentation (see Chapter 11)

▶ NOS administrator manuals

▶ Miscellaneous software manuals

▶ Miscellaneous hardware and peripherals manuals

▶ LAN troubleshooting guides

▶ This book, of course!

Follow-up Training

Once you're comfortable that you and everyone else using the network have been adequately trained in the essentials, consider setting up a recurring follow-up training strategy. This strategy will allow for quick skills updates when future revisions to software packages are received from software vendors. Also, having a plan for future training builds upon your goals to not only expand your business, but expand your networking capabilities as well.

As we mentioned earlier, many software and hardware companies offer training opportunities in the form of on-site training, tutorial software, and interactive CD-ROMs, usually available at reasonable rates. There are many independent computer retailers and resellers who offer training classes at their locations. By and large, these training classes have been endorsed by the manufacturers and cater to all skill levels.

Also, look to your local community or college to offer computer skills and software applications training. In many cases, semester-long classes offered by a college or university are credited toward college degrees. These college classes, while more expensive than traditional computer training options, are usually very comprehensive and designed to teach specific disciplines in detail.

Summary

When you train the users of your network, begin with those skills that are essential, build on them, and reinforce them through follow-up sessions. Remember that the more your users know about the LAN and the various applications they use, the more efficient they will be and the less time you will spend answering their questions.

CHAPTER 15

Troubleshooting

Troubleshooting. Just the word invokes fear, trepidation and pain. *Trouble,* as in ""Houston we have a problem." *Shooting,* as in "I'm going to shoot someone if this server crashes again!" The file server is down, a file is corrupted or missing, a workstation is dead, Susan's printer won't print, and the list goes on. "It was working yesterday," you hear. "What are we going to do about the spreadsheet I've been working on all week that the boss is expecting today?" "I have to print these invoices today!" You've heard these cries for help before, or you've been the one crying. Don't panic right away. Today's tools and technicians can work wonders.

LAN technology is generally stable. Some LANs run trouble-free for years, while others need only an occasional repair call. NOSs are getting easier to install and maintain, hardware is becoming more standardized and stable, and application software is now more network compatible than ever. But any technology that is comprised of so many pieces — hardware, cable, and software — has potential for problems. And, of course, when problems occur it is always at the least convenient time.

This chapter is devoted to solving common problems quickly. We begin with practical tips for what to do first if something goes wrong. Then we divide up the probable points of failure and describe both what you can check yourself and what you should leave for a qualified repair technician.

General Troubleshooting Guidelines

As in life, the first thing to remember when something goes wrong with your network is: *don't panic.* Sure, it's frustrating when the printer suddenly stops printing, or the drive doesn't read the disk anymore. Maintaining a cool head and using a step-by-step approach to problems will more than pay for itself. Often the user or network administrator can solve the problem if he or she is armed with the right information.

Problems can be intermittent or constant. The intermittent ones are the hardest to diagnose. If the problem is inconsistent and cannot be duplicated, it will be more difficult to diagnose and fix. Does it appear that a single workstation has the problem, a segment of the network, or the entire network? If one workstation is having the problem, look at the drivers, configuration, hardware, cabling, or software installed on the workstation. Try a different login, or a supervisor login from the workstation. Have the user go to another workstation and see if the problem is still there. If the problem persists, a change to their network rights could be the culprit.

Here are a few basic rules for approaching technical problems.

IDENTIFY THE PROBLEM

The first thing to do is identify the problem. *Really* identify the problem. "The printer won't work." Is it printing unintelligible characters? Is it printing light on one side of the paper? Is it printing Susan's document but not Tom's? Whether you're the one responsible for fixing the problem or you only have to call a technician to fix it, the first step is to isolate the difficulty. Things are not always as they seem.

A workstation that cannot access the server could be caused by buggy software on the workstation, corrupted or erased drivers, a bad network interface card, loose cabling, a bad port on the hub, a problem with the server, another workstation locking a file you need, or a bad login. The list is endless. The more you can identify, eliminate, and isolate, the better off you will be. Have users try to recreate the problem and write down the steps that lead up to the occurrence.

Is the whole network (that is, every workstation) down, a few workstations attached to one particular hub, or only one workstation? Are all printers down, or just one? Prepare a concise and accurate description of the problem.

Do documents print in Word but not Excel? Does one user have problems or do all users? Can the problem be recreated? Ask these questions and investigate all variables before going on a wild goose chase. In the long run, you will save time by identifying the problem before you attempt to fix it.

IDENTIFY WHAT HAS CHANGED

Many times the cause of the problem is that something has changed, such as new equipment or software being installed. Try to remember the last time everything worked and what changed since then. Did it work last night, but is dead this morning? Someone could have set a desk on a cable, or knocked a cable loose.

Every lead is helpful. Don't think any detail is too trivial. Technicians have been overheard muttering to themselves, "I had a suspicion that was the problem at first, but didn't believe it was so simple." Some software installation programs change the AUTOEXEC.BAT and CONFIG.SYS files. This can create conflicts with memory and TSR programs. Network drivers are TSRs, and any change or addition can affect memory allocation.

DISCUSS THE PROBLEM WITH SOMEONE

Talk over the problem with someone else. Often the act of talking out loud will cause the answer to snap into focus immediately and almost by magic. Maybe this is why many network administrators are found talking to themselves. Talk to a colleague. Call your buddy next door who has a similar configuration. Call the vendor that installed or sold the system. They will have suggestions or may have had the same problem happen to another customer.

Bulletin boards, the Internet, and online services such as CompuServe and America Online have software forums where questions can be posted. Either software employees or other users will post answers if they have any. Your network software provider may furnish information on newsgroups that are network-specific.

Use proper bulletin board etiquette when posting questions on forums. Don't be insulting or trite. State your problem concisely and with as many details as possible. Provide information such as NOS version, cabling, topology, hubs, and software installed on the server and workstation. Also include server information such as brand, CPU, memory, installed peripherals, and so on. A sample question may be, "I have a 25-user NetWare 4.1 installed on a Compaq Prosignia Pentium 120, Intel CPU, 32MB memory, 2.1GB Seagate drive, Sony 4GB tape drive, Cheyenne Arcserve, UTP Ethernet, two SMS 12 port unmanaged hubs, and a mixture of 386, 486, and Pentium workstations. Intermittently a volume dismounts itself. I can't determine what events cause it to happen. Anyone with any ideas?" Be patient when using this medium. Answers are not immediate, but almost always forthcoming with time.

LOOK FOR THE OBVIOUS FIRST

Many problems can be solved by a quick check of the fittings on cables and plugs. Repair technicians who've responded to "emergency" calls often walk away after just turning on the power switch or plugging in a loose cable. Are all cables connected, free of kinks, not frayed, and plugged into the correct connector? Just because everything was OK a few minutes ago, doesn't mean that it can't be a cable. The cleaning people could have moved or bumped the equipment during the night. You could have dropped something behind the computer and knocked something loose. A chair may have rolled over the cable and damaged it. Rats have even been known to chew through cables. Accessory cards can wiggle loose. The printer could be out of toner, ribbon, or paper. The power could be in the wall outlet. The surge protector could be blown. The workstation can lose its CMOS setup. Reboot the workstation. Recheck everything.

READ (AND REREAD) THE FRIGGIN' MANUAL

If there's still a problem after you've checked the obvious, locate the manual for the hardware or software that seems to be failing. Here's where things can get confusing. Sometimes what appears to be a hardware problem turns out to be software, or the other way around.

Generally, however, you can find clues. If, for example, you can't get a document to print from Word, but all your spreadsheets print fine from Excel, chances are something has gone astray with the word-processing software, rather than the printer or the cables. Knowing this, you would look for troubleshooting tips in the Word manual.

Often, just skimming through manuals will provide lots of clues. Look carefully at the installation instructions and ask yourself if everything was followed to the letter. Then look at those parts of the manual devoted to troubleshooting. Many software and hardware vendors anticipate potential conflicts and document them in their manuals.

Is the software a network version or a standalone? If it is a network version, is it tested for your network? Was it installed properly? Even if you don't find your specific problem outlined in the manual, you will have eliminated some possibilities and narrowed your search for the cause of the problem.

CHANGE ONLY ONE THING AT A TIME

It's all too easy to reinstall software, change out a driver, slap in a new network card, and change the cable in one fell swoop. If, after this, things start working, then fine, you're set. If they don't, you may have inadvertently introduced new complications into the scenario, confusing your search and adding to your problems. If you want to take this approach, replace the workstation with a working PC. If the problem persists, it isn't the workstation.

If you do change several variables at once and things start working, you'll still never know what went wrong in the first place. The symptoms could reoccur, leaving you to go through that whole time-consuming process to fix it again. You may throw out perfectly good equipment. Experienced network troubleshooters gather up all the clues and take one step at a time to find the right solution, beginning with the most simple fix first. Change the cable before changing a network card. Plug the dead workstation cable into another port on the hub if you suspect a single port on the hub is bad. Boot the workstation from a network floppy disk. If your NIC has lights, check the manual to see what they mean. Turn the printer off and on again.

KNOW YOUR OWN TECHNICAL LIMITATIONS

Don't try to exceed your own technical limitations. While hardware, software, and network vendors make every effort to simplify the installation and configuration processes, sometimes this technology is best left in the hands of experts. Some changes can be destructive and compound the problem. Always save configuration files before changing them. You can then get back to a starting point by reloading the old files. Simply rename them or copy them to a disk for safe keeping. Saving a good configuration disk is always good policy. If the configuration files are inadvertently changed or erased, they can quickly be restored from disk.

Don't try to change *complimentary metal-oxide semiconductor* (CMOS) settings unless you know exactly what you are doing. CMOS settings are the internal computer configurations that sets things such as hard disk type, number and type of floppy drives, time, date, video type, and other more complicated settings. Changing any one of these settings can cause the computer to not boot or not recognize certain peripherals.

Don't change security and access tables in the network if you don't understand how they affect the users, network, and application software. You may be loading software or drivers that conflict with the network operating system. The individual workstations might include other adapter cards, extra boards with extra serial ports, internal modems, scanner boards, game boards, or other devices that conflict with your network board or an unsupported network card. Sometimes that bargain network card or PC isn't a bargain if you calculate the time spent getting it to communicate with the network.

Give yourself a time budget, say thirty minutes or an hour. If you can't solve the problem by then, don't waste valuable time. Call someone who can take care of it quickly. Call someone before the problem gets bigger.

CALL THE MANUFACTURER'S HELP LINE FOR SUPPORT

If you've checked the obvious, not changed more than one thing at a time, read the manual, and still think you can do it within your budgeted time, the next step is to call a help line for support. Be ready to describe the symptoms. Try to paint a complete picture of the problem — it's not very helpful to say, "My printer doesn't work." Instead, tell the support person about the whole problem. It's more helpful to say, "My printer doesn't work in Excel, but it does in PowerPoint." Or, "My printer won't print anything from any software package, and I've already checked the cables, power cord, printer assignment, and print queue."

Often, the manufacturer's help personnel can diagnose and solve your problem in a short time. Support personnel handle hundreds of calls a day similar to yours, and have several solutions to try. They deal similar problems every day, where you may only face the problem once. Don't be shy about asking for a senior help desk person, if you feel your question is beyond the scope of the first person's experience. If you are working in an organization with in-house technical support, it is also an option to get help there.

Many manufacturers no longer provide free support. Many now use 1-900 numbers or bill you directly for any advice given. This makes it important to identify the problem, be succinct on the phone, and be ready to implement the suggestions immediately to save time and money. Be prepared to stick to your guns if you feel the problem is definitely the responsibility of the company you are calling. Help desks are notorious for trying to pass the blame to someone or something else. Keep an open mind, but if all of your network cards of one brand work fine and a different brand has problems in the same computer, it is probably that brand of network card.

CALL IN THE CAVALRY

Some problems just seem to defy detection. No matter how knowledgeable you and your help staff might be, there are times when you have to call in technical experts. At this point, you should contact a local repair facility. Make sure you describe the problem in complete detail so they can dispatch the right kind of expert. A networking guru probably isn't the best person to fix a broken printer. Likewise, a software specialist probably can't tell whether or not the RJ-45 connector on your network cable was improperly made.

Be forewarned, too, that lots of charlatans disguise themselves as LAN consultants. Make sure the technicians are certified for your network. Certifications are available for most network operating systems, and while this doesn't insure a competent technician, it is a good place to start. The best way to find competent practitioners is through personal referral from a satisfied customer.

Aside from that, interview your candidate by phone or in person about his or her previous networking experience. It helps to find a technician or company with similar priorities and one that will respect your wishes. Does the technician always suggest the most expensive solution or is he or she willing to work within your budget without being insulting? It will help if the firm has previous experience with your operating system and hardware.

Don't hire a technician solely on price. Let's try a third grade math word problem to find out why. If a technician charging $150 per hour solves your problem in an hour, and a technician charging $100 per hour takes two hours, which technician will fix your problem for the least amount of money?

It also helps to stay with a single company, if possible, for your repair. The reasons for this are obvious. The technicians are familiar with your setup and don't have to spend time investigating your installation. The service provider is more likely to do a good job if they can expect repeat business. Credit information and other pertinent information is already on file. The service call can be placed on account instead of collected when the job is complete. It's nice to see a familiar face and know everything will be all right. Once you find a good service provider, treat them right. Don't cry wolf every time any little thing happens. There are real emergencies and there are problems that can wait. Most service companies try to provide service within a specified period of time and charge more for expedited service calls. Expect to pay more if a call is after hours or on weekends. Build trust and rapport with your technician and they'll do their best for you. Treat them badly and you'll get excuses and promises that go unfulfilled.

When the Network Is Slow

This is probably the most common complaint, but the most difficult to diagnose. There are so many components that make up a network. An individual component can be the bottleneck or it may be a composite problem. In this section we discuss how the server, server memory, cabling, workstations, and topology affect speed.

"A chain is only as strong as its weakest link" and a network is only as fast as its slowest link. Most networks have evolved over the years. You needed to share files, so you turned a workstation into a file server, loaded the NOS, and ran a few cables, possibly ARCnet, and — *voilà!* — you were networked. Then employees started clamoring for access to the Internet. You ran a few more cables and discovered the NICs that you used for the first workstations weren't available anymore, so you bought different ones. Someone had the bright idea of running the accounting department on the network. "Can't we all fax from the network?" "We need one of those new-fangled laser printers, and let's network it so we can *all* use it." "Oooh, Windows is really neat. We all need Windows." "Wow, this is a really cool Windows program. Let's install it on the network." "I know our network will run faster with a newer, faster, bigger server." Before you knew it, your network was divided and multiplied until you weren't sure what you had or what you should do — and it had slowed to a crawl. Few of us have the luxury of tossing out all the old equipment and starting over from scratch. You have a big investment and you can't afford to scrap it all. Now is the time to step back and look at what you have. Better yet, call in a disinterested third party to review the state of the network and report on ways to improve speed.

REVIEW OF ETHERNET AND TOKEN RING

Ethernet is the most popular type of topology today. Ethernet is theoretically capable of 10Mbps throughput. A single workstation cannot, in practice, use all the bandwidth, but is capable of a throughput of 2–4Mbps. It doesn't take advanced math to calculate how many workstations can use the entire bandwidth. When this happens, the bandwidth is divided between the nodes. Token Ring, on the other hand, only allows a single workstation to transmit at a time, with the others waiting their turn. This happens very quickly and each workstation sends small pieces or frames at a time. Each scheme has its proponents and benefits. While not delving into the intricacies of the data passing, it helps to review the fundamentals.

Ethernet

Ethernet is a *contention network,* which means that each workstation competes to send data across the network. Safeguards are in place that let nodes know when it is OK to send data and resend data if there is a collision. However, Ethernet degrades unpredictably as workstations are added. Only workstations actively transmitting data affect performance. This means that a one hundred-node network with two active logins should give the same performance as a ten-node network with two active logins. Ethernet only transmits when necessary, so this permits large networks of workstations that are not in heavy use. Performance may be adequate when an average number of workstations are active, but can degrade to an unacceptable point when all nodes become very active.

Ethernet can be thicklan (10base5), thinlan (10base2), or UTP (10baseT). Thicklan and thinlan use coax cables. The thinlan looks like TV cable. Thinlan is a single cable running from the server to all the workstations on the network. A T-connector taps the line for each node, and the last node ends the cable with a terminator. Thinlan has the advantage of being able to connect additional workstations easily and inexpensively. You simply add the workstation to the end of the line or between two existing workstations.

Thicklan is a coaxial cable that is larger in diameter than thinlan, hence the name. The main benefits of thicklan are good shielding and long-distance carriage of signals (up to 500 meters). Adding nodes is the same process as with thinlan, except the cable is pierced with a vampire tap and a fifteen-pin cable connects the tap and the NIC.

UTP looks like the telephone cord you use to attach your phone to the phone jack. Each cable from a workstation is run to a hub or concentrator. A single cable is then attached to the server. This is called star topology because all cables fan out from the hub or center of the network. Hubs can be linked together or chained. This makes multiple smaller hubs operate as a larger hub. One disadvantage of UTP cable is that to add an additional workstation, you must have a free port on the hub. If no ports are available, a larger hub or additional hub must be purchased. If you have an eight-port hub that is fully populated (all ports connected to a node), to add a ninth node, you will need a ten- or twelve-port hub, or another eight-port to chain to the first. Hubs should be purchased that have a coax port to link to another hub or the server. Hubs with RJ-45 connectors, used with UTP, lose a port or two when linked together.

The top diagram of Figure 15.1 shows a simple 10BaseT network in a star configuration. The server and all workstations are connected to a central hub or concentrator. Any additional workstations are added to available ports on the hub, and additional hubs are added as needed. The bottom diagram in Figure 15.1 shows a thicklan or thinlan network. Additional workstations are added between existing workstations or at either end. The server can be located anywhere along the line.

Figure 15.2 shows two ways of chaining multiple hubs together. The top diagram uses hubs with coax backbone connections that free all ports for workstations or servers. The bottom diagram demonstrates how hubs without coax connections are chained. Ports from each hub connect to other hubs, reducing the available number of ports. For instance, five ports are lost in this diagram.

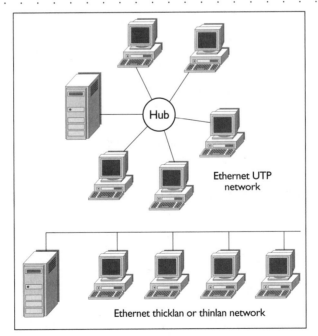

FIGURE 15.1

Simple diagrams demonstrating 10BaseT or UTP Ethernet cabling in a star configuration (top) and an Ethernet thicklan or thinlan network (bottom)

Ethernet UTP network

Ethernet thicklan or thinlan network

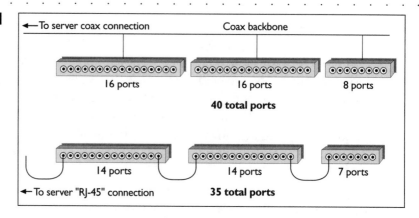

Simple diagrams demonstrating hub wiring topology with a coax backbone (top) and simply chained (bottom)

Token Ring

Token Ring is not a contention network. A single token is transmitted at a time. A token is like a bucket being passed around the network. There is only one bucket. If the bucket is empty, a node can fill it with data. The bucket is passed around the network and each node looks in the bucket to see if the data is for them. If it is, the node empties the bucket and sends it back to the originating bucket to let it know it was received. The originating node then sends the empty bucket around the network again. It circles the network until a node fills it and sends it to another destination. Token Ring networks degrade predictably as nodes are added. Each workstation added to the network drops performance for all other workstations. The ring becomes bigger as nodes are added. The bucket has to go further and more nodes have to look in the bucket to see if the data is for them. This adds time, even if few nodes are active.

CHANGING TOPOLOGY TO INCREASE PERFORMANCE

Learning how data is passed helps you understand what is happening when your network slows down. Is your Ethernet network slow at month's end, or first thing in the morning when everyone is logging on and checking e-mail? Is it necessary to change anything in your Ethernet network, or can you live with short periods of slow network access?

In any case, network topology can be changed to increase network performance. The most common way is to segment the network. This increases the throughput dramatically. Remember, the network is able to pass 10Mbps of data. Segmenting means adding another network card to the server and moving workstations to the new network card. This adds another physical network to your local network. Each segment, or physical network, is now able to pass 10Mbps of data for a total of 20Mbps of potential data. There is only a small overhead associated with the server talking to two network cards. This does not affect server performance. If your server is fully utilized (running as fast as it can, all the time) adding the additional card will do nothing, and possibly even slow the network a bit. If the server is under-utilized, this can dramatically improve performance.

Carefully plan which users are attached to which segment. If all the heavy users are still located on one segment, they will still overload that segment. This is similar to a highway. As growth in a city causes a highway to become congested, lanes are added to the highway. Let's say we take a two-lane road and make it a four-lane highway. When completed, the same number of cars are now on twice the number of lanes, thereby reducing traffic congestion in half. If most of the cars still used the old two lanes, congestion would be the same.

Locating servers and the way they are attached can also affect performance. Multiple servers make up many networks. In Figure 15.3 we have engineering server, accounting, and communication servers, all connected with coax. This type of fragmentation occurs when a network grows one server at a time, and performance is not an issue, most often with thinlan coax networks.

FIGURE 15.3

Multiple servers in a fragmented network

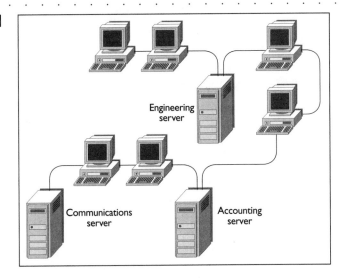

Engineering server

Communications server

Accounting server

These servers are all attached to the same LAN, composed of many internal and physical networks. An *internal network* is created within any file server that has two NICs. Each server in this diagram has two network cards and is therefore an internal network. A *physical network* is each group of workstations attached to a network card. An internal router in each network must locate the correct destination for each packet and route it appropriately. Internal routers can find the address to deliver the packets anywhere on the physical network. Each hop or pass through a router adds the additional time it takes to pass data. The servers in the middle are always routing packets from both ends of the network. In Figure 15.3 a packet from Workstation 1 must make three hops to get to the communication server.

Hops are similar to bus transfers. Buses don't usually run directly from your front door to your destination. You must ride the bus to another stop, get off and wait for a different bus, transfer to another bus, and so on until you get to your destination. Each transfer or hop adds time while you wait for the next bus. Even if the next bus is waiting, you have to wait for the bus to stop, get off it, and get on the next bus. All this takes time. The fewer the transfers, the less time your trip takes. Let's see how we can reduce the number of hops or bus transfers.

Figure 15.4 shows how connecting all servers to a backbone causes fewer hops and therefore increases performance. Connecting the servers to a backbone eliminates much of the hopping. The servers still have two network cards. The only difference is the order in which they are wired or attached. The middle servers are no longer routing data between the other servers. A request from the engineering server can go directly to the communication server without going through the accounting server. The circuitous route the packet had to travel before is now reduced to two hops, and performance is improved.

Improving Server Utilization

A faster server won't help if the cabling can't carry the additional throughput. A faster server won't help if the current server is not being utilized to its fullest, or is being overwhelmed with errors on the network. Network operating system utilities and third-party programs can measure server utilization. Server utilization is the percentage of time the CPU is processing. If the CPU is sitting around most of the time, waiting for something to do, this is called *low utilization*. If the CPU is working as fast as it can all the time, this is called *high utilization*.

FIGURE 15.4

Servers on a backbone

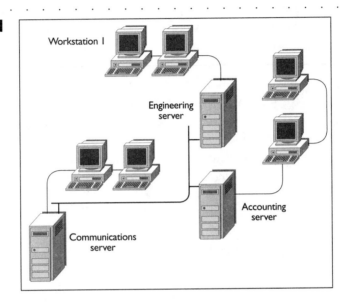

Low server utilization and a slow network indicate that software, cabling, bad components, or the workstation NIC is creating errors and resending packets. If the server has high utilization, it still could be any of the aforementioned reasons. A bad workstation NIC, cable, or hub will create additional network traffic as the packets are sent and resent, trying to connect to the server. Server utilization will be up and the workstations that are OK will slow down. If the cabling and other components are optimum, and the server is working as hard as it can, your network would benefit from more memory or a faster CPU. All factors contribute to network speed, and each component must be matched to get the most performance from your network.

▶ . . . . ◀

Adding Server Memory

The single most cost-effective way to help a slow network that is not hampered by cabling is by adding memory to the network. Networking technicians use formulas to determine the optimum server memory. It's best to let them perform the calculations, because many factors contribute to memory needs. Memory is the fastest storage medium in your server.

Various forms of caching can do much to improve performance. *Caching* is a way of storing files or information in memory instead of the hard drive. The CPU can access the information in a cache much faster than on the drive. A hard drive is mechanical, with a spinning platter or multiple platters, and a head that moves to the area on the disk containing the data requested. Memory is electronic with no moving parts. It is just there, almost instantaneously. Servers use various memory schemes to speed access and execution such as:

- ▶ Directory caching

- ▶ Directory hashing

- ▶ File caching

- ▶ Elevator seeking

- ▶ Memory pools

DIRECTORY CACHING

Networks store information on ownership of files and directories in a directory table. This is similar to the *File Allocation Table* (FAT) on a hard drive. The directory information includes information such as, information about assigned trustee rights, file names and ownership, directory names and ownership, date and time of last update, and the address of the first block on the network disk, if the entry is a file. The server stores the most recently accessed parts of the directory in memory. The directory table is searched each time a file or directory is used. If the information is in memory, the access is quicker than if it is retrieved from the hard drive.

DIRECTORY HASHING

Networks use both the directory table and FAT to store information about files. Both these tables are accessed each time a file is used. *Directory hashing* is an indexing algorithm that stores the directory table and FAT in memory in a specific order, instead of randomly, as in DOS. The search for information is faster because the server knows where to get the information, instead of searching the entire table until it finds it.

FILE CACHING

When parts of files or entire files are stored in server memory, they can be accessed up to ten thousand times faster from memory than from the servers' disks. Files that are not used are replaced by other files that are used. Think of *file caching* as putting files on your desk while you use them. When you need a number of files from a filing cabinet, you retrieve them and set them on your desk until you're finished with them. You don't find each portion of the file and refile it immediately, since you know you'll have to refer to it again in a few minutes. You keep the files on your desk until you know you are finished with them. This is much faster than going to the filing cabinet each time you need a small piece of information. File caching keeps the files ready for quick access until they are no longer needed.

ELEVATOR SEEKING

Files are not stored in contiguous regions of the hard disk. That is, the entire file in one position on the physical media. Not all files are the same size. Files written to an empty disk are usually written in one location. As files are erased and written to the disk, empty places for new files are created that are different sizes. New data is then written in pieces to empty portions of the disk, until the file is completely copied to the disk. This creates files that are spread over the disk in many different places, commonly called *disk fragmentation*. The FAT keeps track of beginning and ending locations of files or portions of files and sends the disk head to those locations until the entire file is retrieved.

Because DOS disks are accessed in order, the action of heads moving over the entire surface of the disk media slows access time. DOS and third-party products provide utilities to defragment disks or reposition data in contiguous areas of the disk. *Elevator seeking* retrieves data differently. The heads are prioritized to retrieve data as they encounter it, even if out of order. The result is less head movement and quicker access.

MEMORY POOLS

Most schemes for increasing speed are performed in memory, and performance-enhancing functions rely on server memory. When the server is originally brought up, all available memory is allocated to file cache buffers. From this point on, all of the server's memory is reallocated to other memory pools as needed. Because all server memory is originally provided to file cache buffers, the memory needed by other memory pools has to be allocated from this memory.

Because each function is assigned a portion of memory to operate in, most applications determine what memory to use so the administrator doesn't really have options for assigning it. This varies among applications. More memory allows more functions to run. Some functions use memory that is left over or not in use. Other functions need protected memory or a set amount of memory that is devoted to its operation. Each server is tuned by assigning available memory to the various functions.

If a server has insufficient memory, it will swap out processes by writing information temporarily to the server's hard disk. Because it is much slower to write operations to a hard disk for later recall, most network professionals try to add RAM so that operations can be processed more quickly. The performance difference can become very noticeable.

It is impossible to give recommendations for memory assignments because each server is different. A lot depends upon the programs that are run on the server.

Increasing Speed or Access Time

Many factors contribute to the speed of the network. Speed is often confused with access time. Retrieving a file from the network hard disk is usually slower than retrieving the file from the workstation hard disk. A really slow workstation will appear to run faster on the network than a stand-alone. Network equipment must be matched to optimize performance. It does no good to have the fastest server and fastest workstations connected to a slow ARCnet network, or install a 100BaseT network with a 386 server.

It also helps to know whether your application software is client-server-based or not. *Client-server* refers to the way the software handles data and processing. The client is the workstation and the server is the central computer, housing the network software, database, and some application programs. A mainframe does all the processing on a central computer with dumb terminals or *video display terminals* (VDTs) simply displaying the results. VDTs have little or no memory, and can only run as fast as the mainframe. Distributed applications spread the processing across many smaller computers, reducing the need for a huge central computer.

Non-client applications transfer the entire database to the workstation, so the workstation does all the processing. A 10,000-record, 1,000-byte-per-record database occupies 10MB of space, and this entire file would be transferred to each user requesting a single record in the file. A client-server application will process the query on the server and pass only the requested record to the workstation or client. This places added processing requirements on the server, but transfers are smaller, reducing network traffic.

Other client-server applications have a database server and an application server. The database server stores the database and the application server does all the processing of data for the workstation. This speeds the processing considerably as the tasks are shared by two processors.

No one method is right for all instances, but each application and process should be optimized by programmers to operate in the most efficient manner. This is a programming concern and usually cannot be changed by the user. Understanding the different processes will help when evaluating software. The bottom line is that your network may be screaming, but your software is slowing it down.

GETTING OUT OF BOTTLENECKS

Other bottlenecks are numerous. Anything that creates network traffic slows down response time. The more users that are attached to the network, the slower it will be. Response time will be slowed any time the server is running disk-, processor-, and memory-intensive tasks. A single, bad, or failing NIC can create so much network traffic that the entire network slows down. Bad hubs can cause collisions, which slow the network. A kinked cable can cause intermittent problems. Network operating systems provide utilities that display statistics on disk space, volumes, frames received and sent, and system resources and utilization. This data can be used to isolate problems or at least furnish a starting point for your investigation.

The best strategy is to hire an experienced technician to provide recommendations for improving network speed. This is a good idea even if you have a technician on staff. The outside technician draws upon experience with many networks in different environments and configurations. Really pesky problems benefit from diagnostic equipment. A PC with a network adapter and diagnostic software is attached to the network and captures frames passed across the network, displaying the results in reports or on-screen graphs and charts. Information such as the addresses creating requests and the type of request, in code, is captured for reference. This makes it possible to see exactly what type of requests are being processed and who is making them. Armed with this information, the technician can make suggestions for segmenting the network, upgrading or replacing hardware, or making software changes. Don't try this at home, kids, unless you really know what the data means. This is best left to a professional.

When Printers Won't Print

Printer problems can be among the most frustrating of LAN maladies. It seems that printers only fail to work when you need them most. Again, we suggest that you take slow and careful steps to debug printing problems. Use common sense techniques first, then look for more technical issues.

First check the obvious. Is the printer plugged in? Are you out of paper? Are there errors on the printer? Is there a paper jam? Is the ribbon, toner, or ink cartridge good? Is the printer cable plugged in? After you check the obvious, you can begin to look at the fun stuff, such as printer queues and print servers.

As discussed earlier in the chapter, identify the problem as carefully as you can. Is the network printer working for some users, but not all? If multiple printers are attached to the server, are all the printers down or just one? Is the printer printing from some applications and not from others? Is the printer printing garbage? What changed since the last time the printer worked? Did a software installation change parameters? Did someone change configurations in the network operating system?

A local printer is a printer attached directly to a workstation and only available to that workstation. Local printer problems are usually easy to fix and most users are experienced at troubleshooting them. A network printer is a printer that multiple users have access to. If the printer is working, most other printer problems can be isolated to cabling, print drivers, print servers, print queues, or user rights to the printer.

Printers are attached to the main server, a workstation, or hardware device acting as a print server, router, or workstation. If a workstation printer is to be accessed by other network users, it must be set up as a remote printer.

Use your powers of deduction and eliminate what is working and what isn't. If all printers on a print server are down, suspect the print server hardware, network cables, print queue, or configuration of the print server. Check to make sure all parameters are set correctly in the network software. If a single printer is down, suspect the cable to the printer, printer port, print driver, or configuration of the printer. A remote printer only works if the workstation it is attached to is up and running. If the user on that workstation removes the TSR from memory, the printer will become unavailable.

If a user or group of users can no longer print, check to make sure they're set up as users in the print server configuration. If you are trying unsuccessfully to get a new software package to print, is the software network-compatible? Are the drivers supplied with the software designed for networks? Is the print server overloaded from excessive print requests? Find out what print activities are causing the overload and defer printing of large jobs to evening hours when users are gone. Distribute users to other printers to balance the load. What use is a new printer if everyone is sending all their requests to the old printer?

Printer problems can be isolated if you understand what makes up the print process and the parts of the network that control printing. Be patient and soon you'll be happily printing again.

Troubleshooting Workstation Problems

Here we focus on those more common glitches that can be inspected by nontechnical personnel, including installation and postinstallation problems and common solutions. Table 15.1 lists some of these basic problems and solutions at a glance.

	PROBLEM	CAUSE / SOLUTION
TABLE 15.1 *Workstation Issues*	PC doesn't power on (or PC powers on, but nothing comes up on the screen) after card is installed.	The NIC has a conflict with some other adapter card in the PC. Remove the network NIC and reconfigure any jumpers or dip switches. Consider running a diagnostics program, such as MSD.EXE, which comes with Windows, to determine which IRQs and base I/O ports memory are available. Newer NICs are software configurable and can be configured with utilities instead of physical dip switches and jumpers. Most PCs have IRQ 5,10,11,15 available. IRQ 5 is used for LPT2, so if you have a second parallel printer, use one of the other IRQs.
	The COM2 port doesn't work anymore.	You have set your NIC for IRQ 3. COM ports usually use IRQ 3 and IRQ 4. Reset the NIC for a different IRQ. If the card supports it, try IRQ 10 or IRQ 11.
	The workstation can't log on to the network.	1. Check network cables to make sure your PC is connected to the network.
		2. Check the hub to make sure the port is OK.
		3. Use a diagnostic utility (usually supplied with your NIC) to make sure your computer can send and receive packets across the network.
		4. Check your installation and make sure you correctly specified the NICs and protocols.
		5. The network administrator may have a security lock on the port or workstation.
		6. Make sure the network drivers are not erased or the batch files and the workstation have not been changed.
		7. The network may be down. This can be due to server problems or simply a backup operation that has locked a file until backed up.

Summary

We have discussed the guidelines for troubleshooting problems on your network. First, identify the problem, check to see what changed, discuss the problem with someone, and then look for any obvious answer. Read the manual and remember to change only one thing at a time. You don't want to introduce new problems. Recognize the limits of your own technical knowledge and don't be afraid to ask for help, either from the manufacturer's help desk, your company's help desk, or from an outside source.

Glossary

3270   A communications protocol that supports online transaction processing and file transference.

56K service (dedicated or switched)   Provided by local telephone companies or long-distance carriers, this service offers customers digital circuits capable of transmitting voice, data, or video at rates of 56Kbps. With switched 56K service, the customer dials up the 56K circuit on demand and pays a per-minute rate based on actual monthly usage.

access charge   A charge paid to a local telephone company for the availability and use of exchange facilities for origination and termination of interexchange services.

active hub   A networking device that connects the wires of a star shaped network. Used most frequently with ARCnet LANs.

analog/digital   Two opposite kinds of communications signals. Analog is a continuously varying electrical signal in the shape of a wave (such as a radio wave), transmitted electronically in a form parallel to the spoken work. Digital is based on a binary code in which the picture or audio information is sent as a series of "on" and "off" signals. This service is more precise and less subject to interference than analog.

analog transmission   A continuous wave transmission expressed by bandwidth, or range of frequencies. Some examples using analog channel transmission include: broadcast television, cable television, and AM/FM radio.

application   A functional system made up of software, hardware, or a combination of both that performs some useful task. Database managers, spreadsheets, word processors, LAN's, fax machines, and so on, are examples of applications.

application icon   A glyph that represents a running application. This icon will appear on your Windows 95 main screen or after you start the application and then minimize (reduce) it.

application switching   Moving from one application to another without closing the first application.

architecture   A set of rules for building programs, networks, and such as structures.

archive   To back up old files and remove them from immediate access. They can be retrieved and used whenever necessary.

ARCnet   A network protocol standard that permits computer data, as well as voice or video information, to be carried across a network. It employs a token-passing star topology and is usually connected using coaxial cable.

ASCII character set   The American Standard Code for Information Interchange 7-bit character set. It consists of the first 128 (0-127) characters of the ANSI (American National Standards Institute) 8-bit character set and most other 8-bit character sets. The ASCII character set is the most universal character-coding set.

association   The relationship between a file type and the application that created or reads the file.

Asynchronous Transfer Mode (ATM)   A high bandwidth, control delay, fixed-size packet switching and transmission system. Because it uses fixed-size packets that are also known as *cells*, ATM is often referred to as *cell relay*. ATM will provide the basis for future broadband ISDN standards.

attributes   Specific information that is maintained about files. Attributes can show that the file is read-only, hidden, or system, and whether it has been changed since it was last backed up. See also *archive attribute, hidden file, read-only file,* and *system file.*

AUTOEXEC.BAT file   A file with a set of commands that is automatically run by the operating system whenever the computer is started or restarted. The file generally contains basic commands that help configure the system.

bandwidth   The range of frequencies over which signal amplitude remains constant as it is passed through a system. This can also be a measure of the information-carrying capacity of a communications channel or the amount of the electromagnetic spectrum that a given signal occupies; the higher (wider) the bandwidth, the greater the information. This is usually expressed in kilohertz (KHz) or megahertz (MHz).

basic rate interface   An ISDN subscriber line consisting of two 64Kbps "B" channels and one 16Kbps "D" channel. This is used for both data and signaling purposes.

baud rate   A measurement of speed that is close to 1bps. It is generally applied to modems. For example, a 2400 baud modem transfers information at approximately 2400bps.

Bell system   A group of affiliated RBOCs (Regional Bell Operating Companies) in the United States that operates under consistent rules and specifications, many of which are set by AT&T.

binary file   A file containing information that is in machine-readable form. The file must have an application capable of reading its format in order for it to make sense.

bisynchronous   A data link protocol for synchronizing transmission of binary coded data.

bit   A binary digit; the smallest unit of information used by a computer represented by a "1" or "0", or by "on" or "off." A single bit is one digital signaling element; one alphabetic or numeric character is typically represented by 10 bits.

bit error rate (BER)   In digital applications, it is the ratio of bits received in error to bits sent. BERs of 10 (one error bit to a billion sent) are typical.

BNC   A type of bayonet-lock coaxial cable connector used for video and communications.

bridge   A device that passes packets between two similar LAN channels; for example, Ethernet-to-Ethernet. This can also be a device which connects three or more telecommunications channels, such as telephone lines.

broadband   A LAN residing on coaxial cable, capable of transporting multiple data, voice, and video channels. Broadband channels have enough bandwidth to carry full motion video, stills, graphics, audio, and text.

Broadband Integrated Services Digital Network (B-ISDN)   A digital signaling network in which equipment interface data rates operate at speeds of 155–622Mbps.

buffer   A place, usually in the computer's memory, used to temporarily store information.

byte   A group of bits, usually eight, handled as a unit by a computer operating system.

cable   An optical fiber, multiple fibers, or fiber bundle. This may include a cable jacket and strength members, fabricated to meet optical mechanical, and environmental specifications. See also *fiber buffer, fiber bundle*.

carrier   A provider of transmission capabilities available to the general public, sometimes referred to as a *common carrier* or a *regulated carrier*, regulated by the FCC.

A current in a communications channel that can be modulated to carry analog or digital signals.

A telephone company or similar non-private telecommunications service supplier.

The radio frequency wave having at least one characteristic that may be varied by modulation.

Carrier Sense Multiple Access/Collision Detection (CSMA/CD) A technique in which a station on a network determines that no other stations are communicating before it transmits data.

CD-ROM Storage technology that can be used to keep information that can be read by a computer or similar hi-tech device. CD-ROMs use the same technology as audio compact discs and laser discs.

channel bank A piece of equipment that typically allows twenty-four analog circuits to be sampled and converted into digital signals having 64Kbps per channel, which are subsequently merged into a time-divided bit format (such as DS1) at a rate of 1.544Mbps for transmission on a single T1 facility between two points. Channel banks are required at both ends of each link, to combine (at one end) and separate (at the other end) the component signals. Using channel banks, slow-scan TV, data, and phone signals can be sent on the same T1 link.

Channel Service Unit/Data Service Unit (CSU/DSU) On some data networks, these are two separate devices. On most networks that use a codec, this is a box that sits between the codec and the data circuit, used to interface and condition the data coming on and off the network. This box may also contain diagnostic testing functions and indicators, and in the case of switched services, will perform all your dialing functions. A CSU/DSU is required for all SW56 and DDS circuits, and is not included with your codec.

client-server network A type of LAN that has at least one computer that is designated as the host computer for some or all of the network's applications.

coax, coaxial cable The copper-wire cable that carries audio and video signals and radio frequency energy, consisting of an outer conductor and an inner conductor that are separated from each other by insulating material. This type of cable can carry a much higher bandwidth than a wire pair.

coder/decoder (codec) Digital encoding/decoding equipment that is necessary to interface analog end-user equipment (such as a television set) to digital transmission facilities. In the case of compressed video, codecs are also used to restore some of the motion which is taken out in the compression process.

COM port A COM port is a serial communication channel on a computer. See also *serial port.*

common carrier A telecommunications company, such as your local telephone company, that provides communication transmission services.

communications settings Settings that specify how information is transferred from your computer to a serial device, such as a printer or modem. See also *serial port*.

concentrator A centrally located device for connecting the wires of a star-shaped topology, contention-based network. Concentrators serve as the traffic cop for managing network data. With a concentrator, all network segments are active at the same time. See also *hub*.

CONFIG.SYS file A text file containing configuration commands used when starting your computer. Commands in the CONFIG.SYS file enable or disable system features, set limits on resources, and extend the operating system's functionality by loading device drivers.

Consultative Committee of the International Telephone and Telegraph Group (CCITT) This committee is working to produce the PX64 standard for compressed video equipment so that the codes of various manufacturers can be used together.

contention-based protocol standard A LAN scheme in which all of the computers can communicate at once. Packets of information can literally collide on the network wire and be destroyed before they are delivered.

continuous audio The audio connection for a switched video network that allows all connected endpoints to speak at the same time, in the same manner as an audio bridge.

CPU The central processing unit of a computer.

customer premises equipment (CPE) Telephone equipment, such as phones and private branch exchanges (PBXs), located on the customers premises.

database Information storage system that can be searched through a number of methods to obtain specific data. "Database" has been associated with computer services, but is now used to refer to general information storage and retrieval systems (e.g. audiotext, teletext, etc.).

data file Any file or document created within an application; for example, a word-processing document, spreadsheet, database file, or chart. See also *text file*.

data path Secondary network consisting of the "overhead" bits above the 36Mbps video channel.

data port The physical and electrical protocol used by the codec and the DSU or TA to transfer data between each other. A codec comes with either V.35 or X.21 protocol built in. These are actually the number of CCITT international standards which specify pinning, levels, and so on. V.35 is common for networks in North America and X.21 is popular on European-manufactured ISDN terminal adapters.

data rate   Analog transmission media is specified in bandwidth (usually in hertz) and signal to noise. Since the principles behind digital transmission are so different, media are specified in different parameters. Rather than how much analog information is passed, a digital user is concerned with how many bits per second can be sent down the channel.

Data Terminal Equipment/Data Computer Equipment (DTE/DCE)   To avoid confusion, the data protocols mentioned above designate equipment and ports as either DTA or DCE. In the case of the codec, the CSU/DSU or TA is always the DCE and the codec is always the DTE. Plugging two DTEs together will not establish communication between them, since the DCE provides all the clocks required to run the data.

dedicated file server   A master computer that directs the network's operation and applications. It may not be used as a user workstation.

dedicated lines   A leased or purchased line that connects two or more data communication sites used exclusively by one vendor or user.

DEMARCATION (Demarc)   A line either side of which determines the contractor's and owner's responsibilities. The location(s) where customer-provided equipment is connected to carrier-provided equipment. For example, the splice block where a telephone line enters most homes is a demarc; everything on the line side of the demarc is the responsibility of the telephone company, and everything on the home side (such as the house wiring and the telephones themselves) is the responsibility of the homeowner.

device   A component of the system's hardware configuration. Examples include the modem, printer, mouse, sound card, or disk drive.

device driver   Software that controls how a computer communicates with a device, such as a printer or mouse. A printer driver, for example, translates information from the computer into information the printer can understand.

Digital Data System   The most common point-to-point, dedicated digital telephone service that works well with the codec. The user pays a flat monthly charge to the phone company for a full time link.

Direct Digital System (DDS)   A network whose component parts and signals (representing information of various types) are all transmitted via standardized digital signaling methods. In a DDS network, no analog-to-digital converters are necessary.

disaster recovery The use of alternative network circuits to reestablish communication channels in the event that the primary channels are disconnected or malfunctioning.

document file A file whose extension has been associated with a specific application. For example, an XLS file is frequently associated with the Excel spreadsheet. Opening a file in the Explore or File Manager causes the associated application to start.

downloading A process that involves transferring information from one device to another over a telecommunications channel (telephone, broadcast, and so on). Information received from the originating source can then be stored by the receiver for future use.

DS0/DS3 Designations given to circuits of different bit rates. A DS0 circuit has a bit rate of 56Kbps (actually, the full width is 64Kbps, but the rest is used for overhead associated with the transfer). A single digital telephone circuit uses a DS0. A DS3 has a bit rate capability of 45Mbps, which is equivalent to 28 T1 circuits, or 672 DS0 circuits.

DS1 See *T1*.

dual 56 Two switched 56K calls made between video conferencing equipment to allow data transfer at 112Kbps. The video conferencing equipment performs a two-channel inverse-multiplexing procedure to assure channel alignment.

duplex On the plain old telephone system (POTS), the audio transmission can be considered half *duplex* because if both parties speak at the same time, their voices will intercept on the single pair of wires on each end of the call. Most digital systems are duplex, having four wires and allowing simultaneous and independent data (or encoded audio) to pass in each direction. Some systems may be *simplex,* which pass digits only in one direction.

duplexer A device that combines transmit and receive signals on one antenna

dynamic allocation The ability to add or remove resources to/from a system based on actual need. The alternative to dynamic allocation is to have a fixed amount of resources for a system, which are always dedicated to that system, regardless of whether they are being used.

Dynamic Data Exchange (DDE) A protocol for the exchange of data between applications.

Electronic Bulletin Boards (EBBs) These are systems in which users can read and post short public messages or announcements stored on a central computer. Messages are sent and received by users with microcomputers equipped with modems and communications software. The messages may be screened and posted within categories established by the system operator.

Electronic Industries Association (EIA) A standards organization specializing in the electrical and functional characteristics of interface equipment.

electronic mail (e-mail) A system by which written messages are entered through a keyboard and distributed to individuals or groups subscribing to the service. Messages are generally stored on a computer and forwarded to recipients when they log on to the e-mail server.

encryption/decryption Special coding or scrambling of a communication signal for security purposes.

Ethernet Baseband protocol and technology developed by Xerox and widely supported by many manufacturers; a packet technology that operates at 10Mbps over coaxial cable and allows terminals, concentrators, workstations, and hosts to communicate with each other.

fault management The process of locating a fault, isolating it, and then fixing it.

fax Electronic technology that transmits documents, usually over telephone systems. Facsimile devices are commonly referred to as fax, telecopies, or datafax.

Federal Communications Commission (FCC) The federal agency responsible for regulating all use of the air waves for broadcast and electrical telecommunications purposes.

Fiber Distributed Data Interface (FDDI) A high-speed protocol standard for sending network data over fiber (not copper) cabling.

fiber-optic link Any optical transmission channel designed to connect two end terminals or to be connected in a series with other channels.

fiber optics Method for transmission of information (voice, video, data). Light is modulated and transmitted over highly-pure, hair-thin fibers of glass. Bandwidth capacity of fiber-optic cable is much greater than conventional cable or copper wire.

firmware Data and/or program software for the codec stored in a nonvolatile form in a semiconductor memory circuit. For codecs, the firmware is often housed in a plug-in module.

flow control The processes used to regulate the transfer of information from one device to another, usually via modems or communication software. One device sends a signal called a *handshake* to the other when information can be transferred.

format   The way text or data is set up on a page, or the way information is structured in a file. Also, to prepare a floppy disk to hold information. Formatting a disk deletes all information that was previously on it. Be careful not to format the hard disk.

fractional T1   Service offering data rates between 64Kbps (DS0 rate) and 1.536Mbps (DS1 rate), in specified intervals of 64Kbps.

frame relay   A form of packet switching using smaller packets and less error checking than traditional forms of packet switching (X.25 i.e.); now a new international standard for efficiently handling high-speed data over WANs.

frequency   The number of cycles per second of an electromagnetic transmission, usually described in hertz. Generally, high frequency transmissions can carry more information at greater speeds than low frequency transmissions.

full duplex   A transmission system, together with its associated equipment, capable of simultaneously transmitting and receiving signals, as opposed to simplex (unidirectional) or half-duplex (one direction at a time) systems.

gateway   Used to describe a device that connects two or more dissimilar networks, and makes communication between/among them possible.

gigabits per second (Gbps)   A rate at which data may be transferred across a communications line. 1Gbps equals 1 billion bits per second, or approximately 125 million characters per second (assuming 8 bits per character).

gigahertz (GHz)   A unit of frequency equal to 1 billion hertz or 1 thousand megahertz per second.

half duplex   A circuit that permits communications in both directions, but not simultaneously.

hertz   A unit of frequency equal to 1 cycle per second (cps). 1 kilohertz equals 1 thousand cps; 1 megahertz equals 1 million cps; 1 gigahertz equals 1 billion cps.

hub   A point or piece of equipment where a branch of a multipoint network is connected. Hubs serve as traffic cops for managing network data. A network may have a number of geographically distributed hubs or bridging points.

hybrid system   A system that combines two or more communication technologies.

IEEE   Institute of Electrical and Electronics Engineers.

in-band signaling   Signaling made up of tones of defined bits which pass within the data transmission stream. Tones sent over digital circuits are encoded into digital PCM bursts and sent as digital data within the data channel.

infrared (IR)   The bank of electromagnetic wavelengths between the visible part of the spectrum and microwaves.

Integrated Services Digital Network (ISDN)   The worldwide standard for digital telephony. WANs are configured with standardized equipment and digital transmission methods that enable voice, data, and video information to be transferred between user resources simultaneously.

interexchange carrier (IXC)   A long-distance supplier.

interface   The connection between two devices. Interfaces carry electronic impulses from one place to another. A hardware interface, for example, would connect a host computer to a computer, a modem, or other device.

interrupt   A signal that a device sends to the computer when the device is ready to accept or send information. Also used when a device needs the computer's attention.

interrupt request line (IRQ)   Hardware line over which devices can send interrupt signals. Usually, each device connected to the computer uses a different IRQ.

inverse multiplexing   The creation of a single higher-speed data channel by combining and synchronizing two or more lower-speed data channels.

ISDN multirate   A network-based ISDN service that allows users' network access equipment to dial network channels of bandwidth in increments of 64Kbps, up to 1536Kbps. Access to ISDN multirate service is obtained over ISDN PRI lines.

I/O address   Input/output locations used by a device such as a modem or printer.

ISO   International Standards Organization

IT   information technologies

jumper   A small set of pins on a computer card that allow for the change of certain settings, such as specifying an IRQ port or address. Jumpers are found on some network interface cards.

kilobits per second (Kbps)   A rate at which data may be transferred across a communications line. 1Kbps equals 1 thousand bits per second, or approximately 125 characters per second (assuming 8 bits per character).

kilohertz (KHz)   A unit of frequency equal to 1 thousand hertz.

laser   Light amplification by stimulated emission of radiation. This highly focused beam of light (or its device) is used in fiber optics and optical video discs.

learning link   A computer bulletin board utilized for education-related services.

leased lines   A circuit rented for exclusive use twenty-four hours a day, seven days a week from a telephone company. The connection exists between two predetermined points and cannot be switched to other locations.

linear bus topology   A network cabling scheme in which all stations are directly connected to one linear cable.

Local Area Network (LAN)   A user-owned, user-operated, high-volume data transmission facility connecting a number of communicating devices (computers, terminals, word processors, printers, mass storage units, and so on) within a single building or campus of buildings.

local exchange carrier (LEC)   A telephone company that provides local service.

LTP port   See *parallel port.*

management protocols   Language used to communicate with and within a given network.

megabits per second (Mbps)   A rate at which data may be transferred across a communications line. 1Mbps equals 1 million bits per second, or approximately 125 thousand characters per second (assuming 8 bits per character).

megahertz (MHz)   A unit of frequency equal to 1 million hertz.

megabyte   An amount of information roughly equivalent to one million characters. Also denoted as *MB.*

memory   A temporary storage area for information/applications, such as ROM, RAM, conventional memory, expanded memory, and extended memory.

memory-resident program   A program loaded into memory that is available while another application is active. Also known as a *terminate-and-stay-resident* (TSR) program.

modem (modulator/demodulator)   An electronic device used to allow a computer to send and receive data, typically over a phone line.

MS-DOS prompt   At the MS-DOS command line, the character or characters that appear at the beginning of the line, indicating the computer is ready to receive input. Also known as the *command prompt.*

multimode fiber   An optical fiber that supports many propagating modes at a given wavelength.

multiplexing   The process of combining a number of individual channels into a common frequency band or into a common bit stream for transmission. The converse equipment or process for separating a multiplexed stream into individual channels is called *demultiplexer.*

multitasking   A feature of the computer and its operating system that enables more than one application to run at the same time.

nano   Prefix meaning one billionth.

network   A group of computers connected by cables or other means and using software to enable them to share printers, disk drives, and information.

network drive   A disk drive, available to users on a network, where data files can be stored.

networking   The tying together of multiple sites for the reception and possible transmission of information. Networks can be composed of various transmission media, including copper wire, terrestrial microwave, or coaxial.

network interface card (NIC)   A printed circuit board installed in a PC that allows network stations to communicate with each other; also called a *network adapter card.*

network operating system (NOS)   The internal set of commands and instructions that directs a network's activities. Novell NetWare, Banyan VINES, Microsoft LAN Managers, and Windows NT are examples of client-server NOSs.

network printer   A printer shared by multiple users over a network.

network topology   A network protocol or design that permits computer data, as well as audio and video information, to be carried across a network. The NICs available for network printers use a variety of topologies, including Ethernet and Token Ring.

node   A termination point for two or more communication links. The node can serve as the control location for forwarding data among the elements of a network or multiple networks, as well as performing other networking, and in some cases, local processing functions.

null modem   A device that interfaces between a local peripheral that normally requires a modem, and the computer near it that expects to drive a modem to interface to that device; an imitation modem in both directions.

Open System Interconnection (OSI)   Emerging standard for a layered architecture which allows data to be transferred among systems through networks.

out-of-band signaling   Signaling that is separated from the channel carrying the information and sent over an independent out-of-band channel.

packet switching   Digital transmissions are broken into data packets that are addressed to their destination and sent by a central switching computer along diverse routes through the network, taking advantage of pauses in voice conversations and interactive data transmissions; the packets are then reassembled at the destination switching center and sent to the end user.

parallel interface An interface between a computer and a printer in which the computer sends multiple bits of information to the printer simultaneously.

parallel printer A printer with a parallel interface connected to a parallel port.

parameter Information added to the command that starts an application, such as a filename or any type of information.

parity A process for error-checking memory chips.

passive hub A small wire connector that can be used to connect certain types of network cables. Usually found on ARCnet LANs.

peripheral device An additional tool that is connected to a computer. Examples include printer, plotter, mouse, and modem.

pigtail A short length of optical fiber permanently fixed to a component, used to couple power between the component and a transmission fiber.

polling LAN managers rely heavily on the network management system to periodically query all devices on the network and determine their status.

port A connection or socket on the computer. Ports are used to connect printers, modems, monitors, or a mouse to your computer. Serial ports (COM) and parallel ports (LPT) are the most commonly used ports.

PostScript A special printing definition language developed by Adobe.

PRI Primary Rate ISDN.

primary rate interface An ISDN subscriber line consisting of twenty-three 64Kbps "B" channels in North America (thirty 64Kbps channels elsewhere) and one 64Kbps "D" channel, used for signaling purposes.

print queue A list of files that have been sent to a printer in the order they are received, including the file currently being printed.

printer driver A program that controls interaction between the printer and computer. This program supplies information such as printing interface, description of fonts, and features of the installed printer.

printer server A network computer that is dedicated to managing requests for a printer.

private branch exchange (PBX) A telephone switch located on a customer's premises that primarily establishes voice grade circuits.

private network A network, usually operated by a single corporate entity, made up of dedicated lines leased from carriers and switching equipment located on the corporate premises.

program file An executable file that starts an application or program. A program file contains a file extension, such as .EXE, .PIF, .COM, or .BAT.

proportional font   A font whose characters have varying widths, such as Times New Roman. Courier font is not a proportional font.

protected mode   A computer's operating mode that is capable of addressing extended memory directly.

protocol   Refers to the communication parameters, such as baud rate and duplex, that are necessary to make a connection between computers.

protocol conversion   The process of translating the protocol that is native to an end-user device, such as a terminal, into a different protocol that is native to another device, such as a computer, so they can communicate with each other.

protocol standard   A standard method for computers to communicate, such as the Ethernet protocol standard or the Token Ring protocol standard.

public network   A network operated by the carriers (IECs and LECs) that includes network-based services and network-based switching.

RAM drive   A portion of memory used as a hard disk drive. RAM drives are much faster than hard disks because computers read information faster from memory than from hard disks. Information on a RAM drive is lost when the computer is turned off. This is also known as a virtual drive. See also *random access memory.*

random access memory (RAM)   The most common computer memory, the contents of which can be altered at any time.

read-only   An attribute given to a file or directory so that others may view the information in the file or directory but not modify it.

read-only memory (ROM) A type of semiconductor memory device that stores unalterable data or program information.

RJ-11   A standard modular telephone jack.

root directory   The top-level or main directory of a disk. The root directory is created when you format the disk, and from this directory you can create files and other directories.

router   An interconnection device that can connect individual LANs. Unlike bridges, which logically connect at the OSI's second layer, routers provide logical paths at the OSI's third layer. Like bridges, remote sites can be connected using routers over dedicated or switched lines to create WANs.

RS-232C   The industry standard for a 25-pin interface that connects computers with various forms of peripheral equipment.

RS-366   An EIA standard for providing dialing commands to network access equipment. It uses RS-232 electrical specifications but different connector pinouts and signal functions.

serial interface   An interface between a computer and a peripheral (like a printer or modem) that allows single bits of information to be transmitted from the computer to the device.

serial port (COM 1)   A connection on a computer where you plug in the cable for a serial device.

serial printer   A printer that uses a serial interface, which you connect to a serial port.

server   A computer that provides disk space, printers, or other services to computers over a network.

smart hub   A wire connector for a LAN with built-in management tools. Smart hubs can generally report statistics about the number of packets they receive or turn themselves off if they detect a problem.

soft font   A font installed in your computer and sent to the printer before it can be printed. They are also referred to as downloadable fonts.

software-defined network (SDN)   A virtually private network in which the network links are assigned to users as needed and are typically invoiced on the basis of bandwidth and time occupancy.

source directory   The directory where files are originally located before you move them.

star-shaped topology   A network cabling configuration in which one computer is designated as a central hub and all other stations are directly connected to it.

subdirectory   A directory within a directory.

switched 56   A service available from local telephone companies that offers a digital channel interface at a 56Kbps rate. It allows the user to place calls between several points and cut costs by only paying for part time service. It's generally used for computer data transmission or compressed video teleconferencing, and is functionally equivalent to a DS0.

switched 64   A dial-up network-based service providing a data channel operating at a rate of 64Kbps.

switched 384   A dial-up network-based service providing a data channel operating at a rate of 384Kbps.

switched 1536 A dial-up network-based service providing a data channel operating at a rate of 1536Kbps.

Switched Multimegabit Data Service (SMDS) A packet-based network service allowing the creation of high-speed data networks (up to 45Mbps).

switching Process of routing communications traffic from a sender to the correct receiver.

SYSTEM.INI file A Windows initialization file that contains settings used to customize Windows for your system's hardware.

T1 Telephone term given to a digital transmission circuit whose bandwidth is equal to twenty-four DS0 voice channels or 1536Kbps (plus 8Kbps bits for overhead).

T3 A carrier of 45Mbps bandwidth. One T3 channel can deliver 28 T1 channels, or 672 voice circuits used for digital video transmission or for major PBX-PBX telephone interconnection.

tail circuit The connection from the central switch location to the individual institution.

tariff A published rate for services provided by a common or specialized carrier, or the means by which regulatory agencies approve such services. The tariff is a part of a contract between customer and carrier.

T-carrier A hierarchy of digital systems designed to carry speech and other signals in digital form, designated T1, T2, and T4. The T1 carrier has twenty-four channels and transmits at 1.544Mbps. The T2 carrier has ninety-six channels equivalent with a 6.312Mbps line rate. The T4 carrier transmits at 274Mbps.

telco Acronym for telephone company.

terminate-and-stay-resident (TSR) program See *memory-resident program.*

time division multiplex/multiple access (TDM/TDMA) A method for combining multiple data circuits into one circuit (or vice versa) by assigning each circuit a fixed unit of time for its data transmission.

token-passing scheme Each computer on the network has an individual turn to accept and relay information.

topology The physical layout of the cable for a network. Popular topologies are linear bus and star-shaped.

TrueType fonts Fonts that are scalable and sometimes generated as bitmaps or soft fonts, depending on the capabilities of the printer. TrueType fonts can be sized to any height, and print exactly as they appear on the screen.

twisted pair   A cable composed of two small insulated conductors twisted together without a common cover. Telephone signals are the most common use of twisted pair technology.

tymnet/telenet   Commercial packet-switched networks available in major cities by direct dialing.

UNIX   A computer operating system.

unshielded twisted pair (UTP)   Wiring with one or more pairs of twisted insulated copper conductors bound in a single plastic sheath.

V.25 bis   An automatic calling and answering command set for use between DTE and DCE which includes both in-band and out-of-band signaling.

V.35   Commonly used to describe electrical and connector characteristics for a high speed synchronous interface between DTE and DCE. Originally, V.35 described a 48bps group band modem interface with electrical characteristics.

value-added service   A communication service utilizing common carrier networks for transmission and providing added data services with separate additional equipment. Such added service features may be store-and-forward message switching, terminal interfacing, and host interfacing.

voice grade channel   Used for speech transmission usually with an audio frequency range of 300–3,300 hertz. It is also used for transmission of analog and digital data. Up to 10Kpbs can be transmitted on a voice grade channel.

VT100   An ASCII character data terminal, consisting of screen and keyboard. Manufactured by Digital Equipment Corporation (DEC), the VT100 has become an industry standard data terminal. VT100 emulation software allows a standard PC to act as a VT100 terminal.

wide area network (WAN)   A data network typically extending a LAN outside a building or beyond a campus, over IXC or LEC lines to link to other LANs at remote sites. Typically created by using bridges or routers to connect geographically separated LANs.

Wide Area Telecommunications Service (WATS)   A bulk rate long-distance telephone service.

WIN.INI file   The initialization file for Windows that contains settings for your specific Windows environment. Certain Windows applications modify the WIN.INI file to add extra information that is used when you run those applications.

wireless cable   The use of frequencies in the MDS, MMDS, OFS, and ITFS ranges, reserved by the FCC for commercial use, to form a transmission service, typically for entertainment programming (usually MMDS-multichannel broadcasting to compete with or fill in a niche not served by cable).

X.21 A set of CCITT specifications for an interface between DTE and DCE for synchronous operation on public data networks. It includes connector, electrical, and dialing specifications.

X.25 A set of packet switching standards published by the CCITT.

Recommended Web Sites

What's the biggest library you've ever been in? Was it the Library of Congress, a university library, or perhaps the New York City Public Library? We agree that all of these are very big libraries housing enormous amounts of information. Now, imagine that all of those libraries and thousands more are available to you without leaving your computer terminal. Well, they are — through the Internet. You don't even need a library card. All you really need is Internet access and the URL of the place you want to go.

Following is our recommended short list of URLs where you can find helpful tips to assist you in gathering more information about network computing and other computing subjects. Each URL will allow you access to the home page for each location. After reaching a home page, where you go from there is purely up to you. We've included the brief descriptions of the company that owns each particular URL to give you an idea of what you'll find at each location.

Network Computing Hardware Companies

Here are some of the major network computing hardware companies whose Web pages you'll find very useful.

COMPAQ COMPUTER CORPORATION

www.compaq.com

Compaq Computer Corporation is the world's largest manufacturer of personal computers. Compaq also offers Internet and enterprise computing solutions, networking products, and commercial PC products.

HEWLETT-PACKARD

www.hp.com

Hewlett-Packard Company designs, manufactures, and services electronic products and systems, with a focus on business, engineering, science, medicine, and education industries.

IBM

www.IBM.com

International Business Machines Corporation is the world's largest computer company. IBM sells an enormous number of mainframes, minicomputers, workstations, and personal computers. To this day, the bulk of the data in most large enterprises still resides in IBM mainframes.

3COM

www.3com.com

3Com manufactures the networking hardware that connects computers to one another across LANs and WANs. These systems, which include adapters, hubs, switches, routers, and remote access platforms, enable users to link into computer network, whether they are in the office, at home, or on the road.

BAY NETWORKS, INC.

www.baynetworks.com

Bay Networks, Inc. is a major provider of internetworking products for businesses, workgroups, small offices, and mobile workers. The company offers LAN and ATM switches, hubs, routers, remote and Internet access solutions, and network management applications, all unified by the BaySIS architecture.

Network Computing Software Companies

Here are some of the major network computing software companies whose Web pages you'll find very useful.

NOVELL

www.novell.com

As the network software leader, Novell connected PCs to create the LAN market, then interconnected those LANs to build the WAN market. With the advent of global computing, Novell is integrating Internet technologies with business networks to create corporate intranets and business-class Internet services. Today Novell is enabling networks (LANs and WANs, intranets and the Internet) to come together into a single, managed Smart Global Network.

MICROSOFT

www.microsoft.com

Microsoft is probably the world's leading software producer. Although best known for the MS-DOS and Windows operating systems and the Microsoft Office business software suite (and the individual applications that comprise it), it is also the leader in developing network software for small and large networks with Windows for Workgroups and Windows NT products.

Search Engines

If you're looking for a Web site about a specific topic, chances are good that it exists. Although finding its location can be a bit of a challenge, if you start your search at one of the following sites, you're bound to find what you're looking for — and then some. These Web sites provide a single staging point for the most common and efficient search engines in use today. You can choose from predetermined and cataloged search topics or build your own specific criteria. It's easy.

www.search.com

www.infoseek.com

www.altavista.com

www.yahoo.com

Index

(continued)

(*continued*)

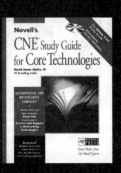